Family Devotions

Family Devotions

A 365-day Devotional
that Uses the Bible
to Teach Your Children
Character

Lauretta Marigny

PathLights Press
O'Fallon, Illinois

Copyright © 2008 by Lauretta Marigny. All rights reserved.

No part of this book may be reproduced, stored in a retrieval system, or transmitted by any means without the written permission of the copyright holder.

Scripture taken from the HOLY BIBLE: NEW INTERNATIONAL VERSION®. NIV®. Copyright © 1973, 1978, 1984 by International Bible Society. Used by permission of Zondervan.

ISBN-10: 0-9798212-0-7
ISBN-13: 978-0-9798212-0-2
LCCN: 2007939510

Published by PathLights Press
an imprint of Unity Press
604 Granite Dr.
O'Fallon, Illinois 62269

To our granddaughter, Elise Ryne Rochman.
Family Devotions is written to help children learn the difference between right and wrong. Elise doesn't need to do that; she is blessed with innocence.

PREFACE

When our children were young, I so wanted a devotion book of this type. In the evenings I tried to have regular devotions. I would look up scriptures that applied to a certain topic and then have each of our girls look up a scripture passage. This book is written so that you will not need that preparation time. *Family Devotions* gives you the tools to consistently teach your children the truths of God's Word. It targets children eight to twelve years old, but can apply to younger and older children as well. By using this book your children will, in a year's time, become familiar with several Biblical characters; they will become familiar with many of the books of the Bible; and they will understand how the Bible applies to everyday life.

God gives us his Word as the source of his revealed truth, and He commands that we teach our children his ways. My hope is that this book will help you in that endeavor.

There is some repetition of scripture and ideas in this book. Consider it intentional.

This book is written for Evangelical Christians. I am working on a Catholic version, entitled *Family Prayer*.

CONTENTS

Devotion Titles xi
Acknowledgements xvii
Introduction xix
Abbreviations of Books of the Bible xxii
Pronunciation of Some Books of the Bible xxiii

Jan	Trust in the Lord	1
Feb	Be Holy/Pure	32
Mar	Forgive One Another	61
Apr	Be Kind	92
May	Humble Yourselves	122
June	Obey Your Parents/Be Good	153
July	Show Proper Respect/Reverence	183
Aug	Do Not Lie	214
Sept	Exercise Self-control	245

Oct	Wisdom	275
Nov	Don't be Selfish	306
Dec	Be Diligent	336

Closing Remarks 367
Index 369

JANUARY
Trust in the Lord

1 In the Beginning
2 We Need Jesus
3 Spiritually Dead
4 Must be Born Again
5 Repent
6 A New Heart
7 Temples of the Spirit
8 A Brood of Vipers
9 God's Family
10 Like Father, Like Daughter
11 Glorify God in Sports
12 Saved Eternally
13 Saved From What?
14 God Created All People
15 Men Who Trusted God
16 All May be One
17 Every Thought Captive
18 Young and Committed
19 Growing Spiritually
20 Big Problems
21 God Protected David
22 God's Care of Joseph
23 Trust God!
24 How God Sees Us
25 Your Name?
26 Count on God
27 Fear Not
28 He Trusted God
29 I'm Bored
30 Think about Good Things
31 Trust God: Pray

FEBRUARY
Be Holy/Pure

1 Dressing Modestly
2 Light: A Symbol of Purity
3 How to Treat Girls
4 God's Purity & Glory
5 Read & Obey
6 God's Word is Perfect
7 God is Holy
8 Gossiping
9 Holy Means Separate
10 On the Net
11 Flee Sin
12 Screen It
13 Kidzone
14 Named after a Priest
15 God's Presence
16 Alligator Head
17 Stinky Behavior
18 Fragrant Sacrifice
19 Hearts Set on God
20 Guard Your Heart
21 Be Pure
22 Elijah is Holy
23 A Double Portion
24 Holy to the Lord
25 Yoga in School
26 Wholesome Talk
27 How to Stay Pure
28 Pure & Pleasing
29 Jesus Never Sinned

MARCH
Forgive One Another

1 Sackcloth and Ashes
2 Deny Yourself
3 Freedom in Forgiving
4 I Don't Know Him
5 In the Nursery
6 Don't Get Even
7 Jesus Can Forgive
8 Healing the Soul
9 A Bitter Root
10 John Mark Quits
11 They Were Envious
12 Too Late
13 A Friend Indeed
14 Bees in the Bible
15 A Thief
16 Esau Still Upset
17 A Missionary
18 Jesus' Example
19 Let's Kill Joseph
20 The Last Supper
21 The Crucifixion
22 Angry Still
23 We Are Forgiven!
24 Forgiven Should Forgive
25 Enough Already!
26 He's a Bully
27 Evil is not Good
28 Repentance Required
29 God is Forgiving
30 Sneaky
31 Produce Good Fruit

APRIL
Be Kind

1 One of Them
2 God Revealed
3 Be Generous
4 Blessed by God
5 Shoeboxes
6 Praying for a Baby
7 The Meanest Girl
8 God is Kind to Jacob
9 Good Gifts from God
10 Maltese Kindness
11 The Promised Land
12 Be Kind at Home
13 Best Friends Forever
14 The Family of a Friend
15 Jonathan's Son
16 Small Acts of Kindness
17 Willing to Listen
18 Egg & Bread
19 The Good Samaritan
20 Bad Shepherds & the Good
21 Showing Compassion
22 Feed the Poor
23 Care for All in Need
24 Jesus Raised the Dead
25 God Cares
26 Swallowed by a Fish
27 God is Kind to People
28 State Tournament
29 Sharing People's Sorrow
30 A Loving Touch

MAY
Humble Yourselves

1 Humility Explained
2 A Humble King
3 A Proud King
4 Tae Kwon Do Break
5 He Saw God
6 Secrets
7 In the Desert
8 Always Messing Up
9 Humble Yourself
10 Washing Feet
11 Humble Promises
12 The Centurion
13 Patrol Boy
14 For God's Eyes Only
15 Down to Earth
16 First Place
17 Donkey Rider
18 Copy Cat
19 Born in a Stable
20 Famous
21 Blue or White?
22 Grazing
23 Eating Pig Food
24 Belshazzar
25 Request of Solomon
26 Admit You are Wrong
27 False Humility
28 Grace to the Humble
29 God is Close
30 Humility Required
31 The Plan of God

JUNE
Obey Your Parents/Be Good

1 Created for Good Works
2 God is Good
3 What Did Jesus Do?
4 Clean Up!
5 He Knows it All
6 Caretakers
7 Hate Evil
8 Jesus Hates Evil
9 Friends: God's Gift
10 Three Monkeys
11 Three Pigs
12 On the Move
13 A Seamstress
14 Blessed to Bless Others
15 Sliced
16 Apple War
17 Farmer in the Dell
18 Church Discipline
19 Thumb Sucker
20 Glass Eye
21 A Good Man
22 Good King, Bad King
23 Bad Man, Good Man
24 Son of Nebat
25 Good or Bad Example?
26 Free Will
27 Turn from Evil
28 For Our Protection
29 Caught
30 Bath Towels

JULY
Show Proper Respect/
Reverence

1 The Fifth Commandment
2 Respect Your Parents
3 Addressing Adults
4 Holy, Holy, Holy
5 Respect Policemen
6 Respect the Elderly
7 Good Manners
8 Respect Worshippers
9 Don't Make Fun
10 Respect Other's Property
11 Don't Litter
12 Fear God
13 Offering Incense
14 Shining Face
15 Date with Dad
16 Hannah's Prayer
17 Hand It Over
18 Here I Am
19 God Reveals Himself
20 Irreverent Priests
21 Samuel Feared God
22 Not Embarrassed
23 God is Jealous
24 Great Salvation
25 The Transfiguration
26 Too Holy to Say
27 Names of God
28 Small Caps
29 God's Name
30 Respect God's Word
31 Glorious God

AUGUST
Do Not Lie

1 Dirty Dishes
2 Garage Cleaning
3 Nothing False
4 On God's Holy Hill
5 Tax Man
6 False Prophets
7 Truth
8 Pay Your Taxes
9 Lying Jerusalem
10 Abraham Lies
11 Isaac Lies
12 Rebekah Deceives
13 Jacob Lies
14 He Believed a Lie
15 God is Honest
16 Carrots or Dirt
17 Vegetable Thief
18 Honest Abe
19 No False Testimony
20 Children are Honest
21 Tempted to Steal
22 A Baggy Fit
23 Wallet Found
24 Keep Your Word
25 Do What You Promise
26 Stolen
27 No Bribes
28 Chronic Liar
29 Truth Tellers
30 Cheating
31 Why Not Lie?

SEPTEMBER
Exercise Self-control

1 Self-control
2 A Gentle Answer
3 Control Your Temper
4 Slow to Anger
5 Excuses, Excuses
6 An Angry King
7 Always Angry
8 The Idol of Food
9 Food & Exercise
10 Kept Safe
11 Because We Love God
12 Accidents
13 Good for All
14 Sprinter
15 Can I Hit Her?
16 Red Beans
17 Control Your Attitude
18 Whining
19 Muttering
20 Rolling the Eyes
21 Smart Remarks
22 God Will Help
23 It's Important
24 Tongue Control
25 Watch What You Say
26 Good Words Welcome
27 Eating Contest
28 Stomach is God
29 Righteous Anger
30 Temper Tantrum

OCTOBER
Wisdom

1 The Wrong Crowd
2 Salvation for All
3 Knowledge & Wisdom
4 Choose Rightly
5 Knowledge Puffs Up
6 Daniel is Wise
7 Tell a Dream
8 Wise Deacons
9 Tired Puppies
10 Jesus is Wise
11 Spiritual Things
12 Avoid the Trap
13 He's a Fool
14 It Brightens the Face
15 Trust & Obey
16 Ezra Knows the Word
17 Girls Feed Lambs
18 Choose to Serve God
19 Wise, Old Man
20 Judging Wisely
21 Wise Men
22 Solomon is Wise
23 A Baby Story
24 Wise to Obey
25 Not a Wise Choice
26 Rich Fool
27 Wise to Follow Jesus
28 No Boasting
29 Wise Words
30 From Idols to God
31 Fisher of Men

NOVEMBER
Don't Be Selfish

1 Greedy Ahab
2 Sharing Heaven
3 Generosity
4 Go Home
5 I'll Stay
6 Giving Up Jesus
7 Think of Others
8 Others above Self
9 Selflessness
10 Care for Others
11 Help Yourself
12 Abraham Tithed
13 Help the Helpless
14 Christ-centered Lives
15 Pray for Others
16 In the Door
17 Out the Window
18 Arguing
19 Me, Me, Me
20 Thanksgiving
21 Feast of Tabernacles
22 Don't Take Anything
23 The Best Animals
24 The 10th Commandment
25 Dirty Face
26 Don't Touch Them
27 Judah is Selfless
28 I Already Told You
29 Suffering for Us
30 Care about Souls

DECEMBER
Be Diligent

1 Jesus is Coming
2 Condi
3 God Worked
4 Work to Eat
5 Lazy Person
6 Undone Chores
7 A Big Job
8 Embarrassed
9 Meditate on the Word
10 Study the Word
11 Gathering Firewood
12 Maker of Tents
13 Two Jobs
14 Care of Pets
15 Eating Dirt
16 Diligence Rewarded
17 Rewarded for Work
18 Changing Jobs
19 Be Prepared
20 Practice, Practice
21 Marble Champion
22 Hit the Beanie Out
23 Santa Claus
24 God's Elves
25 Follow Advice
26 Work, Work, Work
27 Study Hard
28 Making the Bed
29 Brushing Your Teeth
30 Jesus Likes Order
31 God Likes Order

ACKNOWLEDGEMENTS

I would like to thank the following people for their various contributions:

My husband, for giving me the freedom to pursue God in whatever direction He is calling me.

My husband and our girls, for the stories they contributed to this book.

My friends, Leila Smith and Betty Naaden, for their encouragement.

My songwriter, Janelle Brackel, for the accompanying CD.

Kelsch Photography, for the cover picture.

Sarah Warner, for designing the cover.

Kent Quamme, my brother-in-law, for crafting the interior design.

Special thanks goes to my editors: Father James Kilzer and Veronica Sparling, who are my siblings, and Ann Blickensderfer.

INTRODUCTION

How to Use this Devotion Book

This book is written so that your children can actively participate in the devotion. It is written for a leader and four participants. The devotion leader assigns various family members (children/ spouse) a scripture passage (designated by the bold print in each devotion) to look up in their Bible. (It is best to have the participants look up the scriptures before the devotion begins so they can read them as soon as the leader says the reference. If each participant has their own Bible, things go much more smoothly. However, if there is just one shared Bible, the readers should have their scripture bookmarked for easy access, so when the Bible is passed to them they can readily find it.)

This book's use can be adjusted for larger or smaller families. For example, if your family is smaller you might assign a single child a scripture and then you, the leader, in order to save time, could just read the other scriptures from this book.

The devotion leader, preferably the dad, reads aloud from this book and as he approaches each scripture he asks the person assigned that scripture to read it aloud. The leader has all the scriptures written in italics so he can affirm that the correct scripture is being read. Some scriptures references have an "a" or "b" after them. An "a" stands for the first part of a verse and "b" usually means the last part of a verse. (See the November 3rd devotion). In this devotion Prov 21:26b is the third scripture. The reader of that verse reads only the second part of the verse beginning with "but the righteous." The person assigned to read Prov 28:27a reads only the first part of the verse stopping at "will lack nothing." In a few instances scripture references may have an "a," "b" and "c." In these cases "b" is the middle portion of the scripture and "c" indicates the last part. (Look at the May 1st devotion for an example of this.) In this devotion a different person is assigned to read each of the three sentences in I Cor 4:7.

All scriptures in this book are taken from the New International Version of the Bible—the NIV Bible (not the TNIV or the NIrV). If you use an NIV Bible printed before 1984, you will notice slight variations in a few scriptures.

Some words or phrases in this book may be unfamiliar to young children. These words or phrases are marked with an asterisk in the text. They appear at the bottom of that page along with their definitions. (See January 6th devotion for an example of this.) It might be helpful to discuss these words before starting the devotion.

Pronunciation of words is given in square brackets with the accented syllable in italics. Many of the Biblical pronunciations are taken from Unger's Bible Dictionary.

Several stories in this book are taken from our family, the Marigny [*mare* uh nee] family. We are Terry (Daddy), Lauretta (Mommy), Kerri, Gladys, Reyne [ruh *nay*] and Rachael. When the twins were born Kerri was four and Gladys was two.

Terry is African-American, and was raised in New Orleans. Lauretta was raised on a farm in North Dakota. Terry's military career took the family to Washington State, Oklahoma, California, New York, Germany, and Italy.

You will notice a designation under the title on some of some of the pages. For example, turn again to January 6. There you see "Marigny" written under the title. That story is about our family. Other stories in this book may have one of the following designations: "Bible" for Bible stories, "Warren Marigny" for stories about Terry's family, "Kilzer" for stories of Lauretta's family and "Rochman" [*rock* mun] for stories about Kerri's family. The family stories may have details changed or left out for purposes of this book. Some of the undesignated stories in this book are based on true stories.

How to Conduct Family Devotions

Christian devotions should consist of worship, instruction and prayer.

Worship is the first part of family devotions. There is a CD available for use with this devotional book. For ordering information go to www.pathlightspress.com. I highly recommend this CD, as the songwriter exceeded my expectations. The CD contains a scripture put to music for each of the character qualities. For example, every night in January you would play Song #1, Trust in the Lord. By the end of the year, your children should have the 12 scriptures committed to memory without even having to work at it. This song may be used as the worship portion of your devotion time. (If you choose not to order the CD, the 12 memory verses are listed below.)

The second part of family devotions is instruction. After the song, the family would read through the devotion for the day. About one quarter of this instruction material is taken directly from the Bible. These devotions are intended to be used in conjunction with the New International Version of the Bible. This book allows you to give your children a daily portion of God's Word. Some of the devotions teach what God is like and some teach how the Bible can be applied to daily life.

The final part of family devotions is prayer. No ending prayer is included in this material. Prayer may be about something that relates to the devotion or anything that is on someone's heart. Each member of the family should be encouraged to pray aloud.

By following this routine you will be incorporating worship, instruction and prayer in your daily family devotions. If things go smoothly, devotions should take about 10 minutes. My desire is that this book will help you to pass on the faith that you embrace to the children that you love.

Monthly Memory Verses

Jan	Prov 3:5-7	May	Jas 4:10	Sept	Gal 5:22-23
Feb	I Pet 1:16	June	Eph 6:1	Oct	Prov 8:11
Mar	Col 3:13	July	I Pet 2:17	Nov	Phil 2:4
Apr	Eph 4:32	Aug	Col 3:9	Dec	Prov 12:24

ABBREVIATIONS OF BOOKS OF THE BIBLE

Acts of the Apostles	**Acts**	Judges	**Judg**
Amos	**Amos**	1 Kings	**I Ki**
I Chronicles	**I Chr**	2 Kings	**II Ki**
II Chronicles	**II Chr**	Lamentations	**Lam**
Colossians	**Col**	Leviticus	**Lev**
1 Corinthians	**I Cor**	Luke	**Lk**
2 Corinthians	**II Cor**	Malachi	**Mal**
Daniel	**Dan**	Micah	**Mic**
Deuteronomy	**Deut**	Mark	**Mk**
Ecclesiastes	**Eccl**	Matthew	**Mt**
Ephesians	**Eph**	Nahum	**Nah**
Esther	**Est**	Nehemiah	**Neh**
Exodus	**Ex**	Numbers	**Num**
Ezekiel	**Eze**	Obadiah	**Obad**
Ezra	**Ezr**	1 Peter	**I Pet**
Galatians	**Gal**	2 Peter	**II Pet**
Genesis	**Gen**	Philippians	**Phil**
Habakkuk	**Hab**	Philemon	**Phlm**
Haggai	**Hag**	Proverbs	**Prov**
Hebrews	**Heb**	Psalms	**Ps**
Hosea	**Hos**	Revelation	**Rev**
Isaiah	**Isa**	Romans	**Rom**
James	**Jas**	Ruth	**Ruth**
Jeremiah	**Jer**	1 Samuel	**I Sam**
John	**Jn**	2 Samuel	**II Sam**
1 John	**1 Jn**	Song of Songs	**Song**
2 John	**II Jn**	1 Thessalonians	**I Thes**
3 John	**III Jn**	2 Thessalonians	**II Thes**
Job	**Job**	1 Timothy	**I Tim**
Joel	**Joel**	2 Timothy	**II Tim**
Jonah	**Jon**	Titus	**Tit**
Joshua	**Josh**	Zechariah	**Zech**
Jude	**Jude**	Zephaniah	**Zeph**

PRONUNCIATION OF SOME BOOKS OF THE BIBLE

Chronicles	[*kron* ih kulz]	Job	[jobe]
Colossians	[kuh *lah* shunz]	Jonah	[*joe* nuh]
Corinthians	[kor *rin* thee unz]	Lamentations	[lam un *tay* shunz]
Deuteronomy	[doo ter *ron* uh mee]	Leviticus	[luh *vit* ih kus]
Ecclesiastes	[eh kleez ee *ass* teez]	Malachi	[*mal* uh kie]
Ephesians	[ee *fee* zhunz]	Micah	[*my* kuh]
Esther	[*es* ter]	Nahum	[*nay* hum]
Exodus	[*ek* suh dus]	Nehemiah	[nee heh *my* uh]
Ezekiel	[ee *zee* kee ul]	Obadiah	[oh buh *die* uh]
Ezra	[*ez* ruh]	Philippians	[fih *lip* ee unz]
Galatians	[guh *lay* shunz]	Philemon	[fih *lee* mun]
Genesis	[*jen* uh sis]	Proverbs	[*prah* verbz]
Habakkuk	[huh *bak* uk]	Psalms	[salms]
Haggai	[*hag* eye]	Revelation	[rev uh *lay* shun]
Hosea	[hoe *zay* uh]	Thessalonians	[thes uh *lone* ee unz]
Isaiah	[eye *zay* uh]	Zechariah	[zek uh *rye* uh]
Jeremiah	[jare uh *my* uh]	Zephaniah	[zef uh *nye* uh]

Pronunciation Key

Pronounce all words in brackets as if they are English words. When there is no English word for the syllable, pronounce it with the rules of basic grammar. Accented syllables are in italics.

ah—the a sound in father, or the o sound in pot
eh—the e sound in pet   ih—the i sound in pit
oh—the o sound in toe   uh—the u sound in up
zh—the s sound in vision

JANUARY 1

In the Beginning

The Bible tells us that in the beginning God created the world and everything in it. God's last and best creation was a man and a woman, Adam and Eve. After God created Adam and Eve he looked at everything he had made and he said it was very good. Adam and Eve were at peace with God.

God put Adam and Eve in the Garden of Eden and he told them not to eat from one tree in the garden, the tree of the knowledge of good and evil. Adam and Eve disobeyed God; they ate some fruit from that tree. When Adam and Eve disobeyed God they sinned—they did something that God said was wrong. They were no longer at peace with God. God had set up a way for them to live, but they instead chose their own way.

Has anyone ever told you that you look like your mother, or your father? They might say: "Your eyes look like your mother's eyes," or, "You have your dad's nose." We might get certain looks from our parents.

Just like we "inherit" certain looks from our parents, the Bible tells us that every human being has "inherited" Adam's sin. Because every human being came from Adam, every human being tends to want to live his own way, not God's way. That is called "having a sinful nature."

Rom 5:12a *Therefore, just as sin entered the world through one man,* **Rom 5:12b** *and death through sin, and in this way death came to all men, because all sinned.*

Sin entered the world through Adam. Every person since Adam has "inherited" a sinful nature.

Rom 3:23 *For all have sinned and fall short of the glory of God.*

David says it like this:

Ps 51:5 *Surely I was sinful at birth, sinful from the time my mother conceived me.*

TRUST IN THE LORD

JANUARY 2

We Need Jesus
Marigny

The Marignys had several guinea pigs as pets. The girls liked to play with them. The girls thought one of the guinea pigs looked like cookie crumbs, so they named him Crumby [*krum* ee].

One time Gladys was playing with Crumby. She left him somewhere and didn't remember where he was. She had the entire family helping her to find him. Crumby was found sitting on the third shelf of the book case. Gladys remembered she had put him there when she was looking for a book.

It seemed that Crumby was afraid to jump so he was stuck there. He needed someone to help him get out of his situation.

We human beings also need help. We can take care of our physical needs of food, clothing and shelter, but we need God to help us with our sinful nature, our sin problem.

Sin entered the world through Adam. That sin took away man's peace with God. To restore that peace God sent Jesus. Jesus suffered the punishment for our sins.

I Pet 3:18a *For Christ died for sins once for all, the righteous for the unrighteous, to bring you to God.* **I Pet 3:18b** *He was put to death in the body but made alive by the Spirit.*

God knew that Adam would sin. He had a plan for making Adam, and not just Adam, but every person, at peace with God again. God would send his own son to save us.

Rom 5:19a *For just as through the disobedience of the one man the many were made sinners,* **Rom 5:19b** *so also through the obedience of the one man the many will be made righteous.*

Adam passed on his sin to all men. Jesus made a way for all people to get right again with God. People need to trust Jesus as their Savior in order to have their sins taken away.

Just like the guinea pig couldn't get down by himself, we can't be forgiven by God without Jesus.

JANUARY 3

Spiritually Dead

When God placed Adam and Eve in the garden they enjoyed God's creation. God said he was giving them the plants so they would have plenty to eat. The garden was a beautiful place to live.

Adam and Eve were warned by God not to eat the fruit of one tree in the garden.

Gen 2:17 *But you must not eat from the tree of the knowledge of good and evil, for when you eat of it you will surely die.*

Eve did eat fruit from that tree. Then she told Adam that he should try it also. Adam ate some fruit. God said they would die if they ate the fruit. Adam and Eve did not die physically as soon as they ate the fruit, but they died spiritually. How does someone die spiritually?

When God created Adam and Eve they enjoyed the blessing of God's presence. Life was wonderful and they were happy. God gave them a test to see if they would obey him. They failed the test and then they were not happy any more. They felt ashamed because of what they had done. They even hid from God. To be spiritually dead means that something—sin—stands between us and God. When Adam and Eve disobeyed God they died spiritually. They were no longer at peace with God.

The apostle Paul talks about how the Ephesians, and all people, are spiritually dead because Adam passed sin on to us.

Eph 2:1 *As for you, you were dead in your transgressions* and sins.*

Eph 2:4-5 *But because of his great love for us, God, who is rich in mercy, made us alive with Christ even when we were dead in transgressions—it is by grace you have been saved.*

Paul writes to the Colossians that they were dead in their sins also.

Col 2:13 *When you were dead in your sins and in the uncircumcision of your sinful nature,* God made you alive with Christ. He forgave us all our sins.*

Transgressions—another word for sins—things we do wrong against God
Uncircumcision of your sinful nature—lack of dedication to God

TRUST IN THE LORD

JANUARY 4

Must be Born Again

Many people can recite John 3:16 from memory.

Jn 3:16 *For God so loved the world that he gave his one and only Son, that whoever believes in him shall not perish but have eternal life.*

Do you know who Jesus was talking to when he said those words? It was Nicodemus. Nicodemus was a Pharisee. That means he was a religious leader for the Jews. He would be like one of our pastors today.

Nicodemus heard Jesus teach and he saw the crowds that came to Jesus for healing. He wanted to know more about Jesus.

Jn 3:2 *He came to Jesus at night and said, "Rabbi, we know you are a teacher who has come from God. For no one could perform the miraculous signs you are doing if God were not with him."*

After Nicodemus said that, Jesus told him that a person needs to be born again before they can see the Kingdom of God. Nicodemus tried to picture in his mind how a man could be born again. He asks Jesus that question.

Jn 3:4 *"How can a man be born when he is old?" Nicodemus asked. "Surely he cannot enter a second time into his mother's womb to be born!"*

Jesus was patient and explained that babies are born physically from their mothers, but all people need to be born spiritually. That is something you can't see; it happens in a person's spirit. Nicodemus had another question for Jesus.

Jn 3:9 *"How can this be?" Nicodemus asked.*

Jesus was a little disappointed that Nicodemus didn't understand this. He was a religious leader and should know about these things. Jesus explained how he would suffer and die for people's sins. He told Nicodemus that anyone who believes in him will be born again spiritually.

JANUARY 5

Repent

Jesus came to earth to take away the sin that we inherited from Adam. He came to give us a way to be at peace again with God. He came to make us spiritually alive.

When Jesus suffered and died on the cross he took on himself the punishment for our sins. The Bible says that God loved us so much that he gave his only son. That son is Jesus. The Bible says whoever believes in Jesus will have eternal life.

Much of the New Testament tells us that trusting in Jesus is what we need to do to get into heaven. Eph 2:8 says it is by God's grace that we are saved through faith.

However, Jesus and the apostles also preached a message of repentance. Repentance means that we have a complete change in the way we think about our sin and about God. We must understand that we have a sinful nature and that we need God's help. Peter preached that message to the people. The people knew what Peter said was true. They asked Peter what they should do next.

Acts 2:38 *Peter replied, "Repent and be baptized, every one of you, in the name of Jesus Christ for the forgiveness of your sins. And you will receive the gift of the Holy Spirit."*

When Peter was preaching to another group of people he told them to repent also.

Acts 3:19 *Repent, then, and turn to God, so that your sins may be wiped out, that times of refreshing may come from the Lord.*

Paul preached that all people need to repent.

Acts 17:30 *In the past God overlooked such ignorance, but now he commands all people everywhere to repent.*

Acts 26:20 *First to those in Damascus, then to those in Jerusalem and in all Judea, and to the Gentiles* also, I preached that they should repent and turn to God and prove their repentance by their deeds.*

When we repent, we tell God we are sorry for our sins. Then we promise God that we will try to live the way he wants us to.

Gentiles—non-Jews—Jews thought of themselves as God's people and of Gentiles as not God's people

JANUARY 6

A New Heart
Marigny

If anyone is thrifty, it's Mommy Marigny. Reyne watched her mom pick up trash, clean it up good, and actually use it. So when Reyne found a beanie bear down in a culvert* she knew it could be her toy. She took it home and sure enough, Mommy got it to looking nice.

What Reyne's mom did for that beanie bear is what God wants to do for every person in the world. God wants to clean people up. He does that by forgiving their sins. God also wants to make them part of his family by putting his Holy Spirit in them.

Eze 36:25 *I will sprinkle clean water on you, and you will be clean; I will cleanse you from all your impurities and from all your idols.*

In this passage God is prophesying through Ezekiel. He says that he will clean the people up; he will forgive them.

Eze 36:26 *I will give you a new heart and put a new spirit in you; I will remove from you your heart of stone and give you a heart of flesh.*

God doesn't just want to clean people up; He wants to give people a new heart and spirit.

When Jesus came he had the same message of forgiveness. Nicodemus was a good man, but he wanted to know more. Jesus told him what he needed to do.

Jn 3:3 *In reply Jesus declared, "I tell you the truth, no one can see the kingdom of God unless he is born again."*

When a person is born again he receives God's forgiveness.

Acts 13:38 *Therefore, my brothers, I want you to know that through Jesus the forgiveness of sins is proclaimed to you.*

Culvert—a drain crossing under a road

JANUARY 7

Temples of the Spirit

Paul wrote to the people in Corinth these verses:

I Cor 3:16 *Don't you know that you yourselves are God's temple and that God's Spirit lives in you?*

I Cor 6:19 *Do you not know that your body is a temple of the Holy Spirit, who is in you, whom you have received from God? You are not your own.*

What does the Bible mean when it says that your body is a temple of the Holy Spirit?

When you ask Jesus to be your Savior you come to life spiritually. At that moment the Holy Spirit comes to live inside of you. Because God's Spirit is holy, the place where the Holy Spirit lives is also holy.

In the Old Testament, God told Moses to have the people build a tabernacle for God.

Ex 25:8 *Then have them make a sanctuary for me, and I will dwell among them.*

God planned to be present in this tabernacle; it was a holy place set apart for God. All God's people would live in tents around it. Later Solomon planned to build a temple for God. Solomon said the temple would be great.

II Chr 2:5 *The temple I am going to build will be great, because our God is greater than all other gods.*

In the Old Testament the tabernacle and temple were places that people could come to get close to God. People could experience God's presence there.

Today God's presence, his Holy Spirit, is in each person that has asked Jesus to be his Savior. That is why Paul said your body is a temple of the Holy Spirit.

JANUARY

8

A Brood of Vipers

When Jesus lived on the earth he made the Pharisees upset with him. The Pharisees were the people who studied the Scriptures. They tried to live according to God's law. You would think that they would have welcomed Jesus. But no! They were jealous of him and even wanted to stop his preaching. Jesus called the Pharisees "a brood of vipers." A brood is a group of animals born at the same time. Vipers are poisonous snakes. Listen to what Jesus said to the Pharisees:

Mt 12:34 *You brood of vipers, how can you who are evil say anything good? For out of the overflow of the heart the mouth speaks.*

Mt 23:33 *You snakes! You brood of vipers! How will you escape being condemned to hell?*

John the Baptist also called the Pharisees vipers.

Mt 3:7 *But when he saw many of the Pharisees and Sadducees coming to where he was baptizing, he said to them: "You brood of vipers! Who warned you to flee from the coming wrath?"*

In Jesus' time the Jews were expecting the Messiah to come. Because the Pharisees studied God's Word they should have known that Jesus was the Messiah. Jesus told the Jews that they studied the Scriptures, but didn't understand them.

Jn 5:39-40 *You diligently study the Scriptures because you think that by them you possess eternal life. These are the Scriptures that testify about me, yet you refuse to come to me to have life.*

Eternal life is available for those who come to Jesus and ask him for it. Most people learn about this eternal life by listening to the preaching of God's Word. Unfortunately the Pharisees, even though they studied God's Word, did not understand it. Jesus called them vipers. They were evil and refused to believe in him. They missed God's plan for their lives.

Have you asked that Jesus be the ruler and master of your life?

JANUARY 9

God's Family
Marigny

When the Marignys were stationed in Germany, the local towns would often sponsor Volksmarches. People, in groups or alone, would register at the beginning point. They were shown the pathway to begin walking. There were signs along the way telling everyone where to turn. The walks were usually five or ten kilometers, which is about three and six miles respectively. You could run them if you wanted to. At the end of the Volksmarch you could gather in the tent and buy souvenirs or food.

The marches were a very fun time to get the family away and do something together. On one march our family sang the song, "I'm So Glad I'm a Part of the Family of God." (Sing it together if you know it).

We become a part of God's family when we ask Jesus to be our Savior. At that time God's Holy Spirit comes to live inside of us. The following passage tells about our relationship to God. You become God's child when you trust Jesus to be your Savior.

Rom 8:14 *because those who are led by the Spirit of God are sons of God.*

We let the Holy Spirit lead us to do good deeds.

Rom 8:15 *For you did not receive a spirit that makes you a slave again to fear, but you received the Spirit of sonship. And by him we cry, "Abba, Father."*

We can call God "Father" when we become part of his family.

Rom 8:16 *The Spirit himself testifies with our spirit that we are God's children.*

If God is our father, then we are his children.

Rom 8:17 *Now if we are children, then we are heirs—heirs of God and co-heirs with Christ, if indeed we share in his sufferings in order that we may also share in his glory.*

"Heirs" are "those who will inherit." Parents often leave an inheritance to their children; it can be money or property. Because the parents owned those things the children can inherit them from their parents. As God's children, we are heirs of heaven; heaven is "our inheritance" from God.

JANUARY 10

Like Father, Like Daughter
Marigny

On one of the Volksmarches that the Marignys walked, Daddy pulled up some wheat grass. The seed head is attached to a stalk which pulls away from the plant; this stalk is tender. Daddy put the tender part in his mouth and chewed on it.

Rachael pulled a stalk of wheat grass. She put it in her mouth and chewed on it just like Daddy. Later when Daddy pulled up his socks to mid-calf Rachael did the same. Because most of the family had shorts on you could really notice how Rachael looked like Daddy.

God wants to change each of us so that we become more like our heavenly Father, more like him each day.

II Cor 3:18 *And we, who with unveiled faces all reflect the Lord's glory, are being transformed into his likeness with ever-increasing glory, which comes from the Lord, who is the Spirit.*

When we accept Christ, God begins changing us so we act more and more like him.

Paul tells the Colossian Christians that before they believed in Jesus they were doing bad things. Now that they are Christians they should stop doing those things.

Col 3:8 *But now you must rid yourselves of all such things as these: anger, rage, malice, slander, and filthy language from your lips.* **Col 3:9** *Do not lie to each other, since you have taken off your old self with its practices.*

Paul said they should put on the new self, they should start being more like God.

Col 3:10 *and have put on the new self, which is being renewed in knowledge in the image of its Creator.*

Rachael wanted to be just like her Daddy. Christians should want to be just like God.

JANUARY 11

Glorify God in Sports

Kyle loved baseball. His dad had coached his team ever since T-ball. Kyle was a good hitter and he played first base. Kyle got a new glove for Christmas. He made sure he cleaned it after the games. He used a certain type of oil on it to help the leather stay soft. He also put his glove under his mattress at night so that it would close easily over the balls he caught. Kyle loved baseball. Is it possible that Kyle loved baseball too much?

The apostle Paul warns us that people can become very self-centered. He says that in the last days people will be **II Tim 3:4** *treacherous, rash, conceited, lovers of pleasure rather than lovers of God.*

God tells us we should love him more than anything else.

Deut 6:5 *Love the Lord your God with all your heart and with all your soul and with all your strength.*

When someone asked Jesus what the greatest commandment was, Jesus said it was to love God.

Mt 22:37 *Jesus replied: "Love the Lord your God with all your heart and with all your soul and with all your mind."*

How can Kyle make sure that he doesn't love baseball more than he loves God? A good question Kyle can ask himself is: "Am I trying to please God when I play baseball?" God can be honored in all that we do.

I Cor 10:31 *So whether you eat or drink or whatever you do, do it all for the glory of God.*

Kyle can play ball for God's glory. He can be a good sport. He can encourage his teammates. He can control his temper when he makes a bad play. He can forgive his teammates when they make a bad play. He can even help around the house so his parents can come watch his games. In all these ways God will be glorified with Kyle's playing baseball.

JANUARY
12

Saved Eternally
Marigny

When the Marignys lived in northern California they had a chance to experience the aftershock of an earthquake. The girls were playing outside. They said they saw the hanging plants on their friend's house swing back and forth. Nothing was damaged in our area, but a big overpass on the highway in southern California had been broken by the quake.

There is a story in the Bible about an earthquake:

People said Paul and Silas were teaching the citizens of Rome things that were unlawful. The city government believed these people. Paul and Silas were stripped, beaten and put in prison.

Acts 16:25-26 *About midnight Paul and Silas were praying and singing hymns to God, and the other prisoners were listening to them. Suddenly there was such a violent earthquake that the foundations of the prison were shaken. At once all the prison doors flew open, and everybody's chains came loose.* **Acts 16:27-28** *The jailer woke up, and when he saw the prison doors open, he drew his sword and was about to kill himself because he thought the prisoners had escaped. But Paul shouted, "Don't harm yourself! We are all here!"*

Acts 16:29-30 *The jailer called for lights, rushed in and fell trembling before Paul and Silas. He then brought them out and asked, "Sirs, what must I do to be saved?"*

Acts 16:31 & 34 *They replied, "Believe in the Lord Jesus, and you will be saved—you and your household." (34) The jailer brought them into his house and set a meal before them; he was filled with joy because he had come to believe in God—he and his whole family.*

When the jailer asked what he needed to do to be saved, he may have just been asking what he needed to do to be saved from the destruction of the earthquake. Paul told them what they needed to do to be saved spiritually. Paul told them to believe in the Lord Jesus. The jailer did what Paul said. That day the jailer's family all became Christians. They were safe not only from the earthquake but safe from eternal loss.

JANUARY 13

Saved From What?

Jesus is called the Savior of the world. What does Jesus save people from? Jesus saves people from their sins.

The angel Gabriel appeared to Joseph. He told Joseph that the baby Mary would have was conceived by the Holy Spirit. He told Joseph that Mary would have a son. He also told Joseph what name to give the baby.

Mt 1:21 *She will give birth to a son, and you are to give him the name Jesus, because he will save his people from their sins.*

Jesus saves us from our sins. Paul preached that forgiveness of sins comes from Jesus.

Acts 13:38 *Therefore, my brothers, I want you to know that through Jesus the forgiveness of sins is proclaimed to you.*

Jesus saves us from God's anger. God is angry with those who reject the truth and follow evil.

Rom 2:8 *But for those who are self-seeking and who reject the truth and follow evil, there will be wrath and anger.*

Jesus saves us from the fear of death. In Hebrews we read that Jesus died so that he might destroy the devil **Heb 2:15** *and free those who all their lives were held in slavery by their fear of death.*

Many people are afraid to die because they don't know what is going to happen to them. When we believe in Jesus he promises that we have a home in heaven. We don't need to be afraid, because we are saved by Jesus.

Jesus saves us from our sins; he saves us from God's anger; and he saves us from the fear of death.

JANUARY 14
God Created All People

Who is Martin Luther King, Jr.? He was an African-American preacher who was a civil rights leader. As a civil rights leader, Reverend King, also known as Dr. King, worked to get black people the same rights as white people.

There was a time when slavery was legal in America. African-Americans were slaves and were not considered citizens. Some people, because they "owned" their slaves, thought that slaves were property, not human beings equal to themselves.

Martin Luther King saw that black people could not go a lot of places and do certain things because of their skin color. For example, they were not allowed in some restaurants; they had to sit at the back of busses; and they were not allowed to attend certain schools. Dr. King worked hard to change this segregation—separation of the races.

Dr. King believed that African-American people, just like white people, were created by God. The Bible teaches this is true.

Gen 1:27 *So God created man in his own image, in the image of God he created him; male and female he created them.*

God says in the Book of Isaiah that he wants his people to come together, then he addresses them: **Isa 43:7** *everyone who is called by my name, whom I created for my glory, whom I formed and made.*

God has created all people. He formed them; he made them.

Rev 4:11 *You are worthy, our Lord and God, to receive glory and honor and power, for you created all things, and by your will they were created and have their being.*

Ps 100:3 *Know that the Lord is God. It is he who made us, and we are his; we are his people, the sheep of his pasture.*

God created all things. He created every person on earth.

JANUARY 15

Men Who Trusted God

Martin Luther King, Jr. was a very bright young man. He skipped 9th grade and 12th grade, and entered college at the age of 15. He finished college and was ordained a minister when he was only 19. After seven more years of school he had a Ph.D., an advanced and prestigious* [press *tij* us] degree, in theology.

Reverend King spent most of his after-school years working for equal rights. In his time there were laws saying people must remain separate. Dr. King helped to get those laws changed. The Civil Rights Act of 1964 gave black people some of the same opportunities as white people. African-Americans could go to white schools and work at jobs that used to be only for whites. The new law said black people should be treated equally in public places. Dr. King also worked hard to get African-Americans the right to vote.

Under the policy of segregation black people were not allowed these basic rights. They were treated like they were less valuable than white people. But Martin Luther King knew "that all men are created equal."

Martin Luther King, Jr. changed our nation for good in a big way. It was not easy, but he knew it was right. Isaiah prophesied the same thing. He knew he was doing the right thing and trusted God would take care of him.

Isa 50:7 *Because the Sovereign LORD helps me, I will not be disgraced. Therefore have I set my face like flint, and I know I will not be put to shame.*

Isa 50:8 *He who vindicates me is near. Who then will bring charges against me? Let us face each other! Who is my accuser? Let him confront me!*

Isa 50:9 *It is the Sovereign LORD who helps me. Who is he that will condemn me? They will all wear out like a garment; the moths will eat them up.*

Isa 50:10 *Who among you fears the LORD and obeys the word of his servant? Let him who walks in the dark, who has no light, trust in the name of the LORD and rely on his God.*

Prestigious—important in the eyes of other people

TRUST IN THE LORD

JANUARY
16
All May be One

Jamal, an African-American boy, played left field. He noticed something about his little league team. When they weren't on the field all the black boys stood at one end of the dugout and all the white boys stood on the other. When he looked at the parents who came to the games it was almost the same way; the African-American parents and fans sat together and the white parents and fans visited with each other. Jamal wondered why the fans and players on his little league team chose to separate themselves from each other.

Jamal's Sunday School teacher had taught him that Jesus prayed for all of his disciples to be one. He prayed: **Jn 17:21** *that all of them may be one, Father, just as you are in me and I am in you. May they also be in us so that the world may believe that you have sent me.* **Jn 17:22** *I have given them the glory that you gave me, that they may be one as we are one:* **Jn 17:23** *I in them and you in me. May they be brought to complete unity to let the world know that you sent me and have loved them even as you have loved me.*

Jamal didn't see much unity among the players even though most of them went to church. Jamal had an idea. He liked Tanner, the boy that played second base. He decided that he would try to get to know Tanner. Every practice and game Jamal made sure he spoke to Tanner. Over the years the boys became best friends; they spent most of their free time together.

Jamal noticed that some other friendships on their ball team also crossed the color lines.

Jamal changed his community for good. Jamal decided to live God's way; he tried doing what his Sunday School teacher had taught him. He was a doer of the Word, not just a hearer of it.

Jas 1:22 *Do not merely listen to the word, and so deceive yourselves. Do what it says.*

JANUARY 17

Every Thought Captive

Jesus tells us that we are supposed to love him with "all our mind."

Mt 22:37 *Jesus replied: "Love the Lord your God with all your heart and with all your soul and with all your mind."*

How do we love God with "all our mind?" The Apostle Paul says we should take our thoughts captive and make them obedient to Christ.

II Cor 10:5 *We demolish arguments and every pretension that sets itself up against the knowledge of God, and we take captive every thought to make it obedient to Christ.*

Our minds are one of God's most wonderful creations. We can learn and think about thousands of different things and ideas. Paul says we should take captive every thought and make it obedient to Christ. How does that happen?

It should begin when we first wake up in the morning. We can think to ourselves, "Thank you, God, that I am alive today. Help me to do my best for you." That is committing your day to God. Your family might pray together at breakfast.

Studying might be part of your daily schedule. You should ask that God help you have a clear mind so you can learn. When you are not using your mind to study or to read you can turn your mind back to God. If you are doing chores that you don't need to concentrate on, you can put your mind back on God.

Prov 3:5 *Trust in the LORD with all your heart and lean not on your own understanding;*

Prov 3:6 *in all your ways acknowledge him, and he will make your paths straight.*

This scripture tells us to acknowledge God in all we do. We can end our day with this prayer, "Thank you for this day, God. I'm sorry for those things I did that were not pleasing to you. Thank you for helping me do the good things I did. I love you, God. Good night!"

JANUARY 18

Young and Committed
Bible

Timothy was in charge of the church at Ephesus.

I Tim 1:3 *As I urged you when I went into Macedonia, stay there in Ephesus so that you may command certain men not to teach false doctrines any longer.*

Timothy was a young man and yet God had placed him as a leader in the church.

The apostle Paul wrote Timothy two letters, I Timothy and II Timothy. In the first letter he said,

I Tim 4:12 *Don't let anyone look down on you because you are young, but set an example for the believers in speech, in life, in love, in faith and in purity.*

Even though Timothy was young, Paul told him that he could be a good example. Young people can sometimes hear from God even better than older people. If our hearts are open to God, he will make himself known to us. In fact, God is looking for people with receptive hearts.

II Chr 16:9a *For the eyes of the LORD range throughout the earth to strengthen those whose hearts are fully committed to him.*

When God was looking around for someone fully committed to him, God found Timothy.

Ever since he was a baby, Timothy's mother and grandmother had taught him about the scriptures.

II Tim 3:15 *And how from infancy you have known the holy Scriptures, which are able to make you wise for salvation through faith in Christ Jesus.*

Timothy was a Christian for most of his life. He was called by God to preach when he was a young man.

If we give ourselves to God, he will show us how we can best serve him. If we give ourselves to God when we are young, God can use us to accomplish great things.

JANUARY 19

Growing Spiritually

There is a children's song that goes like this:
>Read your Bible, pray every day and you'll grow, grow, grow.
>Read your Bible, pray every day and you'll grow, grow, grow.
>And you'll grow, grow, grow, and you'll grow, grow, grow.
>Read your Bible, pray every day and you'll grow, grow, grow!

Forget your Bible, forget to pray, and you'll shrink, shrink, shrink.
Forget your Bible, forget to pray, and you'll shrink, shrink, shrink.
And you'll shrink, shrink, shrink, and you'll shrink, shrink, shrink.
Forget your Bible, forget to pray, and you'll shrink, shrink, shrink!

When we become Christians we begin a relationship with God. It is like we have found a new best friend. If we want to get to know someone, we spend time with them. We talk to them and they talk to us. Sometimes we don't say anything; we just spend time together.

It is the same way with God as our best friend. We talk to God by praying, and we listen to God by reading his Word. Sometimes we just sit quietly in his presence.

God wants us to tell him what is happening in our lives.

Ps 62:8 *Trust in him at all times, O people; pour out your hearts to him, for God is our refuge.*

God wants our minds to be thinking about him. If we read his Word and memorize it we can meditate on it throughout the day. Psalm 1 says a person is blessed if he delights in God's law.

Ps 1:2 *But his delight is in the law of the Lord, and on his law he meditates day and night.*

Ps 119:97 *Oh, how I love your law! I meditate on it all day long.*

Psalm 46 reminds us to be quiet before God.

Ps 46:10a *Be still, and know that I am God.*

We grow as Christians by praying, reading God's Word, and sitting quietly before God.

JANUARY
20

Big Problems
Rochman

When the Rochman's baby, Elise, was seven months old, they noticed how she wasn't sitting up like other babies did at that age. A lady came to the house to see what Elise could and could not do. She said Elise should: be sitting up, be able to pick things up with her fingers and be able to say consonant sounds. Baby Elise could do none of those things.

Over the next four months the Rochmans took Elise to see many doctors and specialists. The Rochmans were told their baby had Tay Sachs [*tay* sacks]. This disease usually causes the child's death before it reaches the age of five. Because there is no treatment or cure for Tay Sachs, the Rochmans were devastated. They could not bear to think of losing their baby. Kerri, Elise's mom, used a scripture when she emailed people the news. Jesus said to his disciples:

Jn 14:1 *Do not let your hearts be troubled. Trust in God; trust also in me.*

Life is not always easy, but God can be trusted.

David trusted firmly in God.

Ps 108:1 *My heart is steadfast, O God; I will sing and make music with all my soul.*

David rejoiced that God answered his prayers.

Ps 34:4 *I sought the Lord, and he answered me; he delivered me from all my fears.*

When we face troubles too big for us, God is there for us.

Ps 46:1 *God is our refuge and strength, an ever-present help in trouble.*

JANUARY

God Protected David

21

Heidi wished that she was not so different from the other kids in her class. She was the only one who had a daddy in the National Guard. He had to go to Iraq. Life was lonely and strange when he was gone.

Heidi's little brothers always used to wrestle with their daddy. Now, a lot of times they would just get into fights. It didn't seem fair that Daddy had to be away.

Mommy tried to help Heidi understand. She said that many times in the Bible God's people were sent to fight. David loved God, and yet he fought many battles. David often asked God for advice on what to do. Three times we can read how God answered David:

I Sam 30:8 *And David inquired of the LORD, "Shall I pursue this raiding party? Will I overtake them?"*

"Pursue them," he answered. "You will certainly overtake them and succeed in the rescue."

II Sam 5:19 *So David inquired of the LORD, "Shall I go and attack the Philistines? Will you hand them over to me?"*

The LORD answered him, "Go, for I will surely hand the Philistines over to you."

II Sam 5:23 *So David inquired of the LORD, and he answered, "Do not go straight up, but circle around behind them and attack them in front of the balsam trees.* **II Sam 5:24-25** *As soon as you hear the sound of marching in the tops of the balsam trees, move quickly, because that will mean the LORD has gone out in front of you to strike the Philistine army." So David did as the LORD commanded him, and he struck down the Philistines all the way from Gibeon to Gezer.*

Mommy told Heidi that God watched over David, and God would watch over Daddy, too.

JANUARY
22
God's Care of Joseph
Bible

Joseph was not well-liked by his brothers. In fact, because of dreams he had, they thought he acted like a big shot. Joseph's dad, Jacob, favored Joseph over his brothers. The brothers got to the point where they did not like Joseph one bit!

Joseph's brothers sold him to the Ishmaelites [*ish* male ites] as a slave. Though Joseph may have been lonely, he continued to trust in God. In Egypt, the Ishmaelites sold Joseph to Potiphar [*pot* ih fer], one of Pharaoh's [*fare* ohz] officials. The story about Joseph is found in Genesis.

Gen 39:2-3 *The Lord was with Joseph and he prospered, and he lived in the house of his Egyptian master. When his master saw that the Lord was with him and that the Lord gave him success in everything he did,* **Gen 39:4** *Joseph found favor in his eyes and became his attendant. Potiphar put him in charge of his household, and he entrusted to his care everything he owned.*

Potiphar's wife tried to get Joseph to do something he shouldn't. When he wouldn't do it, Potiphar's wife lied. Because of the lie of Potiphar's wife, Joseph was sent to prison. Even in prison God blessed Joseph.

Gen 39:20b-21 *But while Joseph was there in the prison, the Lord was with him; he showed him kindness and granted him favor in the eyes of the prison warden.* **Gen 39:22-23** *So the warden put Joseph in charge of all those held in the prison, and he was made responsible for all that was done there. The warden paid no attention to anything under Joseph's care, because the Lord was with Joseph and gave him success in whatever he did.*

God looked out for Joseph when he was sold as a slave, and even when he was unjustly sent to prison.

No matter how bad things are, God will look out for us if we trust him.

JANUARY 23

Trust God!

Allison's Daddy was only forty-five when he had a stroke. That meant she and her four brothers and sisters were going to have some big changes in their home. Daddy couldn't work anymore because he was no longer able to walk; he sat in a wheelchair. What was the family going to do?

None of us want bad things to happen to us or to the people we love, but sometimes those things do happen. At those times people often feel like God doesn't know or care about them. God does know; he knows all things.

Ps 139:1 *O Lord, you have searched me and you know me.*

Ps 139:3 *You discern my going out and my lying down; you are familiar with all my ways.*

To "discern" means to "know." God knows all about us. He knows when we leave our houses. He knows when we go to bed. He knows that Allison's daddy is in a wheelchair. He knows Allison and her family are sad and worried about what will happen. God knows everything about Allison's family, and he wants them to trust him.

Ps 56:3 *When I am afraid, I will trust in you.*

Ps 25:4-5 *Show me your ways, O Lord, teach me your paths; guide me in your truth and teach me, for you are God my Savior, and my hope is in you all day long.*

Allison is worried about what will happen to her family. She wishes things could go back to the way they were before, but they can't. Allison can put her trust in God and then watch to see how God will take care of them.

JANUARY
24

How God Sees Us
Marigny

Dads are good at giving their children pet names. Pet names usually come from how a child looks or acts or from a time when the father and child shared an event. Kerri didn't have a pet name and wanted one so Daddy asked her, "How's, 'Gumdrop?'" Gladys was called "Bug" because she used to catch green bugs that were common in Italy. Rachael was called, "D" from a movie she and her dad watched, and Reyne was "Skinny Minny" for her thinness as a little girl.

Do any of you have pet names? God gave several people in the Bible new names. Each of these new names meant something, so you might say they were pet names that God gave to people. God gave Abram the title of "father of a multitude" or "Abraham."

Gen 17:5 *No longer will you be called Abram; your name will be Abraham, for I have made you a father of many nations.*

"Abraham" was like a "pet name;" it meant "father of a multitude." This was a name change for Abraham. God changed Abraham's wife's name to Sarah, which means "princess."

Gen 17:15 *God also said to Abraham, "As for Sarai [say rye] your wife, you are no longer to call her Sarai; her name will be Sarah."*

God also changed Jacob's name to "Israel," which means "ruling with God."

Gen 32:28 *Then the man said, "Your name will no longer be Jacob, but Israel, because you have struggled with God and with men and have overcome."*

God called Gideon a "mighty warrior."

Judg 6:12 *When the angel of the Lord appeared to Gideon, he said, "The Lord is with you, mighty warrior."*

I bet none of your pet names are "father of a multitude," "ruling with God," or "mighty warrior." Some of you might be "princess," though.

Your Name?

JANUARY 25

God changed some people's names in the Old Testament. We can also find some names that were given to people in the New Testament.

Jesus gave Simon the name "Cephas" [*see* fuss], in Aramaic [air uh *may* ik], or "Peter," in Greek. These names mean "a rock." In Jn 1:42 Andrew brought Simon to Jesus.

Jn 1:42 *And he brought him to Jesus. Jesus looked at him and said, "You are Simon son of John. You will be called Cephas" (which, when translated, is Peter).*

When Jesus changed Simon's name to Peter, it was like calling him "Rocky" or saying, "You will be strong."

On a different day, Jesus called James and John the "Sons of Thunder."

Mk 3:17 *James son of Zebedee and his brother John (to them he gave the name Boanerges* [boh uh *ner* jehz]*, which means Sons of Thunder).*

These names probably came from the time the Samaritans would not welcome Jesus into their village. James and John asked if they should call down fire from heaven.

Lk 9:54 *When the disciples James and John saw this, they asked, "Lord, do you want us to call fire down from heaven to destroy them?"*

The man we know as Barnabas used to have a different name. His name was Joseph. Because he was good at encouraging people, the apostles called him "Barnabas."

Acts 4:36 *Joseph, a Levite from Cyprus, whom the apostles called Barnabas (which means Son of Encouragement).*

Would you like to be called, "Rock," "Son of Thunder," or "Son of Encouragement?" Peter was probably encouraged when Jesus called him "Rock" and said he would be strong. James and John were zealous—fired up, and Barnabas was an encouragement to others.

What name do you think God might give to you?

JANUARY
26
Count on God

When Reyne and Rachael were very young they had blankets that they took everywhere they went. The girls liked the feel of the slippery tags on the blankets. Rachael sucked her thumb and Reyne sucked her two middle fingers. While they sucked on their thumb or fingers on their right hand they would feel the slipperiness of the tag in their left hand.

Mommy knew the girls liked tags so she sewed an extra one on each of their blankets. They carried these blankets with them. Whenever they got tired it was important to have their blankets ready.

Those blankets gave the girls a sense of security. Children feel secure when they know their parents, or their blankets, will be there when they need them.

God promises to be there for us when we need him.

Heb 13:5b *because God has said, "Never will I leave you; never will I forsake you."*

In Jacob's dream God told him, **Gen 28:15** *I am with you and will watch over you wherever you go, and I will bring you back to this land. I will not leave you until I have done what I have promised you.*

When the Israelites were about to invade the land of Canaan [*kay* nun], God told Moses that he shouldn't be afraid of the Canaanites [*kay* nuh nites]: **Deut 31:6** *Be strong and courageous. Do not be afraid or terrified because of them, for the* LORD *your God goes with you; he will never leave you nor forsake you.*

God spoke those same words to Joshua: **Josh 1:5** *No one will be able to stand up against you all the days of your life. As I was with Moses, so I will be with you; I will never leave you nor forsake you.*

Because God promises never to leave us, we can trust him to take care of us.

JANUARY
27

Fear Not
Marigny

When twins Reyne and Rachael were almost three years old their whole family flew from Germany to the States. A stewardess asked them to sit in their own seats on the plane. Because they were "Mama's babies" they started crying. Mommy reassured them that they would be OK, but the girls didn't think so. Their whimpers became all-out screams. The girls wanted their mother and they wanted the tags on their blankets. They yelled, "Mommy, Mommy, two-tag, two-tag, Ahhhh!"

The stewardess had to give in so that everyone on the plane wouldn't have to listen to the screaming. One of the girls sat on Mommy's lap, and the other one sat beside her.

When children are very young they are often very attached to their parents. The twins were scared to be separated from their mother. Sometimes we let fear control us, but God says our trust should be in him.

Isa 43:1 *But now, this is what the* LORD *says—he who created you, O Jacob, he who formed you, O Israel: "Fear not, for I have redeemed you; I have summoned you by name; you are mine.* **Isa 43:2** *When you pass through the waters, I will be with you; and when you pass through the rivers, they will not sweep over you. When you walk through the fire, you will not be burned; the flames will not set you ablaze."*

Isa 44:2 *This is what the* LORD *says—he who made you, who formed you in the womb, and who will help you: Do not be afraid, O Jacob, my servant, Jeshurun [jesh you run], whom I have chosen.*

Jeshurun is another name for God's people.

Lk 12:6-7 *Are not five sparrows sold for two pennies? Yet not one of them is forgotten by God. Indeed, the very hairs of your head are all numbered. Don't be afraid; you are worth more than many sparrows.*

God is faithful; if we trust him, he'll take care of us.

TRUST IN THE LORD

JANUARY
28

He Trusted God
Bible

Jehoshaphat [jeh *hosh* uh fat] was a king of Judah who found himself with a big problem. Some men came and told him that a huge army was coming to fight against him. The king asked everyone to fast and the people came to the temple in Jerusalem to pray. The king stood in front of the people and prayed. The spirit of God came on a prophet named Jahaziel [juh *hay* zih ul]. He began to speak.

II Chr 20:15 *He said: "Listen, King Jehoshaphat and all who live in Judah and Jerusalem! This is what the LORD says to you: 'Do not be afraid or discouraged because of this vast army. For the battle is not yours, but God's.'"*

II Chr 20:17 *"'You will not have to fight this battle. Take up your positions; stand firm and see the deliverance the LORD will give you, O Judah and Jerusalem. Do not be afraid; do not be discouraged. Go out to face them tomorrow, and the LORD will be with you.'"*

That was the message the prophet spoke. The next morning the king told the people to have faith in God. He put people in the front of the army singing praises to God. They didn't even need to fight that day. The soldiers coming against them began turning on each other until they were destroyed.

II Chr 20:24 *When the men of Judah came to the place that overlooks the desert and looked toward the vast army, they saw only dead bodies lying on the ground; no one had escaped.* **II Chr 20:25** *So Jehoshaphat and his men went to carry off their plunder,* and they found among them a great amount of equipment and clothing and also articles of value—more than they could take away. There was so much plunder that it took three days to collect it.*

Jehoshaphat trusted God when he had a problem. God took care of him.

Plunder—anything taken from the enemy in time of war

JANUARY 29

I'm Bored

Sofia got home from school just in time to get ready for dance lessons. On Mondays, Wednesdays and Fridays she had ballet lessons, and on Tuesdays and Thursdays she had tap lessons. Each evening when she finished her dinner and her homework, she would say, "I'm bored." Mom would try to find something for Sofia to do.

Have you ever heard anyone say that they were bored? Have you ever said that? Children don't always need to be busy. Sometimes it's good just to relax, to read a book, or maybe just to think about God.

When we say we are bored it means that we have nothing to do. We usually want someone to find us something to do, and it better be something fun!

It might be helpful for Sofia to remind herself why she is here. The Apostle Paul says we are here to serve the Lord.

Rom 12:11 *Never be lacking in zeal, but keep your spiritual fervor, serving the Lord.*

Paul gives us another reason why God created us.

Eph 2:10 *For we are God's workmanship, created in Christ Jesus to do good works, which God prepared in advance for us to do.*

God created us so that we could do good works.

When Sofia gets bored she could look for things to do that would make other people happy. She could do something special for her brothers or maybe volunteer to watch her baby sister. She could ask her mother what she could do for her that would be a "good work."

When we are living our lives for God we find contentment.

I Tim 6:6 *But godliness with contentment is great gain.*

I Tim 6:8 *But if we have food and clothing, we will be content with that.*

Being content means we are satisfied. When we say we are bored, we are showing that we are not content. We are unhappy. Instead, we should be content with what God has given us.

JANUARY
30
Think about Good Things

When his dog, Patch, got run over, Tyrone thought he couldn't make it. He was so sad that he didn't want to get out of bed. His mother let him stay there until lunch and then she took a tray to his room, and shared scriptures with him.

Tyrone's mom said she understood his sorrow. She also explained to Tyrone that because Jesus lived on this earth he can understand whatever troubles we go through.

Heb 4:15 *For we do not have a high priest who is unable to sympathize with our weaknesses, but we have one who has been tempted in every way, just as we are—yet was without sin.*

Sometimes people think Jesus doesn't know what it feels like to be sad. When Jesus' good friend, Lazarus, died Jesus was very sad.

Jn 11:35 *Jesus wept.*

Tyrone's mom told Tyrone that God could give him peace if he would trust him:

Isa 26:3 *You will keep in perfect peace him whose mind is steadfast, because he trusts in you.*

Tyrone's mother tried to help her son with this final scripture:

Phil 4:8 *Finally, brothers, whatever is true, whatever is noble, whatever is right, whatever is pure, whatever is lovely, whatever is admirable—if anything is excellent or praiseworthy—think about such things.*

Tyrone's mother suggested he think about good things, maybe even some fun times with Patch. She told him that if thinking about those things made him cry, he should think about good things that were not related to Patch. Tyrone was sad for several days, but by trusting God and thinking about good things he eventually returned to his happy self.

JANUARY

Trust God: Pray

31

Marigny

One day Mrs. Marigny was driving home with three of her daughters. The car was on the interstate and traveling about seventy miles an hour. Mommy didn't know what was happening but for some reason the car started slowing down. It came to a complete stop on the side of the road.

They didn't have a cell phone to call someone, and no one was around to help, so Mommy said, "Girls, let's pray." The four of them bowed their heads as Mommy prayed for the car to start. What do you suppose happened?

Mommy prayed, the car did start, and there were no more problems the rest of the forty miles home.

Now you might be thinking this story is a tall tale, but it really happened!

God wants us to trust him.

Prov 3:5 *Trust in the Lord with all your heart and lean not on your own understanding;*

Prov 3:6 *in all your ways acknowledge him, and he will make your paths straight.*

Prov 3:7 *Do not be wise in your own eyes; fear the Lord and shun* evil.*

Mrs. Marigny could have tried to fix the car herself but that probably wouldn't have worked. Instead she saw this experience as an opportunity to trust God.

A verse in Psalms also talks about trusting in God.

Ps 20:7 *Some trust in chariots and some in horses, but we trust in the name of the Lord our God.*

People put their trust in many different things, but God wants his people to trust in him. The Marignys showed their trust in God by praying. God answered their prayer.

Shun—to avoid or keep away from

FEBRUARY 1

Dressing Modestly

God tells us that everything we do should be done to glorify God.

I Cor 10:31 *So whether you eat or drink or whatever you do, do it all for the glory of God.*

Col 3:17 *And whatever you do, whether in word or deed, do it all in the name of the Lord Jesus, giving thanks to God the Father through him.*

Even the way we dress can glorify God. The Bible tells us how women should dress, and that would include girls.

I Tim 2:9 *I also want women to dress modestly, with decency and propriety, not with braided hair or gold or pearls or expensive clothes,* **I Tim 2:10** *but with good deeds, appropriate for women who profess to worship God.*

Dressing "with propriety" is dressing properly or appropriately. Some ways that girls can dress modestly are:

Wear clothes that cover your lower back even when you bend over.

Wear clothes that cover your stomach even when you turn at the waist or when you raise your arms.

Wear clothes that, when you bend over, people cannot look down your shirt.

Do not wear very short shorts or skirts.

Do not wear very tight-fitting clothes.

Girls, if you follow these rules you will probably be dressed modestly.

In Bible times, maybe men and boys dressed modestly by habit, so we find scripture verses only about women's modest dress. Today, though, some men and boys do not dress modestly. A boy may show off his chest by wearing a tight-fitting tank top, or even no shirt at all. He might wear baggy pants that ride too low, displaying his underwear or bare skin when he sits. Boys, too, should glorify God in how they dress.

God wants us to glorify him in everything we do, even in the way we dress.

FEBRUARY 2

Light: A Symbol of Purity

Light is often a symbol of God's holiness or purity. Let's look at some scriptures that tell us about this light.

When God wanted to get Paul's attention, the Bible says:

Acts 9:3 *As he neared Damascus on his journey, suddenly a* **light** *from heaven flashed around him.* (I emphasized the word "light" by using bold letters.)

Later in his life, Paul writes to Timothy. In a letter, he tells Timothy a little bit about what God is like.

I Tim 6:16 *who alone is immortal and who lives in unapproachable* **light***, whom no one has seen or can see. To him be honor and might forever. Amen.*

Paul says that God lives in unapproachable light. Unapproachable light is light so bright that you can't go near it or even look directly at it. This magnificent light is told about in Matthew 17.

Mt 17:1 *After six days Jesus took with him Peter, James and John the brother of James, and led them up a high mountain by themselves.* **Mt 17:2** *There he was transfigured before them. His face shone like the sun, and his clothes became as white as the* **light***.*

Can you imagine Jesus' face being so bright you couldn't look at it? Can you imagine his clothes being as white as light? Light often is a symbol of God's holiness or purity. God is holy and pure.

FEBRUARY

3

How to Treat Girls

The apostle Paul wrote to Timothy who was a young pastor. Now Timothy was not in elementary school; he was probably in his twenties or thirties, but Paul was older than him and wrote him this advice:

I Tim 4:12 *Don't let anyone look down on you because you are young, but set an example for the believers in speech, in life, in love, in faith and in purity.*

Paul told Timothy to set an example in purity. How does a young man, or a boy, set an example of purity? Probably the best thing you can do is to show respect for women and girls. Don't make fun of them, tease them or look down on them. Be respectful and kind when you talk to them.

In another scripture Paul tells Timothy how to treat others.

I Tim 5:1 *Do not rebuke an older man harshly, but exhort him as if he were your father. Treat younger men as brothers,* **I Tim 5:2** *older women as mothers, and younger women as sisters, with absolute purity.*

Paul says to treat older women like mothers and younger women like sisters. So, if you have women teachers, you should show them respect as if they are someone's mother or even your own. Girls should be treated with respect as if they were your sisters. Paul ends the sentence by saying "with absolute purity." Absolute means complete.

Psalm 119 tells us how young people can live pure lives.

Ps 119:9 *How can a young man keep his way pure? By living according to your word.*

FEBRUARY 4

God's Purity & Glory

Jesus taught us about rising from the dead; that is called "resurrection." We look forward to that day, because then we can go to heaven. I Jn 3:3 says if we have this hope in the resurrection, we should do something.

I Jn 3:3 *Everyone who has this hope in him purifies himself, just as he is pure.*

John says we should purify ourselves even as God is pure.

When someone says God is pure what does that mean? It can mean that God is clean, that God is good, or that God is holy. It can also be a way to describe God's glory.

Some people in the Bible saw some of God's glory. In Exodus, Moses couldn't go into the tabernacle because of God's glory.

Ex 40:35 *Moses could not enter the Tent of Meeting because the cloud had settled upon it, and the glory of the LORD filled the tabernacle.*

Solomon built a temple for God, and God chose to live there. His glory was so wonderful that it filled the temple. The priests were not able to do their work because of God's glory.

I Ki 8:10 *When the priests withdrew from the Holy Place, the cloud filled the temple of the LORD.* **I Ki 8:11** *And the priests could not perform their service because of the cloud, for the glory of the LORD filled his temple.*

People often don't know about God's purity or his glory. The reason we don't experience God's purity or his glory is because we become too interested in things on the earth. If we keep ourselves pure, dedicated to God alone, he will show us his glory.

Wouldn't it be great if God's glory would fill our churches today like it filled the tabernacle and temple in Old Testament times?

FEBRUARY 5

Read & Obey

Yesterday we learned that God is pure. God wants his people to be like him. He wants us to be pure. God tells us that we should purify ourselves.

I Jn 3:3 *Everyone who has this hope in him purifies himself, just as he is pure.*

How do we purify ourselves? We can find the answer in I Peter.

I Pet 1:22 *Now that you have purified yourselves by obeying the truth so that you have sincere love for your brothers, love one another deeply, from the heart.*

Peter tells us that we purify ourselves by obeying the truth. The truth is what we find in God's Word.

When Jesus prayed to God the Father he asked that God would sanctify his disciples. He prayed that God would sanctify them by the truth of his Word.

Jn 17:17 *Sanctify them by the truth; your word is truth.*

"Sanctify" means "to set apart" or "to make holy." Jesus was praying to his Father in heaven. He asked God to make his people holy or pure. He asked God to make us pure with the truth, with God's Word. If we want to be pure we should be reading God's Word every day.

Another scripture that talks about God wanting his people to be holy can be found in the book of Ephesians. This scripture says Jesus loved the church and gave himself up for her. He did this **Eph 5:26** *to make her holy, cleansing her by the washing with water through the word.*

If we want to purify ourselves, we should be reading God's Word and trying to obey it.

God's Word is Perfect

FEBRUARY 6

How can reading and obeying God's Word make us pure? The reason it can make us pure is because God's Word is perfect. In Psalm 19 David says that the law of the Lord is perfect.

Ps 19:7 *The law of the Lord is perfect, reviving the soul. The statutes of the Lord are trustworthy, making wise the simple.*

David says the law of the Lord is perfect.

James also says the law of God is perfect; he says people should look intently into—they should carefully study—the perfect law.

Jas 1:25 *But the man who looks intently into the perfect law that gives freedom, and continues to do this, not forgetting what he has heard, but doing it—he will be blessed in what he does.*

Another word for perfect is flawless. In both Proverbs and Psalms, God's Word is called flawless.

Prov 30:5 *Every word of God is flawless; he is a shield to those who take refuge in him.*

Every word of God is flawless or perfect.

Ps 12:6 *And the words of the Lord are flawless, like silver refined in a furnace of clay, purified seven times.*

When metals are refined that means they are heated until they melt. The impurities are then separated from the metal. The number seven in the Bible is often used as the perfect number. Silver that is refined seven times would be perfect. Psalm 12 says that the words of the Lord are like this silver—they are perfect.

Because God's Word is perfect—flawless, it can make us pure when we read and obey it.

FEBRUARY 7

God is Holy

If someone would describe you, what word would you like them to use? Would you like people to say you are happy, or pretty, or strong, or brave? Which word best describes you? A word that describes God is the word "holy." All through the Bible God is called holy. At the beginning, in the middle and at the end of the Bible, "holy" is a word used by different people to describe God.

Exodus is close to the beginning of the Bible. God is called holy in the Book of Exodus. Moses led the Israelites out of Egypt and then through the Red Sea. When the sea swallowed up Pharaoh [*fare* oh] and his army the people were very excited. Exodus fifteen is a song the people sang in praise to their great God.

Ex 15:11 *Who among the gods is like you, O Lord? Who is like you—majestic in holiness, awesome in glory, working wonders?*

In this song the people said that God was majestic in holiness.

In the middle of the Bible is the book of Isaiah. Isaiah was a prophet, which means he spoke God's word to the people. More than twenty times, God has Isaiah say that God is the "Holy One of Israel." These are two examples:

Isa 12:6 *Shout aloud and sing for joy, people of Zion, for great is the Holy One of Israel among you.*

Isa 48:17 *This is what the Lord says—your Redeemer, the Holy One of Israel: "I am the Lord your God, who teaches you what is best for you, who directs you in the way you should go."*

At the end of the Bible God is still known as a holy God. In the Book of Revelation John tells of a vision he had of heaven. He describes four creatures and he says they never stop saying:

Rev 4:8b *"Holy, holy, holy is the Lord God Almighty, who was, and is, and is to come."*

In the beginning, in the middle and at the end of the Bible, in fact, all through the Bible, God is known as holy. He wants his people to be holy, also.

FEBRUARY 8

Gossiping

Sarah ran into her Sunday School room and blurted out to the other children, "Did you know Marshall got in trouble at school on Friday?" All the other children wanted to know exactly what Marshall did and how he was punished. This is what we call gossip.

When we tell things about someone that might be personal and private we are probably gossiping. When we gossip it can make us feel important because you know something other people don't know. People who listen to gossip are as wrong as the people who tell it. Psalm fifteen, verse one, asks a few questions.

Ps 15:1 *Lord, who may dwell in your sanctuary? Who may live on your holy hill?*

David answers his own question; he tells what kind of people will live on God's holy hill. Included in that list of people is the person who speaks the truth **Ps 15:3** *and has no slander on his tongue, who does his neighbor no wrong and casts no slur on his fellowman.*

If we want to live on God's holy hill, we should not gossip about other people. Two identical scriptures in Proverbs tell us about a gossip—that is someone who gossips.

Prov 18:8 *The words of a gossip are like choice morsels; they go down to a man's inmost parts.*

Prov 26:22 *(same as Prov 18:8)*

When we hear someone gossiping about someone else, we want to hear all about it. Just like we would enjoy eating a piece of chocolate, we enjoy listening to this kind of gossip.

Marshall would not have wanted his classmates talking about how he got in trouble. If his Sunday School classmates were looking out for Marshall's happiness, they would not gossip about him. Instead, they could pray for him.

FEBRUARY 9

Holy Means Separate

God brought his people, the Israelites, out of Egypt and gave them his Law. Many times in the book of Leviticus he tells them he wants them to be holy. Here are four times:

Lev 11:44a & 45 *I am the LORD your God; consecrate yourselves and be holy, because I am holy. (vs 45) I am the LORD who brought you up out of Egypt to be your God; therefore be holy, because I am holy.*

Lev 19:1-2 *The LORD said to Moses, "Speak to the entire assembly of Israel and say to them: 'Be holy because I, the LORD your God, am holy.'"*

Lev 20:7-8 *Consecrate yourselves and be holy, because I am the LORD your God. Keep my decrees and follow them. I am the LORD, who makes you holy.*

Lev 20:26 *You are to be holy to me because I, the LORD, am holy, and I have set you apart from the nations to be my own.*

The word "holy" really means "to be set apart" or "to be separate." Being set apart and separate is not something people usually want. People, especially children, want to fit in and be part of the group. Being part of a group is OK as long as the group we want to be a part of is God's group. Let's look at a sample person.

Maggie is a new girl on the block. Only two other girls on her block go to church with their families. They are nice girls, but they aren't part of the larger group of girls who are more popular.

Maggie has to make a choice. Does she want to be a part of the larger group or does she want to make friends with one or both of the other "church girls?" Maggie decides to be "separate" and make friends with the two girls. She decides to be separate and remain holy like God wants her to. She is still friendly to the other girls, but decides her close friends will be those who love and obey God.

On the Net

FEBRUARY 10

One night Hank stayed up late. He was playing some games on the internet. His mom told him he could stay up another half an hour and then go to bed. She kissed him goodnight and then went to join his dad, who had gone to bed an hour earlier.

Hank really liked playing games on the computer, but a friend had told him he should check out a certain website. Hank played his game for twenty minutes. Then he pulled the paper out of his pocket with the website address written on it. He typed in the address. What Hank saw was something he knew he shouldn't be looking at, but his curiosity got the best of him. He spent the next hour looking at pictures. All the while he was on pins and needles thinking his mom might catch him. He was glad when he finally turned the computer off and went to bed. He was thinking, "I'll never do that again."

The next day Mom looked on the computer's history to see what sites Hank had been looking at. She knew Dad would have to talk to Hank and that they, as his parents, would have to make some computer changes.

There are many bad sites on the internet. God does not want us looking at these sites. Job and David both wrote about being careful what they look at.

Job 31:1 *I made a covenant with my eyes not to look lustfully at a girl.*

Ps 101:3a *I will set before my eyes no vile thing.*

Hank thought no one knew what he had done, but God sees all that we do.

Prov 5:21 *For a man's ways are in full view of the LORD, and he examines all his paths.*

Prov 15:3 *The eyes of the LORD are everywhere, keeping watch on the wicked and the good.*

Vile thing—something that is bad or disgusting

BE HOLY/PURE

FEBRUARY 11

Flee Sin

Hank should have listened to his conscience last night. What does it mean to "listen to your conscience?" It means when you know something is not right you choose to get away from the wrong thing, and you do it fast! In the Bible the word "flee" is used; it means "to run from" what is bad.

Paul wrote two letters to a young pastor named Timothy. In each letter Paul says to flee from sin. First he tells Timothy to flee the love of money.

I Tim 6:11 *But you, man of God, flee from all this, and pursue righteousness, godliness, faith, love, endurance and gentleness.*

Then Paul tells Timothy to flee from evil desires of youth.

II Tim 2:22 *Flee the evil desires of youth, and pursue righteousness, faith, love and peace, along with those who call on the Lord out of a pure heart.*

Hank should have fled from sin. He could have stayed away from sin altogether by showing his parents the name of the website his friend had given him. He could have fled sin by quickly closing the website and going to bed. Finally he could have promised himself before going to bed that he would tell his parents in the morning. Hank wasn't planning on telling his parents anything. If his parents had not found out, Hank would be tempted again and again to visit that site.

God has given us parents to watch over us. It's better to tell our parents what happens than to keep secrets.

Jas 5:16 *Therefore confess your sins to each other and pray for each other so that you may be healed. The prayer of a righteous man is powerful and effective.*

Prov 28:13 *He who conceals his sins does not prosper, but whoever confesses and renounces them finds mercy.*

Hank should have fled and kept away from sin, but he didn't. After Hank committed the sin, the best thing for him to do was to confess it—tell what he did—to his parents.

FEBRUARY 12

Screen It

Www.screenit.com is a website that tells parents what is bad about movies so they can decide if they think it's alright for their children to watch them. They have fifteen headings, but all these can fit into the following questions for parents:

- Is the movie too scary or too violent for our children?
- Does the movie show things or have bad language we don't want our children to see or hear?
- Does the movie show people doing things we do not want our children doing?

When you are grown up you will be able to decide for yourselves what movies you think God would want you watching, but for now that is your parents' job.

We can decide if this is a movie we should see, by asking:

Question #1. Is this movie a "vile" one?

Ps 101:3a *I will set before my eyes no vile thing.*

Some different translations of the Bible translate the word "vile" as "base," "wicked," or "worthless." We could use the word "bad." Some movies are just "bad."

Question #2. Will this movie make it hard for me to be holy?

Paul told the Ephesian church to be different in their attitudes **Eph 4:24** *and to put on the new self, created to be like God in true righteousness and holiness.*

God wants those of us who are serving Jesus to live good and holy lives.

Question #3. Are we offering our eyes to God?

Rom 6:13a *Do not offer the parts of your body to sin, as instruments of wickedness, but rather offer yourselves to God,* **Rom 6:13b** *as those who have been brought from death to life; and offer the parts of your body to him as instruments of righteousness.*

BE HOLY/PURE

FEBRUARY 13

Kidzone

Shan noticed, after Dad had hooked up the TiVo box on top of their television, that she could not watch a lot of the channels and shows that she used to watch. She asked Mom what had happened. Mom explained that TiVo would allow them to record their favorite programs if they were not home to watch them. She told Shan that TiVo also has something called Kidzone. Kidzone allows parents to block certain programs from their TV that they do not want their children to watch. Shan said, "But Mom, you blocked out my favorite show." Shan's mom said that she and her dad would sit down with Shan and watch that program. The people at TiVo KidZone had not recommended it for her age group but maybe Dad and Mom would think it was alright. Mom and Dad wanted to make sure Shan was watching good programs.

God wants us to be holy people, set apart for himself. Paul tells the Corinthian church about being separate and being holy. He quotes promises of God from the Old Testament.

II Cor 6:16 *What agreement is there between the temple of God and idols? For we are the temple of the living God. As God has said: "I will live with them and walk among them, and I will be their God, and they will be my people."* **II Cor 6:17** *"Therefore come out from them and be separate," says the Lord. "Touch no unclean thing, and I will receive you."* **II Cor 6:18** *"I will be a Father to you, and you will be my sons and daughters, says the Lord Almighty."*

God promised to walk among us. He promised to be our God. He promised we would be his people. He promised he would receive us. He promised he would be a father to us. He promised we would be his sons and daughters. After Paul tells about all these promises of God, he tells us we should purify ourselves and be holy.

II Cor 7:1 *Since we have these promises, dear friends, let us purify ourselves from everything that contaminates body and spirit, perfecting holiness out of reverence for God.*

One way to be pure and holy is to be careful about the TV programs we watch.

FEBRUARY

14

Named After a Priest

Valentine's Day

God created Adam as the first man. Adam was lonely, so God created Eve. God gave Eve to Adam as his wife.

Gen 2:18 *The LORD God said, "It is not good for the man to be alone. I will make a helper suitable for him."*

Gen 2:22 *Then the LORD God made a woman from the rib he had taken out of the man, and he brought her to the man.*

Gen 2:24 *For this reason a man will leave his father and mother and be united to his wife, and they will become one flesh.*

God planned that most men and women would get married; marriage is holy, it is good.

Emperor Claudius II was someone who did not think that marriage was holy and good.

He thought that young men would make better soldiers if they didn't have a family to worry about. So the emperor made a law that said Roman soldiers could not get married.

Valentine was a priest during Emperor Claudius' time. History shows that he was martyred* in Rome. Some legends say the reason he was martyred is because he performed marriage ceremonies for soldiers even though he knew the Emperor had made it illegal. Soldiers and their fiancés would come secretly and Father Valentine would marry them.

Emperor Claudius thought marriage was a bad thing for his army. Fr. Valentine knew marriage was a good thing, a holy thing.

Heb 13:4 *Marriage should be honored by all, and the marriage bed kept pure, for God will judge the adulterer and all the sexually immoral.*

About 200 years after Fr. Valentine was martyred, Pope Gelasius named February 14 as St. Valentine's Day.

Martyred—killed for believing certain things about God

BE HOLY/PURE

FEBRUARY
15

God's Presence
Bible

Moses was watching sheep when he noticed that a bush was burning. He thought he'd take a closer look so he went over to see it. God spoke to Moses.

Ex 3:5 *"Do not come any closer," God said. "Take off your sandals, for the place where you are standing is holy ground."*

What made the place where Moses was standing holy? It was holy because God's presence was there. God asked Moses to take his sandals off when he stepped into God's presence.

Later God asked Moses to have the people bring offerings and then build a sanctuary, or a tabernacle for God.

Ex 25:8 *Then have them make a sanctuary for me, and I will dwell among them.*

God's presence among his people was most real in the tabernacle. Later the tabernacle was replaced by a large stone temple; God's presence was there in the temple.

Jesus came to the earth and he started a new way. In Old Testament times the temple was the place where God lived. After Jesus came, God began living in the heart of every person that believes in Jesus. The Holy Spirit comes to live inside of us when we believe that Jesus came and died for our sins.

I Cor 3:16 *Don't you know that you yourselves are God's temple and that God's Spirit lives in you?*

I Cor 6:19 *Do you not know that your body is a temple of the Holy Spirit, who is in you, whom you have received from God? You are not your own.*

God is holy. The Holy Spirit, who is God, lives inside of believers. God's presence within us makes us holy.

Alligator Head
Marigny

One time Aunt Gladys took three of her nieces, Gladys, Rachael and Reyne, swimming. They all noticed the head of an alligator floating on the water. Rachael swam toward it, but then got "creeped out." She turned around and swam away from it, fast! Next Reyne thought she'd be brave and pull the head to shore. She didn't last either; she chickened out and swam away from it.

The alligator head floating on the water was an ugly sight. The girls felt like they didn't even want to touch the thing. That is how God wants us to feel about sin. He wants us to see that it is bad and choose to stay away from it.

Rom 6:23 *For the wages of sin is death, but the gift of God is eternal life in Christ Jesus our Lord.*

The girls probably thought that the alligator head would snap at them. That's the way sin is; if we fool around with sin it will lead to death. We should steer clear of sin.

Rom 6:12 *Therefore do not let sin reign in your mortal body so that you obey its evil desires.*

When Paul says we should "not let sin reign in our mortal bodies," he means that we should not let sin be the thing that rules or controls us.

Rom 6:22 *But now that you have been set free from sin and have become slaves to God, the benefit you reap leads to holiness, and the result is eternal life.*

When we are free from sin and we are living for God, we are becoming holy.

Heb 12:14 *Make every effort to live in peace with all men and to be holy; without holiness no one will see the Lord.*

Just like the alligator head caused Rachael and Reyne to turn away from it, we should turn away from sin when we see it.

(to be cont.)

FEBRUARY
17

Stinky Behavior
Marigny (cont.)

Gladys, Reyne and Rachael finally did get that alligator head to shore. It was really the head of an alligator garfish. An alligator garfish is a fish whose head looks like an alligator. The girls wrapped the head in several plastic bags and decided they wanted to take it with them from New Orleans back to New York, a trip of about thirteen hundred miles. Mommy put the head wrapped in the plastic into a bucket in the back of the van. Before we left the city Daddy said the head had to go—it "stunk too bad." We left the head in New Orleans.

Do you know what "smells bad" to God? It's when his people don't live the way they should. Isaiah said these things about God's people.

Isa 3:8 *Jerusalem staggers, Judah is falling; their words and deeds are against the Lord, defying his glorious presence.*

Isa 3:14 *The Lord enters into judgment against the elders and leaders of his people: "It is you who have ruined my vineyard; the plunder* from the poor is in your houses."*

Isa 3:16 *The Lord says, "The women of Zion are haughty, walking along with outstretched necks, flirting with their eyes, tripping along with mincing steps,* with ornaments jingling on their ankles."*

God's people were not living like he wanted them to; their behavior "stunk." In their words and in their deeds they were not holy. The elders were not acting like shepherds of the people; instead they were taking advantage of them. The women were not pure in heart; they were showing off their physical beauty. Through Isaiah God says he will bring judgment on his people. The people remaining will be holy.

Isa 4:3 *Those who are left in Zion, who remain in Jerusalem, will be called holy, all who are recorded among the living in Jerusalem.*

Plunder—things wrongfully and sometimes forcefully taken
Mincing steps—walking in a way that you show off how fancy you are

FEBRUARY 18

Fragrant Sacrifice

The past two days we talked about things that smell bad. The Bible also talks about some things that smell good. Another word for smelling good is fragrant. Can you think of some things that are fragrant? Some flowers are fragrant. Perfumes are fragrant. Clean clothes just out of the dryer can be fragrant. Some people even think coffee is fragrant.

God says Jesus' death on the cross is a fragrant offering.

Eph 5:2 . . . *and live a life of love, just as Christ loved us and gave himself up for us as a fragrant offering and sacrifice to God.*

Paul says when Jesus died, that his death was a fragrant offering to God. Why would Paul say that? It's probably because in the Old Testament in Leviticus and Numbers God told the people how to offer sacrifices. He said at least thirty times that if sacrifices were made like he wanted, they would be a sweet smell to God. That is a way of saying God would be pleased with them. Let's read two of these scriptures:

Lev 23:18 *Present with this bread seven male lambs, each a year old and without defect, one young bull and two rams. They will be a burnt offering to the Lord, together with their grain offerings and drink offerings—an offering made by fire, an aroma pleasing to the Lord.*

Num 28:2 *Give this command to the Israelites and say to them: "See that you present to me at the appointed time the food for my offerings made by fire, as an aroma pleasing to me."*

Paul said Jesus' death was a fragrant offering to God. That means God was pleased with Jesus' sacrifice of himself.

Heb 10:10 *And by that will, we have been made holy through the sacrifice of the body of Jesus Christ once for all.*

God is pleased with Jesus' sacrifice because by it we are made holy. Jesus' death was a fragrant offering to God.

FEBRUARY

19

Hearts Set on God

Some days Tony was good and some days Tony was bad. I guess that's better than if he would have been bad every day.

God's people are the same way. Sometimes we live like God wants us to and sometimes we do what we want instead of what God wants.

Jeremiah was God's prophet. He told the Israelites, God's people, that they were wrong to let their hearts turn away from God.

Jer 17:5 *This is what the LORD says: "Cursed is the one who trusts in man, who depends on flesh for his strength and whose heart turns away from the LORD."*

God also said through Jeremiah:

Jer 17:7 *"But blessed is the man who trusts in the LORD, whose confidence is in him."*

Because God's people so often turned away from him, Jeremiah said this:

Jer 17:9 *"The heart is deceitful above all things and beyond cure. Who can understand it?"*

People do good things and they do bad things. When they decide they are going to live their lives for God, they will start doing more good things.

God wants us to love Him more than anything else. When we do that, we are pure in heart. Jesus said this about people who are pure in heart.

Mt 5:8 *Blessed are the pure in heart, for they will see God.*

FEBRUARY 20

Guard Your Heart

Matt always used bad words when he was at the park. None of the boys he played with did, though. Most of the boys attended church with their families, but Matt's family didn't go to church. The boys knew that everyone in Matt's family used bad words, so they didn't say anything to Matt.

One day Jeremy got angry and he said some of those bad words that he had heard Matt use. Jeremy's dad was quick to punish him. Jeremy told his dad where he had heard that kind of language. Jeremy's dad decided to have a talk with Matt.

Jesus said that what is in our hearts will come out of our mouths.

Lk 6:45 *The good man brings good things out of the good stored up in his heart, and the evil man brings evil things out of the evil stored up in his heart. For out of the overflow of his heart his mouth speaks.*

Mt 12:34 *You brood of vipers, how can you who are evil say anything good? For out of the overflow of the heart the mouth speaks.*

Proverbs also says that our hearts and our mouths work together.

Prov 22:11 *He who loves a pure heart and whose speech is gracious will have the king for his friend.*

It would have been almost impossible for Jeremy to have said those bad words if he had never heard them. Jeremy and the boys he played with should have asked Matt not to use that kind of language. In that way they would have been guarding their hearts.

Prov 4:23 *Above all else, guard your heart, for it is the wellspring of life.*

BE HOLY/PURE

FEBRUARY
21
Be Pure

Have you ever camped out in a friend's backyard? Logan did one time. When he was unpacking the things in his backpack he found a note from his mom. It read: "Logan, Hope you have a great time. We miss you. Remember to be pure. Love, Mom and Dad."

That's not really what Mom's note said. She didn't write, "Remember to be pure." She wrote, "Remember to be good."

In Paul's letter to Timothy, though, he did tell Timothy to "keep himself pure."

I Tim 5:22 *Do not be hasty in the laying on of hands, and do not share in the sins of others. Keep yourself pure.*

We don't hear many people talk about purity. How do we stay pure? In order to stay pure we need to be careful what we look at. TV shows, movies and even magazines can show things that are not pure.

Paul tells Timothy that love comes from a pure heart.

I Tim 1:5 *The goal of this command is love, which comes from a pure heart and a good conscience and a sincere faith.*

Peter tells the church that they purify themselves by obeying God.

I Pet 1:22 *Now that you have purified yourselves by obeying the truth so that you have sincere love for your brothers, love one another deeply, from the heart.*

In Proverbs we learn that God is pleased with us if we keep our thoughts pure.

Prov 15:26 *The Lord detests the thoughts of the wicked, but those of the pure are pleasing to him.*

FEBRUARY 22

Elijah is Holy

Most people must die in order to go to heaven. However, the Bible tells us of a few people whom God took straight to heaven; they did not die.

Elijah [ee *lie* juh], the Old Testament prophet, is one of these people. He was out taking a walk with another prophet when God took him.

II Ki 2:11 *As they were walking along and talking together, suddenly a chariot of fire and horses of fire appeared and separated the two of them, and Elijah went up to heaven in a whirlwind.*

Why did God take Elijah to heaven like that? It could be because Elijah was a holy man.

Elijah listened to God and whenever God gave him a message to deliver to someone, Elijah would go.

God sent Elijah to tell Ahab that there would be no rain for three and a half years.

I Ki 17:1 *Now Elijah the Tishbite, from Tishbe in Gilead, said to Ahab, "As the LORD, the God of Israel, lives, whom I serve, there will be neither dew nor rain in the next few years except at my word."*

After the time of no rain, God sent Elijah to tell Ahab that he was sending rain.

I Ki 18:1 *After a long time, in the third year, the word of the LORD came to Elijah: "Go and present yourself to Ahab, and I will send rain on the land."*

Later God sent Elijah to Ahab's son, Ahaziah [ay huh *zie* uh]. Ahaziah had sent someone to consult Baal-Zebub, the god of Ekron. God sent Elijah to give Ahaziah a message.

II Ki 1:3 *But the angel of the LORD said to Elijah the Tishbite, "Go up and meet the messengers of the king of Samaria and ask them, 'Is it because there is no God in Israel that you are going off to consult Baal-Zebub, the god of Ekron?'"*

Each time God sent him, Elijah went. Because Elijah listened to God and did what God asked of him he was a holy man.

BE HOLY/PURE

FEBRUARY 23

A Double Portion

Yesterday we learned that Elijah was a holy man. He walked closely with God; God's spirit was with him.

God told Elijah that Elisha [ee *lie* shuh] would be the next prophet of Israel.

Elijah found Elisha working in the fields. Elijah threw his mantle—his outer garment, probably a sheepskin—around Elisha. Elisha understood what that meant. He knew God was calling him to be Israel's next prophet. Elisha quit farming and followed Elijah. Elisha must have owned his equipment because the Bible says he butchered his oxen and burned his plow.

When Elijah was about to be taken by God to heaven, he asked Elisha if there was anything he could do for him. They had just crossed the Jordan River.

II Ki 2:9 *When they had crossed, Elijah said to Elisha, "Tell me, what can I do for you before I am taken from you?"*

"Let me inherit a double portion of your spirit," Elisha replied.

II Ki 2:10 *"You have asked a difficult thing," Elijah said, "yet if you see me when I am taken from you, it will be yours—otherwise not."*

This is when the chariot and horses of fire took Elijah in a whirlwind to heaven.

II Ki 2:12 *Elisha saw this and cried out, "My father! My father! The chariots and horsemen of Israel!" And Elisha saw him no more. Then he took hold of his own clothes and tore them apart.*

Elisha saw Elijah taken to heaven. He was given double the spirit of God that Elijah enjoyed. He did some amazing things. You can read about him in II Kings, chapters 2-13. People knew that Elisha was a holy man. A wealthy woman of Shunem welcomed Elisha into her home.

II Ki 4:9 *She said to her husband, "I know that this man who often comes our way is a holy man of God."*

Elisha was given twice the spirit of God that Elijah had; he was holy, just as Elijah was.

FEBRUARY 24

Holy to the Lord

Corey caught himself daydreaming when he was working on his arithmetic assignment. He was thinking back on last year's Christmas play. He had been one of the three wise men. He had been given the most lines, so his mother went out of her way to prepare his costume. Corey thought about how he looked that day. He wore a full-length robe that had fur down the front. He wore some high top boots that came almost to his knees. The best part of his costume, the part that made him feel most like a king, was the crown he wore on his head. He looked fabulous!

Corey had a special wise man costume. In the same way, God's priests in the Old Testament had special clothes. God told Moses what clothes the people should make for them.

Ex 28:4 *These are the garments they are to make: a breastpiece, an ephod,* a robe, a woven tunic, a turban and a sash. They are to make these sacred garments for your brother Aaron and his sons, so they may serve me as priests.*

Everyone in Israel knew who the priests were because their clothes set them apart. Aaron was the leader of the priests so he had some things that set him apart from the other priests. His ephod was fancier. He wore the breastplate and the robe and his turban had a gold plate on it.

Ex 28:36-37 *Make a plate of pure gold and engrave on it as on a seal:* HOLY TO THE LORD. *Fasten a blue cord to it to attach it to the turban; it is to be on the front of the turban.*

God has always wanted his people to be holy. The plate on Aaron's turban was to remind the people of this. When people see how you live can they tell that you are "holy to the Lord?"

Eph 1:4 *For he chose us in him before the creation of the world to be holy and blameless in his sight. (In love)*

II Pet 3:11 *Since everything will be destroyed in this way, what kind of people ought you to be? You ought to live holy and godly lives.*

Ephod [*ee* fodd]—a full-length sleeveless garment worn by Jewish priests in Old Testament times

BE HOLY/PURE

FEBRUARY 25

Yoga in School

Pastor Dan heard that the school was going to be teaching Yoga to his second grade daughter, Kim. He asked that Kim be allowed to participate in an alternate activity.

The yoga instructor explained that the class was mostly relaxing and stretching activities. Pastor Dan replied that most Yoga classes are taught with the children sitting in the lotus position—sitting on the floor with their legs crossed. This is the position of prayer for many eastern religions, e.g., Buddhism and Hinduism. In fact, the dictionary says Yoga is a Hindu practice that trains people to have spiritual insight and peace.

God does not want his people to practice other religions. He wants us to serve only him.

Deut 6:13 *Fear the LORD your God, serve him only and take your oaths in his name.*

Almost twenty times in the book of Deuteronomy God warns his people not to worship false gods. Here are three of those warnings:

Deut 6:14 *Do not follow other gods, the gods of the peoples around you.*

Deut 8:19 *If you ever forget the LORD your God and follow other gods and worship and bow down to them, I testify against you today that you will surely be destroyed.*

Deut 28:14 *Do not turn aside from any of the commands I give you today, to the right or to the left, following other gods and serving them.*

Many people, even some Christians, believe that Yoga is not a religious practice. They believe that the techniques taught in Yoga classes, such as sitting still and quietly, and breathing deeply and slowly are not harmful. Some would even say this is a healthy exercise that can teach children how to be comfortable with solitude or to be quiet before God, rather than children always needing to be busy.

Pastor Dan, however, didn't want it to appear that his daughter was following a different God. He didn't allow her to participate in the Yoga classes.

FEBRUARY 26

Wholesome Talk
Warren Marigny

Terry was raised by his godmother,* his "nannand" [nuh *nand*], since he was a baby. Each night they knelt beside the bed and prayed. Terry's nannand taught him to respect his elders.

Terry often got to go along when his godmother went to play cards. Sometimes Terry's Uncle Minot [mih *no*] would cheat. When Uncle Minot cheated, the other people playing with him would call him a bad name.

Terry was about thirteen when he began playing cards with the grown-ups. Uncle Minot peeked at Terry's hand. He told Terry he knew what cards he had; he said that's why he hadn't played a certain card earlier. Terry called Uncle Minot the same name he had heard everyone else call him when he cheated. The name just came tumbling out.

Terry's nannand was a big woman. She stood up, took a few steps toward Terry, and excused him from the table. Later she made Terry apologize to his uncle.

Terry's nannand knew she was responsible for Terry. She could not let him talk like that even if others did.

As God's people we should act different than those who are not a part of God's family.

Eph 4:29 *Do not let any unwholesome talk come out of your mouths, but only what is helpful for building others up according to their needs, that it may benefit those who listen.*

The name that Terry had called Uncle Minot was not wholesome.

Paul tells the Ephesians how God's holy people should behave.

Eph 5:1 *Be imitators of God, therefore, as dearly loved children.*

Eph 5:3 *But among you there must not be even a hint of sexual immorality, or of any kind of impurity, or of greed, because these are improper for God's holy people.* **Eph 5:4** *Nor should there be obscenity, foolish talk or coarse joking, which are out of place, but rather thanksgiving.*

Godmother—in some faiths, a godmother is a woman who sponsors a child at its baptism

BE HOLY/PURE

FEBRUARY 27

How to Stay Pure

How can a young man keep his way pure? That question is asked in the Bible. The answer is also given.

Ps 119:9 *How can a young man keep his way pure? By living according to your word.*

This scripture says if young people want to be pure they should live the way the Bible says to.

If you decide today that you want to live according to God's Word, what are some things you should do? Many families do devotions together each day, but God also wants to speak personally to each of us through his Word. Christians should take time each day to read God's Word, even if it's just a few minutes. Because God's Word is "alive" it can speak to each one of us. When we know what the Bible says, we can live according to it.

The person who wrote Psalm 119 says several times that he loves God's law.

Ps 119:47 *. . . for I delight in your commands because I love them.*

Another time the psalm writer says he meditates on God's law all day long.

Ps 119:97 *Oh, how I love your law! I meditate on it all day long.*

Close to the beginning of Psalm 119, the writer says by hiding God's Word in his heart—that means memorizing Scripture—he is kept from sin.

Ps 119:11 *I have hidden your word in my heart that I might not sin against you.*

By reading, memorizing, and meditating on God's Word, young people can live pure lives.

FEBRUARY

28

Pure & Pleasing
Marigny

It was a rule in the Marigny family that the girls wear only one-piece bathing suits. That was the rule, until the rule changed. Mommy went with the girls to the store and decided that some of the two-piece tank-top style bathing suits were more modest than the skimpy one-piece suits. She would rather have a little of the girls' stomach showing, than have the legs cut up high on the sides and the top cut down low in the front with the back open.

Gladys, however, found out that the tank-top bathing suits can be "dangerous." When she dove off the diving board, the bottoms didn't have tight elastic on the waist and they came off a little bit. Girls concerned about dressing modestly, should choose bathing suits wisely.

I Tim 2:9a *I also want women to dress modestly, with decency and propriety.*

Another way we can say "dress modestly" is to say "cover our bodies." You wouldn't run naked in the street, because that would not be modest. Neither should girls wear clothes that show too much skin or are skin-tight. Some girls seem to think this means they should wear baggy clothes. That is not true either. When other people see how we dress they should know that we are looking the best we can for God.

The Bible in Genesis, chapter 1 makes this statement five times, "And God saw that it was good." Each time God created something new, he thought it was good. Let's read about one of these times. God had just created the sun, moon and stars.

Gen 1:17 *God set them in the expanse of the sky to give light on the earth,* **Gen 1:18** *to govern the day and the night, and to separate light from darkness. And God saw that it was good.*

After God created Adam and Eve he said something else.

Gen 1:31a *God saw all that he had made, and it was very good.*

When God added people to his creation he said it was very good. If we dress to please God he will be pleased with us.

BE HOLY/PURE

FEBRUARY

29

Jesus Never Sinned

Have you ever known someone that you thought was perfect? You might have thought that you wanted to be just like that person. It is good for us to have people we admire and want to be like.

The person we admire is not perfect, though. The only person who has ever lived a perfect life is Jesus Christ.

John is talking about Jesus when he says,

I Jn 3:5 *But you know that he appeared so that he might take away our sins. And in him is no sin.*

Jesus never sinned. Because he is God, Jesus is perfect and he is holy.

The writer of Hebrews says this about Jesus:

Heb 7:26 *Such a high priest meets our need—one who is holy, blameless, pure, set apart from sinners, exalted above the heavens.*

The writer of the letter to the Hebrews says that Jesus is holy. Not only writers of the Bible said Jesus was holy; even a demon-possessed man said Jesus was the Holy One of God. This demon-possessed man was in the synagogue. When he saw Jesus, he said, **Mk 1:24** *"What do you want with us, Jesus of Nazareth? Have you come to destroy us? I know who you are—the Holy One of God!"*

When Jesus walked on this earth he was holy. He wants his followers to be holy, also.

I Pet 1:16 *. . . for it is written: "Be holy, because I am holy."*

MARCH 1

Sackcloth and Ashes
Ash Wednesday

Ash Wednesday is the seventh Wednesday before Easter. It is the first day of Lent. Some churches celebrate this day. People come forward during the church service and the clergyman* [*klur* jee mun] uses ashes to make a cross on their foreheads. This cross of ashes is a way for people to show they are sorry for their sins. As the clergyman makes the cross he might say these words, "Remember man that you are dust and unto dust you shall return." These are the words God said to Adam after Adam ate the forbidden fruit:

Gen 3:19 *By the sweat of your brow you will eat your food until you return to the ground, since from it you were taken; for dust you are and to dust you will return.*

Receiving ashes shows sorrow for sins. In the Old Testament people showed they were sorry for their sins by wearing scratchy clothes called sackcloth. They might also sit in ashes or put ashes on themselves to show that they were sorry for their sins. Jesus told his disciples about how the people in Tyre [*tire*] and Sidon [*sy* don] would have repented if they too had seen Jesus work miracles.

Lk 10:13 *Woe to you, Korazin* [koe *ray* zin]*! Woe to you, Bethsaida* [beth *say* ih duh]*! For if the miracles that were performed in you had been performed in Tyre and Sidon, they would have repented long ago, sitting in sackcloth and ashes.*

Job put on sackcloth when he had suffered through many hard things.

Job 16:15 *I have sewed sackcloth over my skin and buried my brow in the dust.*

At the end of the book of Job, God revealed his glory to Job. Job realized how sinful he was, and how holy God was. Job said he "hated himself" because of his sin.

Job 42:6 *Therefore I despise myself and repent in dust and ashes.*

The practice of having ashes put on your forehead is a way to show sorrow for sin. It is much easier than wearing sackcloth and sitting in ashes.

Clergyman—a religious leader, e.g., a pastor or priest

MARCH
2

Deny Yourself
Lent

Lent is about six and a half weeks long. It begins on Ash Wednesday and ends on Easter Sunday. Many Christians "give something up" during this time. For example, some people have said they won't eat any chocolate or drink sodas during Lent. Other people do things like only listening to Christian radio or not eating any sweets. Why would anyone do these things? They do it to deny themselves. Jesus told us to deny ourselves. The apostles Matthew, Mark and Luke all remember this teaching of Jesus:

Mt 16:24 *Then Jesus said to his disciples, "If anyone would come after me, he must deny himself and take up his cross and follow me."*

Mk 8:34 *Then he called the crowd to him along with his disciples and said: "If anyone would come after me, he must deny himself and take up his cross and follow me."*

Lk 9:23 *Then he said to them all: "If anyone would come after me, he must deny himself and take up his cross daily and follow me."*

Sometimes when people decide to "give something up" during Lent, that thing is something they like a lot. When people do this, it is like saying to God, "God, I love you more than anything else." They remind themselves that, even if they like something a lot, they love God more.

No matter what we give up, it doesn't compare to what God gave up so that we might be forgiven.

Jn 3:16 *For God so loved the world that he gave his one and only Son, that whoever believes in him shall not perish but have eternal life.*

Freedom in Forgiving

MARCH 3

Anna asked her mom why her little brother, Javier, was always breaking things. She was still angry at him and it had been a week since he had pulled her Barbie's head off. It was not one of the kind that could just be pushed back on and it would stay. Javier must not have known that, but Anna was still angry about it.

Anna had not enjoyed being around Javier since. When they went to the park she thought about how upset she was. When they played at home she kept thinking about her doll and it made her angry.

Anna's mom said Javier didn't intentionally ruin her doll. Her mom told Anna that she should forgive Javier.

Eph 4:32a *Be kind and compassionate to one another,* **Eph 4:32b** *forgiving each other, just as in Christ God forgave you.*

Anna didn't really want to forgive Javier, but she didn't want to continue to be angry either.

Col 3:13a *Bear with each other* and forgive whatever grievances* you may have against one another.* **Col 3:13b** *Forgive as the Lord forgave you.*

Anna decided that she would forgive Javier. She noticed that after she had forgiven him, spending time with him was more fun.

Bear with each other—be patient with others
Grievances—things that people do that make you upset

FORGIVE ONE ANOTHER

MARCH 4

I Don't Know Him
Bible

Peter was a disciple of Jesus. At the Last Supper Jesus had told his disciples that they would all fall away from him. Peter said that even if everyone else left Jesus, he never would. Jesus told Peter that before the rooster crowed he would deny him—say he didn't know him—three times. That same night Jesus was arrested and taken to a trial at the high priest's house. Peter followed closely, but he was not allowed in the house. He stayed in the courtyard, where people were warming themselves around a fire.

Lk 22:55 *But when they had kindled a fire in the middle of the courtyard and had sat down together, Peter sat down with them.* **Lk 22:56-57** *A servant girl saw him seated there in the firelight. She looked closely at him and said, "This man was with him."*

But he denied it. "Woman, I don't know him," he said.

Lk 22:58-59 *A little later someone else saw him and said, "You also are one of them."*

"Man, I am not!" Peter replied.

About an hour later another asserted, "Certainly this fellow was with him, for he is a Galilean."

Lk 22:60-62 *Peter replied, "Man, I don't know what you're talking about!" Just as he was speaking, the rooster crowed. The Lord turned and looked straight at Peter. Then Peter remembered the word the Lord had spoken to him: "Before the rooster crows today, you will disown me three times." And he went outside and wept bitterly.*

Peter felt terrible about what he had done. He never got a chance to tell Jesus he was sorry.

When Jesus rose from the dead he took Peter alone on the beach. Jesus let Peter know that he was forgiven. If Jesus could forgive Peter after Peter disowned him, we can trust Jesus to forgive us too, when we have done wrong and we ask his forgiveness.

MARCH 5

In the Nursery

Jerrod and Max were playing on a toy in the nursery. It was a square "house" that had shapes cut out of the sides so that children could crawl in and out of it. Off of one side a slide came down. Children could also get inside the "house" if they slid through a hole from the top. Max climbed into that hole. He got half-way in and realized maybe he didn't want to go down there.

Jerrod had many times gone down there and he thought Max should hurry up and do the same. Jerrod started stepping on Max's head and shoulders to get him to go. Max cried!

The nursery worker saw what happened. She asked Jerrod why he stepped on Max. Jerrod was not mean, nor did he want to hurt Max.

The nursery worker asked Jerrod to tell Max he was sorry for hurting him. Jerrod said he was sorry. Max said it was OK, and they played for the rest of the time.

Why should we forgive others? One reason is because Jesus said we should.

Lk 17:3 *So watch yourselves. If your brother sins, rebuke him, and if he repents, forgive him.* **Lk 17:4** *If he sins against you seven times in a day, and seven times comes back to you and says, "I repent," forgive him.*

Another reason we should forgive others is because God will forgive us our sins if we forgive other people.

Mt 6:14 *For if you forgive men when they sin against you, your heavenly Father will also forgive you.* **Mt 6:15** *But if you do not forgive men their sins, your Father will not forgive your sins.*

FORGIVE ONE ANOTHER

MARCH 6

Don't Get Even

What does it mean to forgive someone? Does it mean that you tell the little boy who was mean to you yesterday, that it's alright for him to be mean to you anytime he wants to? No! That is not what forgiveness means! Some people say forgiveness means you give up your right to get even.

Forgiveness is a hard thing to do, but God can help us with it. In the book of Exodus, God revealed himself—God showed what he is like—to Moses. He told Moses that he is kind and that he is slow to anger. God also told Moses that he forgives "wickedness, rebellion and sin."

Ex 34:6 *And he passed in front of Moses, proclaiming, "The Lord, the Lord, the compassionate and gracious God, slow to anger, abounding in love and faithfulness,* **Ex 34:7a** *maintaining love to thousands, and forgiving wickedness, rebellion and sin."*

Moses reminded God about this revelation in the book of Numbers. He said, **Num 14:18a** *The Lord is slow to anger, abounding in love and forgiving sin and rebellion.*

God is a forgiving God. He wants us to be like him and learn to forgive. When we find it hard to forgive someone, we should ask God for help. When God's people asked him for help this is what a psalmist wrote:

Ps 99:8 *O Lord our God, you answered them; you were to Israel a forgiving God, though you punished their misdeeds.*

It is probably best to avoid a person that is being mean to you just to be mean. You should tell an adult if someone is going out of his way to find you in order to be mean to you.

If you give up your right to get even with that person, you have learned part of what it means to forgive.

MARCH 7

Jesus Can Forgive
Bible

One time Jesus was preaching in someone's house. The house was full of people, and even more people were crowded around outside the house.

Mk 2:2 *So many gathered that there was no room left, not even outside the door, and he preached the word to them.*

A paralyzed man* had four friends who had heard how Jesus could heal people. They brought him to that crowded house. Let's read the story:

Mk 2:3 *Some men came, bringing to him a paralytic, carried by four of them.* **Mk 2:4** *Since they could not get him to Jesus because of the crowd, they made an opening in the roof above Jesus and, after digging through it, lowered the mat the paralyzed man was lying on.*

Mk 2:5 *When Jesus saw their faith, he said to the paralytic, "Son, your sins are forgiven."*

Why would Jesus tell the man that his sins were forgiven? Those men didn't bring their friend to get his sins forgiven; they brought him so that Jesus would heal him. These friends of the paralyzed man were probably surprised by what Jesus said. The religious leaders were not only surprised, but they were angry with what Jesus said.

When the religious leaders heard Jesus say, "Your sins are forgiven," they immediately thought, "Only God can forgive sins." They thought, "This man, Jesus, is claiming to be God."

These men were right in their thinking. Jesus was claiming to be God. Jesus is God. Therefore, Jesus can forgive sins.

Tomorrow we'll learn what happened to the paralyzed man.
(to be cont.)

Paralyzed man—a man who can't move certain parts of his body

MARCH 8

Healing the Soul
Bible (cont.)

A paralyzed man was brought to Jesus by four of his friends; four people were carrying a fifth person on a mat. They knew they would not be able to get to Jesus through the crowd. They decided to take the man on the roof. A roof in Bible times was often just a covering of straw. The four men somehow were able to get their friend on the roof of the house. They removed the straw over the place where Jesus was preaching, and they let the man down.

Jesus didn't heal the man right away. Instead he said, "Son, your sins are forgiven you." The religious leaders were thinking bad things about Jesus, but Jesus said,

Mk 2:9 *"Which is easier: to say to the paralytic, 'Your sins are forgiven,' or to say, 'Get up, take your mat and walk'?* **Mk 2:10** *But that you may know that the Son of Man has authority on earth to forgive sins . . . ." He said to the paralytic,*

Mk 2:11 *"I tell you, get up, take your mat and go home."*

Then we see what happened next.

Mk 2:12 *He got up, took his mat and walked out in full view of them all. This amazed everyone and they praised God, saying, "We have never seen anything like this!"*

Jesus has the power to heal every disease or sickness. He knows that healing our souls is even more important than healing our bodies. Jesus heals our souls by forgiving all our sins and letting us start a new life with him. Jesus healed the paralyzed man's soul. Jesus is willing to heal anyone else's soul. All a person needs to do to receive healing for her soul is to ask for Jesus' forgiveness.

MARCH 9

A Bitter Root

Jack was fed up. His little brother, Alex, had just gotten into his stuff one too many times. This time it was his science project that he had been working on for a few months. It was a week before the science fair, and Jack would have to spend several hours getting the project back in shape.

Perhaps someone had made Peter angry like Jack was. One day Peter asked Jesus a question about forgiveness.

Mt 18:21 *Then Peter came to Jesus and asked, "Lord, how many times shall I forgive my brother when he sins against me? Up to seven times?"*

Mt 18:22 *Jesus answered, "I tell you, not seven times, but seventy-seven times."*

If you look in the footnotes of your Bible it says "seventy-seven times" might also be translated as "seventy times seven times." That would be four hundred and ninety times that you should forgive someone when they repent.

Jack thought, "You know, Alex is so little he doesn't even know how to repent." The science project was a big deal, though, so Jack was very angry with Alex.

Heb 12:14 *Make every effort to live in peace with all men and to be holy; without holiness no one will see the Lord.*

God wants us to live in peace with all people. He wants Jack to forgive Alex. When Jack decides to forgive Alex, they will once again be at peace.

Heb 12:15 *See to it that no one misses the grace of God and that no bitter root grows up to cause trouble and defile many.*

If Jack continues to hold on to unforgiveness it can turn into a bitter root. That bitter root can hurt not only Jack's relationship with Alex, but Jack's relationships with other people as well.

FORGIVE ONE ANOTHER

MARCH 10

John Mark Quits
Bible

A young man named John Mark went with the apostle Paul and Barnabas on Paul's first missionary trip. It was exciting for them to travel to new places. They traveled by ship and first preached on the island of Cyprus [*sy* prus]. Then they sailed again and landed at Perga.

Acts 13:13 *From Paphos [pa foss], Paul and his companions sailed to Perga in Pamphylia [pam fill ee uh], where John left them to return to Jerusalem.*

The Bible doesn't tell us why John Mark went back to Jerusalem. Paul finished the missionary trip, but John Mark wasn't there to help.

Paul went back to his home church of Antioch [*an* tee ahk] for a while. Then he decided he would like to go and check on all the churches his team had started during their first missionary trip.

Acts 15:37-38 *Barnabas wanted to take John, also called Mark, with them, but Paul did not think it wise to take him, because he had deserted them in Pamphylia and had not continued with them in the work.* **Acts 15:39-40** *They had such a sharp disagreement that they parted company. Barnabas took Mark and sailed for Cyprus, but Paul chose Silas and left, commended by the brothers to the grace of the Lord.*

On this, Paul's second trip, he did not think it was right to take John Mark. John Mark had quit on the first trip.

Later, Paul did forgive John Mark. The Bible doesn't tell us this, but it says that Paul told Timothy to bring Mark with him. We find this in Paul's second letter to Timothy. This letter was written about twenty years after John Mark left the missionary team.

2 Tim 4:11 *Only Luke is with me. Get Mark and bring him with you, because he is helpful to me in my ministry.*

When we get into disagreements we might be angry with people for a while. We should try to forgive them. If they later prove that they are faithful, we may trust them once again.

MARCH 11

They Were Envious

Marcia whispered to Valerie, "Did you hear about Gloria?" Valerie said, "No, what?"

Marcia said that Gloria had made the gym team. The girls started talking about how Gloria thought she was better than everyone else.

Gloria was at the top of their class. She was not a "snob." She worked hard to get good grades and to make the gym team. Marcia and Valerie were probably envious of Gloria, and they gossiped about her.

Moses was faced with the same kind of trouble. It wasn't his friends that were gossiping about him. It was his brother and sister, Aaron and Miriam.

Num 12:1 *Miriam and Aaron began to talk against Moses because of his Cushite* wife, for he had married a Cushite.* **Num 12:2** *"Has the LORD spoken only through Moses?" they asked. "Hasn't he also spoken through us?" And the LORD heard this.*

Moses didn't deserve this kind of treatment, so God stepped in. God allowed Miriam to be struck with leprosy.*

Aaron begged Moses to forgive them for how they had talked about him.

Num 12:11 *. . . and he said to Moses, "Please, my lord, do not hold against us the sin we have so foolishly committed."*

Moses could have said, "It's her fault. She shouldn't have been gossiping about me." Moses didn't say that; instead he forgave Miriam. He prayed that God would heal her.

Num 12:13 *So Moses cried out to the LORD, "O God, please heal her!"*

Cushite—a descendant of Cush, son of Ham—probably a dark-skinned person

Leprosy—a disease that causes people's skin and flesh to rot

FORGIVE ONE ANOTHER

MARCH
12

Too Late

Rita had probably eaten her burger too fast. Dad was driving the family home when Rita said, "I feel like I'm going to throw up."

Dad knew they were only about ten minutes from home. He thought maybe Rita could wait that long so he kept driving. A few minutes later Gwen said, "Daddy I think you should pull over. Rita is going to throw up."

Before Dad could pull over, Rita threw up. It's good they were close to home.

Daddy apologized for not listening more closely. Rita forgave her Daddy. Rita said she was sorry for throwing up in the car. Everyone forgave Rita, even Mom who spent an hour cleaning the car.

Forgiveness is the Bible's central message; God has forgiven us because of what Jesus endured on the cross.

Col 1:13 *For he has rescued us from the dominion of darkness and brought us into the kingdom of the Son he loves,* **Col 1:14** *in whom we have redemption, the forgiveness of sins.*

We have forgiveness for our sins because Jesus died for us.

Col 2:13 *When you were dead in your sins and in the uncircumcision of your sinful nature, God made you alive with Christ. He forgave us all our sins.*

When we ask Jesus to be our Savior, he forgives our sins and lets us start over again.

Col 3:13 *Bear with each other and forgive whatever grievances you may have against one another. Forgive as the Lord forgave you.*

We should forgive others, because God has forgiven us.

A Friend Indeed

MARCH 13

Jamison had liked school at first. He learned how to read very well. But Jamison's classmates had been teasing him since kindergarten. His ears stuck out from his head so they called him "Dumbo." Dumbo is an elephant in cartoons. The teasing became worse and worse. Every day someone would make a smart remark directed at him.

Jamison's grades began to drop; then he started getting into trouble. He had been to the principal's office four times for disrupting class. Finally, he was suspended for fighting with another student. When Jamison returned to school, the teasing continued and now they made fun of him for getting suspended.

Things changed for the better when a family moved into the house next door. Abdul was about Jamison's age. Abdul and Jamison would walk together to school every day. Because Jamison now had a friend he once again enjoyed going to school. He overlooked the teasing of the other students. He began studying and it was not hard for him to get good grades.

Abdul invited Jamison to go to church with his family. Jamison enjoyed being with Abdul so he was happy to go to church with him. Jamison listened to the pastor's message about forgiveness. The pastor said that no matter what we have done, that God is willing to forgive.

Ps 130:3 *If you, O LORD, kept a record of sins, O Lord, who could stand?*

If God kept a record of everyone's sins, no person would be found perfect. Because God is merciful, he is willing to forgive us.

Ps 130:4 *But with you there is forgiveness; therefore you are feared.*

To be "feared," means to be respected or revered.

Ps 103:2 *Praise the LORD, O my soul, and forget not all his benefits.*

Ps 103:3 *Who forgives all your sins and heals all your diseases.*

At the end of the church service Jamison asked Abdul if he would go forward with him to accept Jesus' forgiveness. The two boys walked to the front of the church and Jamison received forgiveness for all the bad things he had done.

MARCH 14

Bees in the Bible

The Bible only uses the word "bees" four times. Let's look at the four times where the word "bees" is used. The Bible says Samson saw some bees. When Samson was going to the place where he planned on getting married, he saw a lion's carcass* full of bees and honey.

Judg 14:8 *Some time later, when he went back to marry her, he turned aside to look at the lion's carcass. In it was a swarm of bees and some honey.*

The other three times we see the word "bees," God is talking about nations who fight against Israel. It's probably because when armies came against Israel, they were difficult to deal with, like a swarm of bees attacking a person.

Ps 118:12 *They swarmed around me like bees, but they died out as quickly as burning thorns; in the name of the LORD I cut them off.*

Often these nations—these "bees"—are a form of God's judgment on his people. Because the Israelites rebelled against God, God sent the Amorite army against them.

Deu 1:44 *The Amorites who lived in those hills came out against you; they chased you like a swarm of bees and beat you down from Seir* [see er] *all the way to Hormah* [hor mah].

In Isaiah's time the people of Israel did not trust God, so God sent armies against them.

Isa 7:18 *In that day the LORD will whistle for flies from the distant streams of Egypt and for bees from the land of Assyria* [uh *sear* ee uh].

God is ready to forgive, but if we refuse to repent we can expect his judgment.

Carcass—the dead body of an animal

FORGIVE ONE ANOTHER

MARCH 15

A Thief
Bible

Jacob and Esau [ee saw] were twins, but Esau was the one born first. The firstborn in Bible times was given a double portion of the inheritance from their family; the firstborn usually got the father's blessing.

Esau was the firstborn. When they were young men Esau came home and he was "oh, so hungry."

Gen 25:29 *Once when Jacob was cooking some stew, Esau came in from the open country, famished.*

Esau was famished; that means he was extremely hungry. He wanted some of Jacob's stew. Jacob said before Esau could have any of it, Esau had to give Jacob his birthright. Esau was so hungry, that all he could think about was food.

Gen 25:32 *"Look, I am about to die," Esau said. "What good is the birthright to me?"*

Jacob took Esau's birthright. Later he also took the blessing that their father was going to give to Esau. Esau knew he had been cheated. He told his father what Jacob had done.

Gen 27:36 *Esau said, "Isn't he rightly named Jacob? He has deceived me these two times: He took my birthright, and now he's taken my blessing!" Then he asked, "Haven't you reserved any blessing for me?"*

Isaac, the father of these twin boys, said that he didn't have another blessing for Esau. Esau was very angry with Jacob.

Gen 27:41 *Esau held a grudge against Jacob because of the blessing his father had given him. He said to himself, "The days of mourning for my father are near; then I will kill my brother Jacob."*

Sometimes when we offend others, they feel like doing harm to us in return. Rebekah, their mother, heard what Esau planned to do. She sent Jacob away to safety in the land of Haran.

(to be cont.)

FORGIVE ONE ANOTHER

MARCH 16

Esau Still Upset
Bible (cont.)

Esau was angry because Jacob had taken his birthright and his blessing. Esau planned to kill Jacob, but Jacob fled to the land of Haran.

Jacob worked in Haran for his Uncle Laban [*lay* bun]. God blessed Jacob; he had many children, he had large flocks of livestock, and he had many servants. Jacob worked for his Uncle Laban for 20 years. Then God told Jacob to return to Canaan, where he had been born.

As Jacob traveled, he remembered how angry Esau was toward him, and he was afraid. He hoped Esau would not hate him for the things he had done when he was younger. Jacob was afraid that Esau would kill him and his whole family. Jacob prayed for help.

Gen 32:11 *Save me, I pray, from the hand of my brother Esau, for I am afraid he will come and attack me, and also the mothers with their children.*

Jacob sent flocks of sheep, goats, camels and donkeys ahead of him. They were gifts for Esau. Jacob told the servant in charge of each herd to space themselves from each other. Each one was to tell Esau that these animals were a gift from "his servant, Jacob."

That night Jacob went to spend the night alone, but the Bible says he wrestled with a man until daybreak. Jacob realized in the morning that the man was really God.

Gen 32:30 *So Jacob called the place Peniel* [pea *nie* ul]*, saying, "It is because I saw God face to face, and yet my life was spared."*

Later Jacob looked up and saw Esau coming with four hundred men. He put the women and children in groups and then he went ahead to meet Esau.

Gen 33:3 *He himself went on ahead and bowed down to the ground seven times as he approached his brother.* **Gen 33:4** *But Esau ran to meet Jacob and embraced him; he threw his arms around his neck and kissed him. And they wept.*

Even though Jacob had stolen his birthright—his inheritance—and his blessing, Esau still forgave Jacob these wrongs and they were at peace.

FORGIVE ONE ANOTHER

MARCH 17

A Missionary
St. Patrick's Day

St. Patrick's Day falls on March 17th. Patrick was born to a rich Christian family in Great Britain about the year 389. That is over 1600 years ago. When Patrick was sixteen years old he was captured and sold as a slave in Ireland. He worked as a shepherd for six years. Often alone and cold, Patrick turned to God. He spent most of his time praying. When he turned twenty-four, Patrick escaped back to Great Britain.

Patrick wanted to return to Ireland as a missionary. He prepared by doing some studying. When he was fifty-two he finally went back to Ireland. He worked in a place where Christianity had never been preached. It is believed that he started over three hundred churches and baptized more than 120,000 people.

Patrick could have hated the Irish people because he was enslaved by one of their ranchers for six long years. However, Patrick forgave the men that mistreated him and allowed God to use his experience for good.

Mt 6:14 *For if you forgive men when they sin against you, your heavenly Father will also forgive you.* **Mt 6:15** *But if you do not forgive men their sins, your Father will not forgive your sins.*

Patrick forgave those Irishmen who had kept him as a slave.

Rom 8:28 *And we know that in all things God works for the good of those who love him, who have been called according to his purpose.*

God can turn things that we think are bad, into things that are good. Joseph learned this lesson. He was sold as a slave by his brothers, but God worked it out for good. Joseph said:

Gen 50:20 *You intended to harm me, but God intended it for good to accomplish what is now being done, the saving of many lives.*

Patrick's enslavement as a boy turned out to be a good thing; he would return there as a missionary and bring about the conversion of Ireland.

FORGIVE ONE ANOTHER

MARCH 18

Jesus' Example

The word "gospel" means "good news." The good news is that Jesus came and died for our sins so that we could go to heaven and live forever with God. The word "gospel" can also mean the story of Jesus' life, death and resurrection. This story about Jesus was written by four different men. Their stories are called "the four gospels."

Do you know the names of the four gospels? They are Matthew, Mark, Luke and John. All four gospels talk about Jesus' life, his death and his resurrection. Let's look at parts of the crucifixion story. We will read from each of the four gospels.

Jn 19:17-18 *Carrying his own cross, he went out to the place of the Skull (which in Aramaic is called Golgotha)* [gol gah thuh]. *Here they crucified him, and with him two others—one on each side and Jesus in the middle.*

Mk 15:26 *The written notice of the charge against him read:* THE KING OF THE JEWS.

Mt 27:39-40 *Those who passed by hurled insults at him shaking their heads and saying, "You who are going to destroy the temple and build it in three days, save yourself! Come down from the cross, if you are the Son of God!"*

Lk 23:34 *Jesus said, "Father, forgive them, for they do not know what they are doing." And they divided up his clothes by casting lots.*

Even when Jesus was being nailed to the cross, he forgave the people who were doing it. When Jesus was suffering great pain he forgave those who were causing it.

The reason Jesus lived and died was so that he could save us from our sins. God's great love for us is shown in the sacrifice he made of his Son, Jesus Christ.

MARCH 19

Let's Kill Joseph
Bible

Joseph's brothers were angry that Joseph was their daddy's favorite son. They didn't like when he told them about his dreams where they were bowing down to him. The brothers let their anger grow until they hated Joseph. They wanted to kill him.

Joseph's brothers were out on the hills herding sheep. Jacob sent Joseph to check on them. Joseph's brothers saw him coming.

Gen 37:18 *But they saw him in the distance, and before he reached them, they plotted to kill him.*

Reuben did not want to kill Joseph. He said to the rest of the brothers,

Gen 37:22 *"Don't shed any blood. Throw him into this cistern* here in the desert, but don't lay a hand on him." Reuben said this to rescue him from them and take him back to his father.*

Gen 37:26-27 *Judah said to his brothers, "What will we gain if we kill our brother and cover up his blood? Come, let's sell him to the Ishmaelites* [ish male ites] *and not lay our hands on him; after all, he is our brother, our own flesh and blood." His brothers agreed.*

The brothers sold Joseph to the Ishmaelites. Joseph was taken to Egypt.

Joseph could have hated his brothers for what they did to him. Instead, Joseph chose to trust in God.

When Jacob died Joseph's brothers thought that Joseph would try to get even.

Gen 50:15 *When Joseph's brothers saw that their father was dead, they said, "What if Joseph holds a grudge against us and pays us back for all the wrongs we did to him?"*

Joseph told his brothers that God turned their harmful actions into a good thing.

Joseph did not hold a grudge against his brothers; he forgave them.

Are you angry at someone for what they have done to you? God wants you to forgive that person.

Cistern– a hole dug in the ground to catch and store rainwater

FORGIVE ONE ANOTHER

MARCH
20

The Last Supper
Maundy Thursday

Maundy Thursday is also called Holy Thursday. This is the day that Jesus ate the Last Supper with his disciples. The Last Supper was a celebration of the Passover.

The Jew's big celebration every year was the Passover. Jewish families, but especially the men, would come from all over the Roman Empire to Jerusalem to celebrate this feast. Because Jesus was a Jew, he celebrated this annual feast.

All four gospels, Matthew, Mark, Luke and John, tell us about the Last Supper. At the Last Supper Jesus celebrated the very first communion service. Let's read about it from the gospel of Matthew.

Mt 26:26 *While they were eating, Jesus took bread, gave thanks and broke it, and gave it to his disciples, saying, "Take and eat; this is my body."*

Mt 26:27 *Then he took the cup, gave thanks and offered it to them, saying, "Drink from it, all of you.* **Mt 26:28** *This is my blood of the covenant, which is poured out for many for the forgiveness of sins.* **Mt 26:29** *I tell you, I will not drink of this fruit of the vine from now on until that day when I drink it anew with you in my Father's kingdom."*

Jesus said that his blood would be poured out for the forgiveness of sins. That forgiveness of sins is for every person in the whole world. Whoever asks for God's forgiveness receives it because of what Jesus suffered on the cross.

Do you remember what the other name for Holy Thursday is? It's Maundy Thursday.

The Crucifixion

Good Friday

MARCH 21

Good Friday is the Friday before Easter. We celebrate Good Friday because it is the day we remember Jesus' death on the cross—his crucifixion.

Crucifixion is the punishment that the Romans used to put to death criminals who were very bad. Some things a person could be crucified for are: piracy—using ships or boats to steal; highway robbery—robbery that is outside or in a public place; assassination—killing an important person; forgery—signing someone else's name or making something counterfeit; false testimony—lying; mutiny—when sailors or soldiers rebel against their commanders; high treason and rebellion. High treason and rebellion can mean people are being very disloyal to their country, like maybe trying to start a war against it or trying to overthrow the leader.

Jesus never did any of these things. In fact, Jesus never did anything wrong. He is the only person who has never sinned. Then why was Jesus crucified? The Bible says he died on a cross because God loves us.

Jn 3:16 *For God so loved the world that he gave his one and only Son, that whoever believes in him shall not perish but have eternal life.*

When we put our faith in Jesus, the Bible says we receive forgiveness for our sins.

Eph 1:7 *In him we have redemption through his blood, the forgiveness of sins, in accordance with the riches of God's grace.*

The apostle Paul said that through Jesus we hear about forgiveness.

Acts 13:38 *Therefore, my brothers, I want you to know that through Jesus the forgiveness of sins is proclaimed to you.*

Ps 86:5 *You are forgiving and good, O Lord, abounding in love to all who call to you.*

God is a forgiving God. He sent Jesus to die on the cross so we could be forgiven.

FORGIVE ONE ANOTHER

MARCH
22
Angry Still

Marquis and Shanice were brother and sister. One time Shanice stayed mad at Marquis for a whole week. Marquis didn't know what he had done wrong, but he figured Shanice would get over it. On Sunday, Marquis' Sunday School teacher, Mrs. Johnson, talked about Jesus' teaching.

Mt 5:23 *Therefore, if you are offering your gift at the altar and there remember that your brother has something against you,* **Mt 5:24** *leave your gift there in front of the altar. First go and be reconciled to your brother; then come and offer your gift.*

Mrs. Johnson explained that we don't offer gifts to God like the Jews did in Jesus' time. We do give offerings in church, though, and we sing songs of worship to God. Mrs. Johnson said Jesus today might say, "If you are worshipping and remember someone is angry with you, go and see if you can settle the matter with each other. After you have settled things, then come back to me." Why is Jesus concerned about how we relate to other people? It is because all believers are part of the body of Christ.

I Cor 12:27 *Now you are the body of Christ, and each one of you is a part of it.*

Rom 12:5 *So in Christ we who are many form one body, and each member belongs to all the others.*

Marquis decided he would do what the Bible teaches. After Sunday School he found Shanice and asked if they could go outside and talk.

Marquis said, "Shanice, I know you are angry with me about something."

Shanice blurted out, "You embarrassed me in front of all my friends."

Marquis remembered what he had said. He didn't think it was a big deal, but he knew it was a big deal to his sister. He said, "I'm sorry Shanice. I didn't mean to embarrass you."

Shanice forgave Marquis. They both felt better as they walked into church.

MARCH 23

We Are Forgiven!
Easter

The Bible says that Jesus died, that he was buried and that on the third day he rose again.

Luke tells us that at three o'clock in the afternoon Jesus called out to God and then he died.

Lk 23:46 *Jesus called out with a loud voice, "Father, into your hands I commit my spirit." When he had said this, he breathed his last.*

Joseph of Arimathea asked Pilate if he could take Jesus' body. Pilate said he could.

Mk 15:46 *So Joseph bought some linen cloth, took down the body, wrapped it in the linen, and placed it in a tomb cut out of rock. Then he rolled a stone against the entrance of the tomb.*

When some women came to take care of Jesus' dead body an angel appeared to them. He told them not to be afraid. He said he knew they were looking for Jesus. Then he said that Jesus had risen.

Mt 28:6 *He is not here; he has risen, just as he said. Come and see the place where he lay.*

Paul says if Jesus had not risen from the dead—had he not been God, but only an ordinary person—we would not be forgiven.

I Cor 15:17 *And if Christ has not been raised, your faith is futile; you are still in your sins.*

Jesus did rise from the dead. His resurrection proves he is God and that all he taught us is true. We are forgiven.

MARCH 24

Forgiven Should Forgive

Mt 18:23-25 *Therefore, the kingdom of heaven is like a king who wanted to settle accounts with his servants. As he began the settlement, a man who owed him ten thousand talents was brought to him. Since he was not able to pay, the master ordered that he and his wife and his children and all that he had be sold to repay the debt.*

Mt 18:26-28 *The servant fell on his knees before him. "Be patient with me," he begged, "and I will pay back everything." The servant's master took pity on him, canceled the debt and let him go.*

But when the servant went out, he found one of his fellow servants who owed him a hundred denarii [dih nare ee eye]. *He grabbed him and began to choke him. "Pay back what you owe me!" he demanded.*

Mt 18:29-31 *His fellow servant fell to his knees and begged him, "Be patient with me, and I will pay you back."*

But he refused. Instead, he went off and had the man thrown into prison until he could pay the debt. When the other servants saw what had happened, they were greatly distressed and went and told their master everything that had happened.

Mt 18:32-35 *Then the master called the servant in. "You wicked servant," he said, "I canceled all that debt of yours because you begged me to. Shouldn't you have had mercy on your fellow servant just as I had on you?" In anger his master turned him over to the jailers to be tortured until he should pay back all he owed.*

This is how my heavenly Father will treat each of you unless you forgive your brother from your heart.

Jesus uses this parable to teach us a lesson: Since God has forgiven our sins, we should forgive those who sin against us.

Enough Already!

MARCH 25

"Tattle tale, tattle tale!" Hannah yelled after her little sister, Kaitlyn. Kaitlyn was going to tell Mommy for the "umpteenth" time that Hannah was picking on her. Mom was getting tired of listening to it all. She decided to get the girls' older brothers, Hunter and Scott, involved.

Mom got all the children together. She looked up Matthew, chapter 18. She found the place where Jesus said how to deal with someone who is sinning against someone else. Kaitlyn thought that Hannah was picking on her. We might say that Kaitlyn thought Hannah was "sinning against her."

Mt 18:15a *If your brother sins against you, go and show him his fault, just between the two of you.* **Mt 8:15b** *If he listens to you, you have won your brother over.*

Mt 18:16 *But if he will not listen, take one or two others along, so that "every matter may be established by the testimony of two or three witnesses."*

Mt 18:17 *If he refuses to listen to them, tell it to the church; and if he refuses to listen even to the church, treat him as you would a pagan or a tax collector.*

Hunter asked, "Are we going to treat Hannah like a pagan or a tax collector?"

Mom said this is how she wanted things to go: First, Kaitlyn needs to tell Hannah that she is feeling sinned against. Maybe the two of them can work it out. Second, if that doesn't work, then Kaitlyn needs to go get Hunter and/or Scott. If they cannot settle the disagreement between the girls, then and only then will Kaitlyn be able to tell Mom.

If Kaitlyn came to Mom, Mom would ask, "Have you talked to Hannah? Have you talked to your brothers? Did your brothers talk to Hannah? They couldn't settle it? Alright then, what's the problem?"

This three-step process freed Mom up to get other things done. Under this plan Kaitlyn worked things out with Hannah much more quickly.

MARCH 26

He's a Bully

Children can be very mean. Mitch was teased almost every day because he talked with a lisp. It got so bad that Mitch couldn't stand it. He refused to go back to school. Mitch's dad listened as Mitch told him what was happening.

Dad asked if there was one child who was doing most of the teasing. Mitch nodded. It was Allen. Dad knew that at the playground there were other boys much bigger than Allen. Dad went and talked to one of them; his name was Brandon. Brandon agreed to look out for Mitch. Dad convinced Mitch that Brandon wouldn't let Allen tease him. When Allen started to tease Mitch, Brandon told him, "You'd better stop that." Allen quickly found something else to do.

Some people think Christians should put up with any and all meanness. They say Jesus told us to forgive. Jesus also said to do something else.

Lk 17:3 *So watch yourselves. If your brother sins, rebuke him, and if he repents, forgive him.*

Allen was sinning by being mean to Mitch. Jesus says we should rebuke that person. Rebuke is a way to say "correct with strong words" or "let them know you mean business." Brandon rebuked Allen, and Allen stopped the teasing. When Allen stopped teasing Mitch, all the other children did the same.

Lev 19:17 *Do not hate your brother in your heart. Rebuke your neighbor frankly so you will not share in his guilt.*

Prov 15:31 *He who listens to a life-giving rebuke will be at home among the wise.*

Prov 27:5 *Better is open rebuke than hidden love.*

Bullies do not just need to be forgiven; they need to be rebuked.
(to be cont.)

MARCH 27

Evil is not Good
(cont.)

Remember yesterday? Brandon rebuked Allen; and Allen stopped teasing Mitch?

Allen never came and told Mitch he was sorry. That was alright with Mitch. He was just glad the teasing had stopped.

Allen may not even think he did anything wrong, really. He was popular and when he made fun of people the other kids laughed.

In Isaiah, the prophet warns people who sin and do wicked things. When God says "woe" to certain people, he means that bad things are going to happen to them.

Isa 5:18 *Woe to those who draw sin along with cords of deceit, and wickedness as with cart ropes.*

God warns people who call evil good.

Isa 5:20 *Woe to those who call evil good and good evil, who put darkness for light and light for darkness, who put bitter for sweet and sweet for bitter.*

God warns of woe to those who are dishonest and unfair, **Isa 5:23** *who acquit the guilty for a bribe, but deny justice to the innocent.*

Allen, by making fun of Mitch, was denying justice to the innocent.

After God says "woe" to all these people, he says what will happen to them.

Isa 5:24 *Therefore, as tongues of fire lick up straw and as dry grass sinks down in the flames, so their roots will decay and their flowers blow away like dust; for they have rejected the law of the LORD Almighty and spurned the word of the Holy One of Israel.*

God will one day judge those who have done evil.

(to be cont.)

MARCH 28

Repentance Required
(cont.)

Mitch never told Allen that he forgave him. When does the Bible say that Mitch must forgive Allen?

Lk 17:3 *So watch yourselves. If your brother sins, rebuke him, and if he repents,* forgive him.*

Mitch should forgive Allen if he repents. That means that Allen says he is sorry and really tries not to tease him again.

If Allen would come to Mitch and say he was sorry, do you think it would be easy for Mitch to forgive him? No, it would be very hard for Mitch. Maybe Mitch will not be able to forgive right away. It might take some time. If Allen is serious that he is sorry, he will not tease Mitch anymore. Mitch might wait to see if Allen is truly sorry or if he just said that because Brandon is bigger than he is.

God extends his forgiveness to all people, but if people refuse to repent, then God's forgiveness does not take place.

Acts 3:19 *Repent, then, and turn to God, so that your sins may be wiped out, that times of refreshing may come from the Lord.*

Acts 3:26 *When God raised up his servant, he sent him first to you to bless you by turning each of you from your wicked ways.*

Mk 1:4 *And so John came, baptizing in the desert region and preaching a baptism of repentance for the forgiveness of sins.*

Repents—says he is sorry

MARCH 29

God is Forgiving
Bible

When God revealed himself to Moses, he told Moses what he was like.

Ex 34:6 *And he passed in front of Moses, proclaiming, "The LORD, the LORD, the compassionate and gracious God, slow to anger, abounding in love and faithfulness,* **Ex 34:7a** *maintaining love to thousands, and forgiving wickedness, rebellion and sin."*

God wanted Moses to know what he was like. He said he was compassionate, gracious, slow to anger, loving, faithful, and last, but not least important, forgiving. God is a forgiving God. We can find that truth in other scriptures.

Neh 9:17b *But you are a forgiving God, gracious and compassionate, slow to anger and abounding in love. Therefore you did not desert them.*

Nehemiah puts forgiving at the beginning of the list rather than at the end. He probably did this because he was asking God to forgive the sin of his people. Nehemiah was "reminding" God that he was a forgiving God so that he would forgive their sins.

Daniel also confesses that God's people are sinful and he prays that God will forgive them. He "reminds" God that he is forgiving.

Dan 9:9 *The Lord our God is merciful and forgiving, even though we have rebelled against him.*

The Bible clearly tells us that God is a forgiving God. If we want to be forgiven we must confess our sins* and ask God to forgive us.

Confess our sins—to admit we have done something wrong

MARCH 30

Sneaky
Warren Marigny

Terry came in late one night. Why he decided to look in the oven, he doesn't know. It might have been because the members in his family often hid food items they didn't want someone else to consume. He saw a glass bottle of coke setting there. He figured it belonged to his older sister, Gladys. He quickly closed the oven, looking around to see if anyone else had seen it. Then he peeked down the hall to see if anyone else was awake. The house was still; it seemed that everyone was asleep.

Terry carefully raised the sides of the metal cap on the coke bottle, then he pushed the cap off gently with his thumbs. He put some ice in a tall glass and poured the coke over it. He sat down and enjoyed the ice-cold drink. When he finished he thought, "Now what do I do?" He took some coffee that was left in the coffeepot, added a little water and filled the bottle with it. He put the top back on and placed it carefully back in the oven. Then he was off to bed.

Terry was trying to make the "owner of the coke" think that he had not done anything. He was trying to deceive. The Bible often talks about deception. That means you try to make someone think something is true, when it isn't, just like Terry did. In the Bible, Jacob deceived his father Isaac; he made him think that he was Esau.

Gen 27:15 *Then Rebekah took the best clothes of Esau her older son, which she had in the house, and put them on her younger son Jacob.* **Gen 27:16** *She also covered his hands and the smooth part of his neck with the goatskins.*

Gen 27:22 *Jacob went close to his father Isaac, who touched him and said, "The voice is the voice of Jacob, but the hands are the hands of Esau."* **Gen 27:23** *He did not recognize him, for his hands were hairy like those of his brother Esau; so he blessed him.*

Deception or deceiving someone is like lying without using words. Terry was trying to deceive the person who hid the coke in the oven. He wanted them to think coke was still in the bottle.

(to be cont.)

MARCH 31

Produce Good Fruit
Warren Marigny (cont.)

Mama got up about 3:00 AM to work in the bakery. She put some ice in a tall glass and pulled her "coke" out of the oven. She poured the "coke" over the ice and swished it around to get it good and cold. Then she took a few big swallows. The taste finally hit her and she sprayed the coffee water out of her mouth and all over the room. Mama went to work and Terry heard about it later.

Terry would never have taken the soda if he would have known it was his mother's. He bought a soda to replace the one he had taken. Sometimes it is not enough to just say we are sorry, we should show we are sorry by trying to repay the damage we have done. When the people came to John the Baptist to be baptized he said,

Mt 3:8 *Produce fruit in keeping with repentance.*

Lk 3:8 *Produce fruit in keeping with repentance. And do not begin to say to yourselves, "We have Abraham as our father." For I tell you that out of these stones God can raise up children for Abraham.*

John the Baptist was telling the people if they wanted to be baptized they should change their ways. They should start doing good rather than bad things.

Mt 3:10 *The ax is already at the root of the trees, and every tree that does not produce good fruit will be cut down and thrown into the fire.*

John the Baptist said that if people were going to say they were sorry for their sins they needed to show it by "producing good fruit" which means by doing good deeds.

Acts 26:20b *I preached that they should repent and turn to God and prove their repentance by their deeds.*

Terry proved his repentance by buying another coke for his mother.

APRIL

1

One of Them

There were four people in class with whom no one wanted to be friends. When one of these four got on the bus, the other kids would scramble to get a partner in their seats lest they get stuck sitting with one of these kids.

Ordinarily Alberto didn't have a friend to sit with. He often sat alone and played his hand-held computer games. But when one of the four students who were tagged as "no one's friends" got on, Alberto was offered to fill the seat beside someone else. Both boys were happy that they weren't forced to sit with one of "those four."

Have you ever had something like that happen to you? Have you been tempted to treat people unkindly? It helps to remind ourselves that God created all people.

Gen 1:26 *Then God said, "Let us make man in our image, in our likeness, and let them rule over the fish of the sea and the birds of the air, over the livestock, over all the earth, and over all the creatures that move along the ground."*

Gen 1:27 *So God created man in his own image, in the image of God he created him; male and female he created them.*

If we are in a situation where we are tempted to be unkind to people, what does God want us to do?

Eph 4:32 *Be kind and compassionate to one another, forgiving each other, just as in Christ God forgave you.*

Col 3:12 *Therefore, as God's chosen people, holy and dearly loved, clothe yourselves with compassion, kindness, humility, gentleness and patience.*

God Revealed

APRIL 2

Bible

Moses was a man who walked closely with God. The Bible says:

Ex 33:11a *The LORD would speak to Moses face to face, as a man speaks with his friend.*

Moses had received the Ten Commandments from God. He came down from the mountain carrying the stone tablets on which they were written. When he saw that the people were worshipping a golden calf, he was so angry that he threw the tablets down and broke them.

Ex 32:19 *When Moses approached the camp and saw the calf and the dancing, his anger burned and he threw the tablets out of his hands, breaking them to pieces at the foot of the mountain.*

Moses really wanted to see what God looked like, so he asked God if he could see him. God told Moses to chisel out another set of stone tablets and then come up the mountain again.

Ex 34:5 *Then the LORD came down in the cloud and stood there with him and proclaimed his name, the LORD.* **Ex 34:6-7a** *And he passed in front of Moses, proclaiming, "The LORD, the LORD, the compassionate and gracious God, slow to anger, abounding in love and faithfulness, maintaining love to thousands, and forgiving wickedness, rebellion and sin."*

This doesn't sound very impressive; but it must have been, because Moses bowed to the ground and worshipped.

When God revealed himself to Moses, the first word God used to describe himself was "compassionate." That is another word for being kind. When someone is compassionate, he cares for the best interests of others. If a person is compassionate, he is also kind. Since God is compassionate, God is kind.

APRIL 3

Be Generous
Bible

The Apostle Paul went on three missionary trips. His home church was Antioch, but he knew that Christianity had its true beginnings in the church of Jerusalem. Many people in the Jerusalem church were suffering because of a famine in the land. A famine is when there is not enough food for people to eat.

The Jews at Jerusalem were poor, so Paul and Barnabas collected money in Antioch. They took it to Jerusalem where the church would give it to the poor people who were in need.

Acts 11:29-30 *The disciples, each according to his ability, decided to provide help for the brothers living in Judea* [jew *dee* uh]. *This they did, sending their gift to the elders by Barnabas and Saul.*

Saul's name was changed to Paul. It was Barnabas and Paul who took this offering to Jerusalem.

In the second letter of Paul to the Christians in the city of Corinth, Paul talks about another offering that he would take to Jerusalem. The people in the churches of Macedonia were not wealthy people. Yet they gave generously to the offering for the poor people of Jerusalem. Paul said their generosity was a display of God's grace.

II Cor 8:1 *And now, brothers, we want you to know about the grace that God has given the Macedonian* [mass eh *doe* nee un] *churches.* **II Cor 8:2** *Out of the most severe trial, their overflowing joy and their extreme poverty welled up in rich generosity.* **II Cor 8:3-4** *For I testify that they gave as much as they were able, and even beyond their ability. Entirely on their own, they urgently pleaded with us for the privilege of sharing in this service to the saints.*

We don't need to be rich in order to give to the poor. These Macedonians were poor themselves, yet they gave what they could.

APRIL 4

Blessed by God
Bible

Abram, who was later called Abraham, grew up in the city of Ur. Ur was a city full of people who believed in other gods. God spoke to Abram.

Gen 12:1 *The Lord had said to Abram, "Leave your country, your people and your father's household and go to the land I will show you."*

When Abram arrived in Canaan God spoke to him again:

Gen 12:7a *The Lord appeared to Abram and said, "To your offspring I will give this land."*

Why did God make this promise to Abram? Because God is kind! Abram had served the one true God, and God wanted to bless him. God wants to bless us, too, if we choose to obey Him.

Deut 7:12-14 *If you pay attention to these laws and are careful to follow them, then the Lord your God will keep his covenant of love with you, as he swore to your forefathers. He will love you and bless you and increase your numbers. He will bless the fruit of your womb, the crops of your land—your grain, new wine and oil—the calves of your herds and the lambs of your flocks in the land that he swore to your forefathers to give you. You will be blessed more than any other people; none of your men or women will be childless, nor any of your livestock without young.* **Deut 7:15-16** *The Lord will keep you free from every disease. He will not inflict on you the horrible diseases you knew in Egypt, but he will inflict them on all who hate you. You must destroy all the peoples the Lord your God gives over to you. Do not look on them with pity and do not serve their gods, for that will be a snare to you.*

God was kind to Abraham and his family because Abraham obeyed God. God will also be kind to us if we obey Him.

APRIL 5 — Shoeboxes

Franklin Graham began a project that he calls "Operation Christmas Child." It is an opportunity for children in wealthier countries like the United States to care for, or show compassion for, children in poor countries. Children pack a shoe box with small items such as soap, pencils, paper, a hair brush, small toys, candy, etc. They take these boxes to their local church. The boxes are sent to a gathering point for shipment to poor countries. It is a good opportunity for children to perform an act of kindness.

The Bible has some things to say about giving. Paul was addressing some church leaders in Ephesus [*ef* uh sus] when he wrote:

Acts 20:35 *In everything I did, I showed you that by this kind of hard work we must help the weak, remembering the words the Lord Jesus himself said: "It is more blessed to give than to receive."*

We are blessed by God when we give.

II Cor 9:7 *Each man should give what he has decided in his heart to give, not reluctantly or under compulsion, for God loves a cheerful giver.*

Giving "under compulsion" means we are being forced to give. When we give cheerfully, we are loved by God.

Jesus gives us some advice about giving:

Mt 6:1-2 *Be careful not to do your "acts of righteousness" before men, to be seen by them. If you do, you will have no reward from your Father in heaven. So when you give to the needy, do not announce it with trumpets, as the hypocrites do in the synagogues and on the streets, to be honored by men. I tell you the truth, they have received their reward in full.*

Mt 6:3-4 *But when you give to the needy, do not let your left hand know what your right hand is doing, so that your giving may be in secret. Then your Father, who sees what is done in secret, will reward you.*

If we give secretly, God will reward us. We should give, not to show off, but to be kind to others.

APRIL 6

Praying for a Baby
Bible

God promised Abraham that he would make his descendants as numerous as the stars in the sky, or as numerous as the sands on the seashore.

Gen 22:17a *I will surely bless you and make your descendants as numerous as the stars in the sky and as the sand on the seashore.*

When Isaac, Abraham's son, got married, his wife Rebekah was barren. That means she could not bear children. Isaac probably knew of God's promise to his father; God had promised to give Abraham many, many descendants. Isaac prayed that his wife would be able to have children.

Gen 25:21 *Isaac prayed to the LORD on behalf of his wife, because she was barren. The LORD answered his prayer, and his wife Rebekah became pregnant.*

God showed kindness to Isaac by answering his prayer. Better yet, Rebekah did not just have one baby; she had twins!

Ps 34:15 *The eyes of the LORD are on the righteous and his ears are attentive to their cry.*

Ps 34:17 *The righteous cry out, and the LORD hears them; he delivers them from all their troubles.*

God showed kindness to Isaac in answering his prayer, and he will show kindness to us in answering our prayers.

APRIL 7

The Meanest Girl

Mary thought Sally was the meanest girl she knew. Sally had lots of friends, but she treated Mary like she wasn't even there. Mary would say something and Sally would just keep talking. Sally also looked down on Mary because of the way she dressed.

When people ignore us and look down on us, we often want to be hurtful in return. But God has a different plan.

I Thes 5:15 *Make sure that nobody pays back wrong for wrong, but always try to be kind to each other and to everyone else.*

God says we should not do evil to others, or even wish evil on them. Instead, he says we should be kind to everyone. That is hard when people are mean to us, but God asks us to do hard things.

I Pet 3:9a *Do not repay evil with evil or insult with insult, but with blessing.*

How can you return a blessing on someone who is unkind to you? You can pray for them. That is not easy either, but you can do it.

God is talking to his people when he says:

Hos 11:4a *I led them with cords of human kindness, with ties of love.*

This scripture means that God is kind to his people. Because God wants us to be like him, we should be kind.

Lk 6:35 *But love your enemies, do good to them, and lend to them without expecting to get anything back. Then your reward will be great, and you will be sons of the Most High, because he is kind to the ungrateful and wicked.*

When we are kind to others, we are truly sons and daughters of God.

APRIL 8

God is Kind to Jacob

God enjoys giving his people good things. This is the promise he made to Abraham:

Gen 12:2 *I will make you into a great nation and I will bless you; I will make your name great, and you will be a blessing.* **Gen 12:3** *I will bless those who bless you, and whoever curses you I will curse; and all peoples on earth will be blessed through you.*

God promised to give Abraham the land of Canaan so his children and grandchildren would have a good place to live. God promised to make Abraham into a great nation. God promised to make Abraham's name great. God also promised to make Abraham a blessing.

Abraham's son was Isaac and Abraham's grandson was Jacob. Just like God blessed Abraham, he wanted to bless his grandson, Jacob. When Jacob was a grown man, he had a dream of a ladder going up to heaven. The Bible says Jacob saw someone at the top of the ladder.

Gen 28:13 *There above it stood the Lord, and he said: "I am the Lord, the God of your father Abraham and the God of Isaac. I will give you and your descendants the land on which you are lying.* **Gen 28:14** *Your descendants will be like the dust of the earth, and you will spread out to the west and to the east, to the north and to the south. All peoples on earth will be blessed through you and your offspring.*

God was kind to Jacob. He promised him many of the same things he had promised to his grandfather, Abraham.

God also wants to be kind to us and give us good things. He requires that we obey him.

APRIL 9

Good Gifts from God

Acts 7:9-10 *Because the patriarchs* [pay tree arks] were jealous of Joseph, they sold him as a slave into Egypt. But God was with him and rescued him from all his troubles. He gave Joseph wisdom and enabled him to gain the goodwill of Pharaoh king of Egypt; so he made him ruler over Egypt and all his palace.*

According to this scripture passage, God did three things for Joseph. He rescued him, he gave him wisdom and he enabled him to gain the goodwill of Pharaoh.

Joseph was working for Potiphar. Potiphar's wife lied about Joseph, so Joseph was thrown in prison. While he was in prison he interpreted some dreams. When the Pharaoh had a dream, he sent for Joseph to interpret it. Because Joseph interpreted the Pharaoh's dream about a coming famine, the Pharaoh freed Joseph from prison. Pharaoh put Joseph in charge of all Egypt. God rescued Joseph from prison by giving Joseph the ability to interpret dreams.

God also gave Joseph wisdom.

Gen 41:39 *Then Pharaoh said to Joseph, "Since God has made all this known to you, there is no one so discerning and wise as you."*

God enabled Joseph to gain the goodwill of Pharaoh. Pharaoh said this about Joseph:

Gen 41:40 *You shall be in charge of my palace, and all my people are to submit to your orders. Only with respect to the throne will I be greater than you.*

Gen 41:41 *So Pharaoh said to Joseph, "I hereby put you in charge of the whole land of Egypt."*

Joseph listened to God and chose to live God's way, so God showed him great kindness. God will do the same for us. If we listen to God and live according to his ways, he will bless us.

Patriarchs—the sons of Jacob

APRIL 10

Maltese Kindness
Bible

On the island of Malta the people knew there was a terrible storm at sea. The winds were high and the surf was hitting the beach hard. One evening they were surprised to see people coming inland from the shore. It was cold and raining and the islanders wanted to do what they could to help. The people of Malta found out there had been a shipwreck. On the ship was the missionary team of the Apostle Paul. Luke, who wrote the Book of Acts, says:

Acts 28:2 *The islanders showed us unusual kindness. They built a fire and welcomed us all because it was raining and cold.*

They showed unusual kindness by caring for the hungry, shivering people. The story continues in verse seven.

Acts 28:7 *There was an estate nearby that belonged to Publius [pub lih us], the chief official of the island. He welcomed us to his home and for three days entertained us hospitably.*

Acts 28:8-9 *His father was sick in bed, suffering from fever and dysentery. Paul went in to see him and, after prayer, placed his hands on him and healed him. When this had happened, the rest of the sick on the island came and were cured.* **Acts 28:10** *They honored us in many ways and when we were ready to sail, they furnished us with the supplies we needed.*

Many acts of kindness were done in this story. The islanders were "unusually" kind to the people who had been shipwrecked. Publius welcomed into his own home those who had been shipwrecked. Paul healed Publius' father and then other people. When the people got ready to leave, the islanders sent supplies with them.

Taking care of people, inviting them over to your house, praying for people and giving gifts to people are all acts of kindness that we can do.

APRIL
11
The Promised Land

Since the creation of the world we have a written record of the history of God's people. That written record is the Bible.

In chapter 9 of Nehemiah [nee heh *my* uh] the author praises God, because God cares about people.

Neh 9:19 *Because of your great compassion you did not abandon them in the desert. By day the pillar of cloud did not cease to guide them on their path, nor the pillar of fire by night to shine on the way they were to take.*

God showed his people how to get to the Promised Land. During the day a cloud led them, and during the night it turned into a pillar of fire so they could see it.

Neh 9:20-21 *You gave your good spirit to instruct them. You did not withhold your manna from their mouths, and you gave them water for their thirst. For forty years you sustained them in the desert; they lacked nothing, their clothes did not wear out nor did their feet become swollen.*

God gave his people food and water in the desert. He made their clothes to last a long time so that they had what they needed.

Neh 9:24 *Their sons went in and took possession of the land. You subdued before them the Canaanites, who lived in the land; you handed the Canaanites over to them, along with their kings and the peoples of the land, to deal with them as they pleased.*

God gave his people the land he had promised them.

Neh 9:25 *They captured fortified cities and fertile land; they took possession of houses filled with all kinds of good things, wells already dug, vineyards, olive groves and fruit trees in abundance. They ate to the full and were well-nourished; they reveled in your great goodness.*

God's goodness to his people was better than what they could have imagined. God wants to be kind to his people today, the way he was kind to his people back then.

Be Kind at Home

APRIL
12

Everyone thought Carly and Emma were very close as sisters. When their mom dropped Carly off at school every day, Carly would give Emma a big hug and kiss. Then Emma was dropped off at Head Start. When Carly and Emma went to daycare after school, they stood up for each other and played together so well.

Mom felt good about how her daughters were very loving in public. Mom didn't feel good that the girls fought most of the time they were at home. Why do children do that? Maybe it's because they feel safe at home and around Mom.

God wants us to be kind even, or should we say, especially to our families. **Ps 68:6a** *God sets the lonely in families.*

Families are one of the greatest ideas that God had. Because of families we don't need to be lonely. Because of families everyone should have someone that loves them. God planned for family members to be the people that care for helpless, newborn babies.

Jesus said in **Jn 15:12**, *"My command is this: Love each other as I have loved you,"* and he said the same thing in **Jn 13:34**, *"A new command I give you: Love one another. As I have loved you, so you must love one another."*

Jesus says we should love other people. We should especially love our families. Families are the people God has given us to help us show His love to the world.

Jn 15:13 *Greater love has no one than this, that he lay down his life for his friends.*

Carly and Emma showed love for each other in public. They should do the same when they are at home.

APRIL 13

Best Friends Forever

In the Bible, David and Jonathan were best of friends.

I Sam 18:1 *After David had finished talking with Saul, Jonathan became one in spirit with David, and he loved him as himself.*

I Sam 18:3 *And Jonathan made a covenant with David because he loved him as himself.*

Jonathan loved David as he loved himself.

Some young girls wear bracelets that say BFF. BFF stands for "Best Friends Forever." We could probably say that David and Jonathan were Best Friends Forever.

Many people knew that David would one day be king because Samuel had anointed him. Saul, Jonathan's father, was the king. Saul wanted to kill David because he knew that David had been anointed to be the next king. Jonathan protected David and made plans for when David would be king.

I Sam 23:16 *And Saul's son Jonathan went to David at Horesh and helped him find strength in God.* **I Sam 23:17** *"Don't be afraid," he said. "My father Saul will not lay a hand on you. You will be king over Israel, and I will be second to you. Even my father Saul knows this."*

Jonathan showed kindness to David by being his friend and by encouraging him. You can show kindness to people by being their friend and by encouraging them.

APRIL 14

The Family of a Friend
Bible

David and Jonathan were close friends. Then David lost his dear friend Jonathan. When The Israelites fought against the Philistines, Jonathan was killed in the battle.

I Sam 31:2 *The Philistines pressed hard after Saul and his sons, and they killed his sons Jonathan, Abinadab and Malki-Shua.*

David was very sad about losing his closest friend. He and his men showed their sadness.

II Sam 1:12 *They mourned and wept and fasted till evening for Saul and his son Jonathan, and for the army of the Lord and the house of Israel, because they had fallen by the sword.*

David said how much he missed Jonathan:

II Sam 1:26 *I grieve for you, Jonathan my brother; you were very dear to me. Your love for me was wonderful, more wonderful than that of women.*

Because David and Jonathan were such good friends, David wanted to do something for Jonathan even though he had already died.

II Sam 9:1 *David asked, "Is there anyone still left of the house of Saul to whom I can show kindness for Jonathan's sake?"*

King David wanted to show kindness to Jonathan's family because Jonathan was a member of that family. If you have a really good friend you can show kindness to them by doing kind things for their family.

(to be cont.)

BE KIND

APRIL
15

Jonathan's Son
Bible (cont.)

David wanted to show kindness to Jonathan's family. A man who had been a servant in Saul's house was contacted. His name was Ziba. King David asked him a question.

II Sam 9:3 *The king asked, "Is there no one still left of the house of Saul to whom I can show God's kindness?"*

Ziba answered the king, "There is still a son of Jonathan; he is crippled in both feet."

An earlier chapter in II Samuel tells us how Jonathan's son became crippled.

II Sam 4:4 *(Jonathan son of Saul had a son who was lame in both feet. He was five years old when the news about Saul and Jonathan came from Jezreel. His nurse picked him up and fled, but as she hurried to leave, he fell and became crippled. His name was Mephibosheth* [meh *fib* oh sheth].*)*

David sent someone to bring Mephibosheth to his royal palace.

II Sam 9:6 *When Mephibosheth son of Jonathan, the son of Saul, came to David, he bowed down to pay him honor.*

David said, "Mephibosheth!"

"Your servant," he replied.

II Sam 9:7 *"Don't be afraid," David said to him, "for I will surely show you kindness for the sake of your father Jonathan. I will restore to you all the land that belonged to your grandfather Saul, and you will always eat at my table."*

It didn't matter to David that Mephibosheth was crippled; David showed him kindness anyway. Are you kind to those who have handicaps?

Small Acts of Kindness

APRIL 16

A potluck had been planned for after church. All the moms had brought food to church to share. Everyone formed a line to eat, but four year-old Jorge said he would stay back and watch his friend Elena's doll until she got her food. Jorge was showing kindness to Elena.

This may not seem like Jorge really did very much, but Jesus notices even our small acts of kindness. Let's read a story about how Jesus noticed a small act of kindness.

Lk 21:1 *As he looked up, Jesus saw the rich putting their gifts into the temple treasury.* **Lk 21:2** *He also saw a poor widow put in two very small copper coins.*

Lk 21:3 *"I tell you the truth," he said, "this poor widow has put in more than all the others.* **Lk 21:4** *All these people gave their gifts out of their wealth; but she out of her poverty put in all she had to live on."*

This woman didn't have much but she wanted to give it to God's work. When all the money that was given was counted, this woman's two small coins didn't look like much in comparison.

No one else probably cared that this woman gave what she could have spent on food. But Jesus noticed and God noticed. The woman probably went hungry because she gave what little she had to God. The woman gave what she could. Jesus noticed that, and he notices all our little acts of kindness.

Jesus even noticed Jorge's act of kindness when he volunteered to "baby-sit" Elena's doll.

APRIL
17
Willing to Listen

Kerri and Gladys were just two years apart. They would often argue. One time, when they were riding in the van, they started fighting. Gladys scratched Kerri's arm with her fingernails.

Kerri yelled and Mommy came from the front seat of the van. Kerri couldn't believe what Mommy said. She accused Kerri of scratching her own arm to make it look worse than it really was.

Older children often are held responsible for things their younger siblings do. Kerri was no longer just angry with Gladys; she was angry at Mommy, also. Kerri was glad she had a dad who understood her. She knew that now was not a good time to talk to him because he was driving. But when they were alone together he would listen and understand.

Kerri's dad is very much like God. God is always ready to listen to us, and he understands our troubles.

Ps 120:1 *I call on the LORD in my distress, and he answers me.*

Ps 3:4 *To the LORD I cry aloud, and he answers me from his holy hill.*

Ps 4:3 *Know that the LORD has set apart the godly for himself; the LORD will hear when I call to him.*

Ps 5:3 *In the morning, O LORD, you hear my voice; in the morning I lay my requests before you and wait in expectation.*

If people are not listening to you, know that God hears your every prayer.

APRIL 18

Egg & Bread
Warren Marigny

Terry grew up in a Catholic family. He wasn't allowed to eat meat on Fridays; every Friday he took two boiled eggs and two slices of bread for his lunch. His schoolmates gave him the nickname "Egg and Bread." Terry didn't mind the nickname Egg and Bread, because he knew the children were not trying to be mean when they said it.

There are some nicknames children have that they don't like. Have you ever heard anyone called "fatso" or a boy called "sissy?" Are there other nicknames you have heard that you know children don't like being called?

If we call people names they don't like, we are being unkind. God tells us to be kind.

Eph 4:32 *Be kind and compassionate to one another, forgiving each other, just as in Christ God forgave you.*

God also tells us we should look out for other people:

Phil 2:4 *Each of you should look not only to your own interests, but also to the interests of others.*

If someone is being called a name they don't like, we could try to be friends with that person. You could also tell the name caller to stop being mean.

God looks out for people who are having trouble. In the Bible these people are often called "the afflicted" or "the oppressed."

Ps 10:17 *You hear, O Lord, the desire of the afflicted; you encourage them, and you listen to their cry,* **Ps 10:18** *defending the fatherless and the oppressed, in order that man, who is of the earth, may terrify no more.*

Because God cares for the afflicted and the oppressed—those who are being called names—we should care for them also.

APRIL 19

The Good Samaritan

The story of the Good Samaritan is found in Luke, chapter ten.

Lk 10:30-31 *In reply Jesus said: "A man was going down from Jerusalem to Jericho, when he fell into the hands of robbers. They stripped him of his clothes, beat him and went away, leaving him half dead. A priest happened to be going down the same road, and when he saw the man, he passed by on the other side.* **Lk 10:32-33** *So too, a Levite, when he came to the place and saw him, passed by on the other side. But a Samaritan, as he traveled, came where the man was; and when he saw him, he took pity on him.* **Lk 10:34-35** *He went to him and bandaged his wounds, pouring on oil and wine. Then he put the man on his own donkey, took him to an inn and took care of him. The next day he took out two silver coins and gave them to the innkeeper. 'Look after him,' he said, 'and when I return, I will reimburse you for any extra expense you may have.'*

Lk 10:36-37 *"Which of these three do you think was a neighbor to the man who fell into the hands of robbers?"*

The expert in the law replied, "The one who had mercy on him."

Jesus told him, "Go and do likewise."

When Jesus says, "Go and do likewise," he means we should help people who are in need. Jesus wants his followers to be kind to other people, just like the Samaritan was kind to the man who got beaten up. When we see someone who needs our help, we should do what we can to help him.

Bad Shepherds & the Good

APRIL 20

God set up a plan in the Old Testament that the Levites would be shepherds for the people. By the time Ezekiel began his work for God, many of these shepherds no longer cared for the people. God told Ezekiel to warn the shepherds:

Eze 34:2 *Son of man, prophesy against the shepherds of Israel; prophesy and say to them: "This is what the Sovereign Lord says: Woe to the shepherds of Israel who only take care of themselves! Should not shepherds take care of the flock?"*

God wanted the Levites to take care of the spiritual needs of his people. They were not doing that; they were just looking out for themselves.

Over five hundred years later, when Jesus was preaching, he saw the same thing happening. People did not have shepherds who were looking out for them.

Mt 9:36 *When he saw the crowds, he had compassion on them, because they were harassed and helpless, like sheep without a shepherd.*

Mk 6:34 *When Jesus landed and saw a large crowd, he had compassion on them, because they were like sheep without a shepherd. So he began teaching them many things.*

These scriptures say that Jesus had compassion on the people. That means Jesus saw people who had needs; he felt badly for them and he wanted to help them. He cared for them like a shepherd cares for his sheep. Jesus says that he is the Good Shepherd.

Jn 10:11 *I am the good shepherd. The good shepherd lays down his life for the sheep.*

APRIL 21

Showing Compassion

We learned yesterday that Jesus, as the good shepherd, had compassion on the people. Having compassion means not only feeling badly about people in need, but also doing something about it. What did Jesus do about it?

Mt 14:14 *When Jesus landed and saw a large crowd, he had compassion on them and healed their sick.*

Mk 1:40-42 *A man with leprosy came to him and begged him on his knees, "If you are willing, you can make me clean."*

Filled with compassion, Jesus reached out his hand and touched the man. "I am willing," he said. "Be clean!" Immediately the leprosy left him and he was cured.

Mt 20:29-31 *As Jesus and his disciples were leaving Jericho, a large crowd followed him. Two blind men were sitting by the roadside, and when they heard that Jesus was going by, they shouted, "Lord, Son of David, have mercy on us!"*

The crowd rebuked them and told them to be quiet, but they shouted all the louder, "Lord, Son of David, have mercy on us!"

Mt 20:32-34 *Jesus stopped and called them. "What do you want me to do for you?" he asked.*

"Lord," they answered, "we want our sight."

Jesus had compassion on them and touched their eyes. Immediately they received their sight and followed him.

Jesus had compassion on people. He healed them. If we have compassion on people we will try to make their lives better like Jesus did.

APRIL

22

Feed the Poor

Many people came to listen to Jesus as he was teaching. They also brought sick people to Jesus, and he healed them.

One time the people had stayed and listened to Jesus teach for three days. Jesus knew they didn't have any more food. He thought that if he sent them home, many people would pass out on the way.

Mt 15:32 *Jesus called his disciples to him and said, "I have compassion for these people; they have already been with me three days and have nothing to eat. I do not want to send them away hungry, or they may collapse on the way."*

Mt 15:33 *His disciples answered, "Where could we get enough bread in this remote place to feed such a crowd?"*

Mt 15:34-35 *"How many loaves do you have?" Jesus asked.*
"Seven," they replied, "and a few small fish."
He told the crowd to sit down on the ground. **Mt 15:36-37** *Then he took the seven loaves and the fish, and when he had given thanks, he broke them and gave them to the disciples, and they in turn to the people. They all ate and were satisfied. Afterward the disciples picked up seven basketfuls of broken pieces that were left over.*

Jesus felt badly that the people were hungry. He didn't just let them go home hungry. He performed a miracle and fed them.

There are many hungry people in our world today. Some live in other parts of the world. Some may even live in the towns and cities where we live. We probably can't perform a miracle to feed these hungry people, but we can give time and money to help feed the poor.

BE KIND

APRIL 23

Care for All in Need

Jesus doesn't only want us to have compassion on the hungry and try to help by feeding them. He wants us to care for all kinds of people who are in need.

Jesus was telling the people how it will be on judgment day. He told them he will separate the "sheep" from the "goats." The sheep are the people who have believed in him and have done good deeds to show their faith. Jesus says he will place the sheep at his right hand.

Mt 25:34-35 *Then the King will say to those on his right, "Come, you who are blessed by my Father; take your inheritance, the kingdom prepared for you since the creation of the world. For I was hungry and you gave me something to eat, I was thirsty and you gave me something to drink, I was a stranger and you invited me in,* **Mt 25:36-37** *I needed clothes and you clothed me, I was sick and you looked after me, I was in prison and you came to visit me."*

Then the righteous will answer him, "Lord, when did we see you hungry and feed you, or thirsty and give you something to drink? **Mt 25:38-39** *When did we see you a stranger and invite you in, or needing clothes and clothe you? When did we see you sick or in prison and go to visit you?"*

Mt 25:40 *The King will reply, "I tell you the truth, whatever you did for one of the least of these brothers of mine, you did for me."*

Whenever we care for someone because of our faith in God, we are showing compassion.

Do you know anyone who is new in your neighborhood that might feel like a stranger? Do you know anyone who is sick or anyone who is in prison? Jesus says if we visit and care for these people we are caring for him.

APRIL

24

Jesus Raised the Dead

Do you know how many people Jesus raised from the dead? The gospels tell us about three.

Jesus raised Jairus' daughter. He took her by the hand and told her to get up.

Mk 5:41-43 *He took her by the hand and said to her, "Talitha koum!" (which means, "Little girl, I say to you get up!"). Immediately the girl stood up and walked around (she was twelve years old). At this they were completely astonished. He gave strict orders not to let anyone know about this, and told them to give her something to eat.*

Jesus also raised a widow's son. The people carrying his coffin were taking him to be buried.

Lk 7:14-15 *Then he went up and touched the coffin, and those carrying it stood still. He said, "Young man, I say to you, get up!" The dead man sat up and began to talk, and Jesus gave him back to his mother.*

The third person Jesus raised from the dead was Lazarus. Before Jesus raised Lazarus he said a prayer.

Jn 11:43-44 *When he had said this, Jesus called in a loud voice, "Lazarus, come out!" The dead man came out, his hands and feet wrapped with strips of linen, and a cloth around his face.*

Jesus said to them, "Take off the grave clothes and let him go."

One of the reasons Jesus raised people from the dead was because of the compassion he felt for their families. The Bible says Jesus felt compassion when he met the widow whose son had died.

Lk 7:13 *When the Lord saw her, his heart went out to her and he said, "Don't cry."*

BE KIND

APRIL
25
God Cares

The Bible tells us that at the beginning of time Jesus was with the Father. Together they created the world and everything that is in it. The Bible also tells us that the church will be the bride of Christ. If the church is the bride of Christ, then Jesus is the church's husband. That is why Isaiah can say to the people, "Your Maker is your husband."

Isa 54:5 *For your Maker is your husband—the Lord Almighty is his name—the Holy One of Israel is your Redeemer; he is called the God of all the earth.*

Isaiah continues prophesying; he is talking for God. Listen for how many times the word "compassion" is used in the following scriptures.

Isa 54:7 *"For a brief moment I abandoned you, but with deep compassion I will bring you back.* **Isa 54:8** *In a surge of anger I hid my face from you for a moment, but with everlasting kindness I will have compassion on you," says the Lord your Redeemer.*

Isa 54:10 *"Though the mountains be shaken and the hills be removed, yet my unfailing love for you will not be shaken nor my covenant of peace be removed," says the Lord, who has compassion on you.*

How many times did you hear the word "compassion?" It was in each of these scriptures once, for a total of three times. God says "with deep compassion" he'll bring the people back to himself. He says "with everlasting kindness" he will have compassion on his people. Finally, Isaiah describes God as "the Lord who has compassion on his people."

God is a God of compassion. He cares about his people.

Swallowed by a Fish

APRIL 26

Bible

God told Jonah to go and preach to the people of Nineveh [*nin* eh vuh]. Jonah didn't want to do what God told him to. He ran away from God. He got on a boat and went the opposite direction from where God had sent him. The boat sailed into a big storm. The people on the boat threw Jonah into the sea because they thought he was the reason for the storm.

Jonah was swallowed by a big fish and then vomited out onto dry land. God told Jonah again to go to Nineveh. God told Jonah to tell them that because their city was so wicked it would be destroyed in forty days. This time Jonah went.

When the people of Nineveh heard the warning that their city was going to be destroyed, they repented.

Jon 3:5 *The Ninevites [nin eh vites] believed God. They declared a fast, and all of them, from the greatest to the least, put on sackcloth.*

The king also repented.

Jon 3:6 *When the news reached the king of Nineveh, he rose from his throne, took off his royal robes, covered himself with sackcloth and sat down in the dust.*

Then the king sent out a message to the people:

Jon 3:8-9 *"But let man and beast be covered with sackcloth. Let everyone call urgently on God. Let them give up their evil ways and their violence. Who knows? God may yet relent and with compassion turn from his fierce anger so that we will not perish."*

Jon 3:10 *When God saw what they did and how they turned from their evil ways, he had compassion and did not bring upon them the destruction he had threatened.*

God showed compassion for the people of Nineveh; he forgave them.

APRIL 27

God is Kind to People

Paul told the Ephesian church that God raised us up with Jesus **Eph 2:7** *in order that in the coming ages he might show the incomparable riches of his grace, expressed in his kindness to us in Christ Jesus.*

How did God express his kindness toward us? He did it by allowing Jesus, his one and only Son, to die for our sins.

In the letter to the Romans, Paul says it is God's kindness that leads us to repentance.

Rom 2:4 *Or do you show contempt for the riches of his kindness, tolerance and patience, not realizing that God's kindness leads you toward repentance?*

How does God's kindness lead us to repentance? The Bible tells us that God is the one who "first loved us." God loved us when we were still sinners. He sent Jesus to die for us. Even before we ever heard this "good news" God loved us. When we really understand how much God loves us, then we want to turn from our sins and follow him.

Paul also wrote a letter to Titus. In it he says that the people in Crete, before they believed in Jesus, were doing a lot of bad things. When they heard about believing in Jesus they changed the way they were living. Paul says when this change happened, it was like the kindness of God appearing.

Tit 3:4 *But when the kindness and love of God our Savior appeared,* **Tit 3:5** *he saved us, not because of righteous things we had done, but because of his mercy. He saved us through the washing of rebirth and renewal by the Holy Spirit.*

The salvation God offers through Jesus is how God shows kindness to people. God gives people a chance to start over.

APRIL 28

State Tournament
Marigny

Reyne and Rachael were pretty good softball players. They were asked by the coach of the team in a neighboring town if they would like to play on his team at the state tournament. Anyone who got a team together could compete. The girls were excited for the chance, and so was Mommy. Mommy was a fan to the core; she was the only mom to watch some of the girls' practices. Daddy was happy to make the three-hour trip to the tournament.

During the second game of the tournament, Reyne was running for third base. The play was close, so Reyne decided to slide. She had not been taught how to slide into base, so she hit her right knee hard on the ground. Reyne's knee was scraped even though she was wearing jeans. Coach looked at the scrape and decided Reyne needed to come out of the game.

Reyne's dad came out on the field and carried her to the bench. Daddy performed an act of kindness for Reyne.

In Peter's second letter he tells us how Christians are given the opportunity to become like God. He says we should try to stay away from bad things in the world. Then he tells us that we should try to add good things to our lives.

II Pet 1:5 *For this very reason, make every effort to add to your faith goodness; and to goodness, knowledge;* **II Pet 1:6** *and to knowledge, self-control; and to self-control, perseverance; and to perseverance, godliness;* **II Pet 1:7** *and to godliness, brotherly kindness; and to brotherly kindness, love.* **II Pet 1:8** *For if you possess these qualities in increasing measure, they will keep you from being ineffective and unproductive in your knowledge of our Lord Jesus Christ.*

By doing acts of kindness we grow in the knowledge of our Lord Jesus Christ.

APRIL 29

Sharing People's Sorrow
Bible

David was a man who knew God as a compassionate and gracious God. In three of the Psalms David wrote, he tells us that God is compassionate.

Ps 86:15 *But you, O Lord, are a compassionate and gracious God, slow to anger, abounding in love and faithfulness.*

Ps 103:8 *The Lord is compassionate and gracious, slow to anger, abounding in love.*

Ps 145:8-9 *The Lord is gracious and compassionate, slow to anger and rich in love.*

The Lord is good to all; he has compassion on all he has made.

David loved God. David wanted to be like God. Just as God is compassionate, David also was a man of compassion.

King Nahash [*nay* hash] of the Ammonites [*am* mun ites] had been kind to David. When King Nahash died David wanted to return the kindness that had been shown to him. David sent some people to tell King Nahash's son, Hanun [*hay* nun], how sorry he was to hear about his father's death.

II Sam 10:2a *David thought, "I will show kindness to Hanun son of Nahash, just as his father showed kindness to me." So David sent a delegation to express his sympathy to Hanun concerning his father.*

David did not just send a sympathy card to the king's son. David sent a group of men who would personally bring a message of sympathy.

When we share in other people's sorrow, we show them compassion. We might send a sympathy card, or we can go personally and tell people how sorry we are that they are suffering.

A Loving Touch

APRIL 30

Lk 18:15a *People were also bringing babies to Jesus to have him touch them.*

Why do you think people wanted Jesus to touch their babies? It is probably because the people knew that Jesus was a holy man. They knew God was with him. They wanted the best for their children. They may have thought if Jesus touched them, their children would be holy.

Jesus didn't only touch babies. He touched those who were sick. The Bible says that some people brought to Jesus a deaf man who could hardly talk. People might have made fun of the man because of his handicap. Jesus didn't make fun of him.

Mk 7:33 *After he took him aside, away from the crowd, Jesus put his fingers into the man's ears. Then he spit and touched the man's tongue.*

Jesus looked up to heaven and said, "Be opened!" The man could hear and speak plainly after that. Jesus touched this man; he put his fingers in his ears and touched his tongue.

Jesus also touched a man with leprosy. A Bible footnote explains that he may have had a skin disease that was not leprosy. Anyway, Jesus was not worried about getting whatever kind of disease this man had.

Mk 1:41-42 *Filled with compassion, Jesus reached out his hand and touched the man. "I am willing," he said. "Be clean!" Immediately the leprosy left him and he was cured.*

On another day, Jesus even touched the bloody face of the servant who had his ear cut off in the Garden of Gethsemane.

Lk 22:51 *But Jesus answered, "No more of this!" And he touched the man's ear and healed him.*

When Jesus touched people he often healed them. Our touching people can also be healing for them. It might not be miraculous like when Jesus touched people, but touching people can make them feel loved.

MAY 1 — Humility Explained

I Pet 5:5 *Young men, in the same way be submissive to those who are older. All of you, clothe yourselves with humility toward one another, because, "God opposes the proud but gives grace to the humble."*

What do the words "humility" and "humble" mean? This story will show us.

Wyatt was the best hitter on the T-ball team. He and everyone else knew that he was. Even the teams they played against knew it, because all those playing in the outfield would back up when Wyatt came up to bat.

Everyone liked Wyatt. He didn't brag about how good he was and he always encouraged the other players to do their best. Wyatt had something called humility. Humility means you recognize that all your talents come from God. Wyatt knew he wasn't a better hitter than the other children because of something he had done; he practiced the same amount of time as everyone else. He was given his talent by God.

Wyatt had humility. Another way you can say that is, "Wyatt is humble," or "Wyatt is a humble person." Every one of us should be humble because all we have comes from God.

In I Corinthians 4:7 Paul asks three questions.

I Cor 4:7a *For who makes you different from anyone else?*

The answer to that question is, "God makes us different from other people."

I Cor 4:7b *What do you have that you did not receive?*

All that we have, and all the talents we possess, we have received from God.

I Cor 4:7c *And if you did receive it, why do you boast as though you did not?*

We shouldn't be boastful about our talents; God has given them to us. Instead, we should be humble like Wyatt.

MAY 2

A Humble King
Bible

David was the youngest of eight boys in his family. His father's name was Jesse. David often looked after his father's sheep.

Samuel, the prophet, was sent by God to Jesse's house. God wanted Samuel to anoint the new king of Israel. Samuel started with David's oldest brother, then the next in age, and so on, waiting for God to tell him which one it would be.

I Sam 16:6 *When they arrived, Samuel saw Eliab and thought, "Surely the Lord's anointed stands here before the Lord."*

I Sam 16:7 *But the Lord said to Samuel, "Do not consider his appearance or his height, for I have rejected him. The Lord does not look at the things man looks at. Man looks at the outward appearance, but the Lord looks at the heart."*

It wasn't the oldest brother, Eliab, or the second oldest, Abinadab, or the next oldest, Shammah, that God wanted to be king. After these three sons, four more sons of Jesse passed in front of Samuel, but God did not tell him that any of these was the one. Samuel asked Jesse a question.

I Sam 16:11 *So he asked Jesse, "Are these all the sons you have?"*

"There is still the youngest," Jesse answered, "but he is tending the sheep."

Samuel said, "Send for him; we will not sit down until he arrives."

I Sam 16:12 *So he sent and had him brought in. He was ruddy, with a fine appearance and handsome features.*

Then the Lord said, "Rise and anoint him; he is the one."

David was anointed by Samuel to be the next king of Israel. Why did God choose David? It was because David had a good and humble heart.

MAY

3

A Proud King

Pride is the opposite of humility. When someone is full of pride, it is not a good thing. Proud people think they are special and that other people are not as important as they are. The Bible talks about a man like that. His name was King Herod.

Acts 12:21 *On the appointed day Herod, wearing his royal robes, sat on his throne and delivered a public address to the people.*

Acts 12:22 *They shouted, "This is the voice of a god, not of a man."*

Acts 12:23 *Immediately, because Herod did not give praise to God, an angel of the Lord struck him down, and he was eaten by worms and died.*

King Herod thought he was someone great. He wore his kingly robes and sat on his royal throne. He gave a regal speech. The people also thought King Herod was someone great; they probably cheered at the end of his speech. Then they shouted that Herod's voice was like the voice of a god.

People over the years have given many speeches. I'm sure many of them have been prideful, but we don't often hear of an angel of the Lord striking them down. Herod must have been a very prideful man!

There are many people today who do not give praise to God, just as Herod did not. The Bible tells us that God would like all people to humble themselves. This scripture in I Timothy says God is the one **I Tim 2:4** *who wants all men to be saved and to come to a knowledge of the truth.*

When people accept God's plan of salvation for their lives, they must humbly ask for Jesus to forgive them of their sins. A proud person often refuses to accept God's plan. He thinks he can get into heaven on his own; he might think he can get in by being good, but no one can be that good. Everyone needs forgiveness for sins committed.

MAY 4

Tae Kwon Do Break

Jason was ten and he had been in Tae Kwon Do as far back as he could remember. Today he was testing for his junior black belt along with two of his good friends. All the parents were there which only added to his nervousness. Jason made it through all his routines, but he didn't make his break. The tester gave him an extra try. The board still didn't break. Jason knew he hadn't passed.

Jason was so disappointed. Both his friends had earned their junior black belts and he felt like a failure. Jason's dad knew how important this was to him. He reminded Jason that he could be thankful that God had given him other gifts. He reminded his son that many kids in school were struggling to get B's and C's, but when Jason worked hard he could get all A's.

If Jason remembers that God is the giver of all good things he will do well.

I Thes 5:18 *Give thanks in all circumstances, for this is God's will for you in Christ Jesus.*

Jas 1:17 *Every good and perfect gift is from above, coming down from the Father of the heavenly lights, who does not change like shifting shadows.*

I Cor 4:7 *For who makes you different from anyone else? What do you have that you did not receive? And if you did receive it, why do you boast as though you did not?*

Rom 11:29 *For God's gifts and his call are irrevocable.*

This last verse says God's gifts are irrevocable. That means that God will not take back the gifts he has given to us.

Jason felt a little better after his father's encouragement. He had done his best and that's all he could do. The instructor said he could try the break again at the next testing session.

HUMBLE YOURSELVES

MAY 5

He Saw God
Bible

When God asked Moses to lead the Israelites out of Egypt, Moses did not think he could do it. He made four excuses before God became angry with him. God did not remain angry at Moses. In fact, God's Word says that Moses was a humble man.

Num 12:3 *Now Moses was a very humble man, more humble than anyone else on the face of the earth.*

How does a person become more humble than anyone else? A different question might be, "How does one become humble before God?" A person becomes humble before God by accepting God's plan for their life. They accept Jesus as their Savior and ask him to take control of their life.

Moses became humble when he left the riches of Egypt to go and live among his people. He became more humble as he allowed God to lead him. Moses wasn't being humble when he made excuses for not being able to lead God's people, but God changed Moses.

Moses was God's chosen prophet. God told Aaron and Miriam about his prophet, Moses.

Num 12:6 *He said, "Listen to my words: "When a prophet of the LORD is among you, I reveal myself to him in visions, I speak to him in dreams.* **Num 12:7** *But this is not true of my servant Moses; he is faithful in all my house.* **Num 12:8a** *With him I speak face to face, clearly and not in riddles; he sees the form of the LORD."*

God spoke to Moses face to face. At that time Moses was the only person God spoke to like that. God did this because Moses was a humble man.

MAY 6

Secrets

The Bible is God's inspired Word to his people. Most churches gather up what they know of God from his Word—the Bible—and write it into a "catechism." Catechisms—or statements of belief—can be as short as a few paragraphs or as long as eight hundred pages!

Why didn't God just give us a catechism that tells us what to believe? One reason is probably because God is looking for a certain kind of people. God is looking for humble people who are willing to follow him. When people trust Jesus as their Savior and ask him to take away their sins, they pass the humility test. God wants to show humble people hidden things about himself.

II Cor 3:15 *Even to this day when Moses is read, a veil covers their hearts.*

II Cor 3:16 *But whenever anyone turns to the Lord, the veil is taken away.*

The first five books of the Bible are called the law and they were written by Moses. When Paul says "when Moses is read," he means "when people are reading from these first five books of the Bible." When Paul says "a veil covers their hearts," he means that people can't understand what the books written by Moses mean. Paul says that when people turn to God and trust Jesus as their Savior the veil is taken away. That means they can understand the Bible now, but they couldn't before.

Jesus told his disciples about the "secrets of his kingdom."

Mt 13:10 *The disciples came to him and asked, "Why do you speak to the people in parables?"*

Mt 13:11 *He replied, "The knowledge of the secrets of the kingdom of heaven has been given to you, but not to them."*

Only people who have humbled themselves before God can understand the secrets of his kingdom.

HUMBLE YOURSELVES

MAY 7

In the Desert
Marigny

Mr. Marigny had been in the Army a long time. He had reached the rank of E-8, and was working as a First Sergeant. He was in charge of about two hundred soldiers. When they were training in the desert, the First Sergeant needed to use the bathroom. It was pitch black with no moon out. The First Sergeant made it to the bathroom but when he headed back to his tent, he realized that he wasn't sure where it was. In the desert it gets so dark that you can't see your hand even though you hold it in front of your face. The generator noise seemed to be coming not just from one direction; each way the First Sergeant turned the sound seemed to be coming from there.

The First Sergeant began thinking about all the critters he might step on, such as tarantulas, scorpions and snakes. He couldn't imagine spending the night out there with them. He did what any red-blooded American would do. He yelled, "H-E-E-E-L-P!" His soldiers heard the voice and came out to rescue the First Sergeant. They laughed that the man in charge had gotten lost. The First Sergeant laughed, too. It's good when people are humble enough to admit they are not perfect.

Eph 4:1 *As a prisoner for the Lord, then, I urge you to live a life worthy of the calling you have received.* **Eph 4:2** *Be completely humble and gentle; be patient, bearing with one another in love.*

I Pet 5:6 *Humble yourselves, therefore, under God's mighty hand, that he may lift you up in due time.*

Col 3:12 *Therefore, as God's chosen people, holy and dearly loved, clothe yourselves with compassion, kindness, humility, gentleness and patience.*

All of these scriptures tell us to be humble. Mr. Marigny showed humility by laughing about his mistake.

MAY 8

Always Messing Up

Some people get really down on themselves. They might say things like:
- I'm no good.
- I can't do anything right.
- I always mess up.

God knows we are not perfect. He knows we are sinners and that we sometimes feel we are hopeless. Even the apostle Paul struggled with these feelings. He wrote this in his letter to the Romans:

Rom 7:18 *"I know that nothing good lives in me, that is, in my sinful nature. For I have the desire to do what is good, but I cannot carry it out."*

Paul says that he wants to do good, but he keeps doing bad things.

Rom 7:19 *For what I do is not the good I want to do; no, the evil I do not want to do—this I keep on doing.*

Paul says he keeps "messing up;" he keeps doing things he doesn't want to do. Then he says: **Rom 7:24** *What a wretched* [rech id] man I am! Who will rescue me from this body of death?*

Rom 7:25a *Thanks be to God—through Jesus Christ our Lord!*

Paul knew Jesus was his only hope. Paul humbly accepted Jesus' salvation and Jesus' help to live a good life.

With Jesus' help, Paul traveled throughout the known world of his time. He spread the good news of Jesus Christ wherever he went. Paul started several churches in different countries.

Humility is admitting to God that we can't do it on our own. With God's help, though, we can do great things.

Wretched—miserable

MAY 9

Humble Yourself

God's Word tells us we are supposed to humble ourselves.

Jas 4:10 *Humble yourselves before the Lord, and he will lift you up.*

I Pet 5:6 *Humble yourselves, therefore, under God's mighty hand, that he may lift you up in due time.*

How does a person humble himself? Praying this prayer is a big part: "Jesus, I know I'm a sinner. Please forgive me. I trust you to be my Savior. Take control of my life."

Accepting God's plan of salvation is every person's most important way to be humble before God. But then after someone has prayed and decided she will live for God, that person continues to grow in humility. This means she will regularly ask God to show her his plan for her life.

Daily prayer is a good way to humble oneself before God. It shows we are dependent on him.

Serving others is another way to show humility. Paul told the Galatians to serve one another in love.

Gal 5:13 *You, my brothers, were called to be free. But do not use your freedom to indulge the sinful nature; rather, serve one another in love.*

Peter also told believers to serve others. He said we should use whatever gifts God has given us to serve others.

I Pet 4:10 *Each one should use whatever gift he has received to serve others, faithfully administering God's grace in its various forms.*

MAY 10

Washing Feet

Rochman (see Jan 20 for start of Elise's story)

When Elise was just 15 months old, her parents, Tim and Kerri, took her to a Tay Sachs conference in Washington, D.C. They came there to learn more about their daughter's genetic disorder and to meet other families who had children with Tay Sachs. Elise was just beginning to have the seizures that are common with this disease. She vomited right after she finished her meal. Another mother came over and cleaned up the mess. Kerri's eyes met the woman's and she felt that the woman understood her pain. This woman humbled herself in doing this act of kindness.

Jesus also humbled himself. He humbled himself by leaving heaven and being born as a little baby. He humbled himself when he died on the cross. He also humbled himself when he washed the disciples' feet at the Last Supper.

Jesus is God. He is the Creator of the world and the one who will judge all men. Even though Jesus is God, he did the duty of a servant when he washed his disciples' feet.

Jn 13:3 *Jesus knew that the Father had put all things under his power, and that he had come from God and was returning to God;* **Jn 13:4** *so he got up from the meal, took off his outer clothing, and wrapped a towel around his waist.* **Jn 13:5** *After that, he poured water into a basin and began to wash his disciples' feet, drying them with the towel that was wrapped around him.*

After Jesus had finished washing their feet he explained to them why he had done it.

Jn 13:14-15 *Now that I, your Lord and Teacher, have washed your feet, you also should wash one another's feet. I have set you an example that you should do as I have done for you.*

Jesus was telling us that he was willing to do the lowest kind of task for his followers. We should be willing to do the lowest kind of task for other people. The lady who helped Kerri was following Jesus' example of humble service.

HUMBLE YOURSELVES

MAY 11
Humble Promises

Do you know that God makes some promises for people who are humble? The first one is that he will lift us up.

Jas 4:10 *Humble yourselves before the Lord, and he will lift you up.*

God promises to lift us up if we humble ourselves before him. If we are willing to obey God, he will prosper us, if not in this life, then in the next.

Jesus had a child stand up before his disciples and then he said,

Mt 18:4 *Therefore, whoever humbles himself like this child is the greatest in the kingdom of heaven.*

Jesus promised that if we humble ourselves, we will be great in the kingdom of heaven.

God says in Proverbs that he gives grace to those who are humble.

Prov 3:34 *He mocks proud mockers but gives grace to the humble.*

Grace is God's kindness shown toward us. God promises to give grace—to be kind—to those who are humble.

Prov 22:4 *Humility and the fear of the Lord bring wealth and honor and life.*

God promises wealth, honor and life to the person that is humble and fears him. Those are some pretty big promises. Are you humble? Do you fear God? If you can answer "Yes" to those questions, then God will be faithful to you. He is a God who keeps his promises.

If you humble yourself before God, he will bless you in many ways.

MAY 12

The Centurion

In the Roman military, a centurion was an officer who commanded one hundred soldiers. Let's read a story about one of these centurions. Jesus had just entered Capernaum.

Lk 7:2-3 *There a centurion's servant, whom his master valued highly, was sick and about to die. The centurion heard of Jesus and sent some elders of the Jews to him, asking him to come and heal his servant.* **Lk 7:4-5** *When they came to Jesus, they pleaded earnestly with him, "This man deserves to have you do this, because he loves our nation and has built our synagogue."* **Lk 7:6-7** *So Jesus went with them.*

He was not far from the house when the centurion sent friends to say to him: "Lord, don't trouble yourself, for I do not deserve to have you come under my roof. That is why I did not even consider myself worthy to come to you. But say the word, and my servant will be healed. **Lk 7:8-9** *For I myself am a man under authority, with soldiers under me. I tell this one, 'Go,' and he goes; and that one, 'Come,' and he comes. I say to my servant, 'Do this,' and he does it." When Jesus heard this, he was amazed at him, and turning to the crowd following him, he said, "I tell you, I have not found such great faith even in Israel."*

When the people whom the centurion had sent to Jesus returned home, they found that the centurion's near-dead servant had been healed.

This centurion was a very powerful man. He was well-liked by the Jews and he probably had quite a bit of power—he built the Jews a synagogue. The centurion even had power over the elders in his community—he sent them to Jesus.

Even with all this power the centurion was still a humble man; he says he is not worthy for Jesus to enter his house. The centurion knew Jesus was more important than he was.

There are humble people in all types of work. People are humble when they admit they are created by God. People are humble when they admit that the power they have is given them by God. The centurion was a humble man.

HUMBLE YOURSELVES

MAY
13

Patrol Boy
Warren Marigny

Terry was chosen to be patrol boy in third and fourth grade. He wore a shiny badge and made sure that automobile traffic stopped so that the children could cross the street. In fifth grade he was promoted to lieutenant. He then wore a badge with a red center. In sixth grade he became captain and wore a badge with a blue center.

Terry may have been chosen for the job because he liked to be dressed neatly and his godmother helped him to look his best. Some people think that because God looks on the heart that he doesn't care what we look like on the outside. They think it doesn't matter to God whether or not we are neat and clean.

It's true that God does look at our hearts.

I Sam 16:7b *The Lord does not look at the things man looks at. Man looks at the outward appearance, but the Lord looks at the heart.*

God looks at our hearts, but our outward appearance affects what people think of us. We are representatives of the God we serve.

Col 3:17 *And whatever you do, whether in word or deed, do it all in the name of the Lord Jesus, giving thanks to God the Father through him.*

Col 3:23 *Whatever you do, work at it with all your heart, as working for the Lord, not for men.*

I Cor 10:31 *So whether you eat or drink or whatever you do, do it all for the glory of God.*

People who care how they look often dress neatly so that they will feel good about themselves. We Christians should dress neatly because we want people to see what a great God we serve. When we look the best we can we are bringing glory to God. It all comes back to the question, "*Why* are you dressing nicely?" God is looking at your heart and he knows why. He even knows why Terry, the patrol boy, dressed neatly.

MAY 14

For God's Eyes Only

We should be doing good things because we want to please God. Sometimes when we do good things it is because we want people to notice us, or we want them to tell us how good we are.

God knows why we do what we do. We shouldn't do things just to get the attention of other people. Jesus tells us about this in Matthew 6.

Mt 6:1 *Be careful not to do your "acts of righteousness" before men, to be seen by them. If you do, you will have no reward from your Father in heaven.*

Mt 6:2 *So when you give to the needy, do not announce it with trumpets, as the hypocrites do in the synagogues and on the streets, to be honored by men. I tell you the truth, they have received their reward in full.*

Why does Jesus say, "They have received their reward in full?" What reward did they get? It was the praise of other people. When people tell them they have done a good job it makes them feel good about themselves. Jesus is saying the "good feeling" they enjoy because of other people praising them is their reward.

When we do good deeds, we should do them to bring glory to God, not attention to ourselves.

Mt 6:3 *But when you give to the needy, do not let your left hand know what your right hand is doing,* **Mt 6:4** *so that your giving may be in secret. Then your Father, who sees what is done in secret, will reward you.*

Do you really think that when you put something in the offering at church with your left hand, that your right hand won't know you did it? Jesus was just using this exaggeration to make a point. When we do things only God can see, he is pleased by our actions.

HUMBLE YOURSELVES

MAY 15

Down to Earth
Marigny

Jesus is God. Paul wrote about Jesus in a letter to the Colossians.

Col 1:19 *For God was pleased to have all his fullness dwell in him.*

Col 2:9 *For in Christ all the fullness of the Deity lives in bodily form.*

It is hard for us to understand, but when Jesus lived as a human being, he was still God.

Paul also wrote about Jesus in his letter to the Philippians. He said Jesus humbled himself by becoming a man.

Phil 2:7 *. . . but made himself nothing, taking the very nature of a servant, being made in human likeness.*

Phil 2:8 *And being found in appearance as a man, he humbled himself and became obedient to death—even death on a cross!*

Jesus is the God of the entire universe. He humbled himself by becoming a man. He humbled himself by acting as a servant and meeting the needs of people. He also humbled himself by choosing to die on the cross for us.

One of the Marigny's pastors humbled himself. We were getting ready to move and the pastor wanted to help in any way he could. He volunteered to clean our bathroom; he didn't even mind scrubbing the toilet.

If we will humble ourselves like Jesus did, we will be willing to do those things that only servants do. Cleaning seems like one of those jobs. If Jesus became like a servant, we should be happy to be humble servants also.

MAY 16

First Place

Children, especially brothers and sisters, argue about many things. One thing they might argue about is who gets to sit beside dad in church.

James and John were grown men when they had this same kind of idea. They told Jesus they wanted him to do something for them. Jesus asked them what that might be.

Mk 10:37 *They replied, "Let one of us sit at your right and the other at your left in your glory."*

James and John said they wanted "front row seats" in heaven. The other disciples were very upset that James and John asked for the best spots.

Mk 10:41 *When the ten heard about this, they became indignant* with James and John.*

Jesus didn't get upset. He explained to them that in this world, important people—like our president and other leaders—have power over other people. Jesus told his disciples to be different. He said, as Christians, we need to be servants.

Jesus said he didn't come to the earth to be served but to serve.

Mk 10:44 *And whoever wants to be first must be slave of all.* **Mk 10:45** *For even the Son of Man did not come to be served, but to serve, and to give his life as a ransom for many.*

If we are humble like Jesus, we will be willing to give up first place to someone else.

Indignant—angry

HUMBLE YOURSELVES

MAY
17

Donkey Rider

Zechariah was a prophet a very long time ago. He wrote the last part of the book of Zechariah almost five hundred years before Jesus was born.

Zech 9:9 *Rejoice greatly, O Daughter of Zion! Shout, Daughter of Jerusalem! See, your king comes to you, righteous and having salvation, gentle and riding on a donkey, on a colt, the foal of a donkey.*

When Zechariah says "daughter of Zion" and "daughter of Jerusalem" he is talking about God's people. Here Zechariah is telling them that their king will come to them riding on a donkey. How would Zechariah know five hundred years ahead of time that Jesus would come to his people riding on a donkey? Zechariah probably didn't know, but God did. God inspired Zechariah to write these words. They were a prophecy; that means they told something that would happen in the future.

Jesus asked his disciples to bring him a donkey and her colt. Matthew tells us that this is when Zechariah's prophecy came true:

Mt 21:4 *This took place to fulfill what was spoken through the prophet:* **Mt 21:5** *"Say to the Daughter of Zion, 'See, your king comes to you, gentle and riding on a donkey, on a colt, the foal of a donkey.'"*

Mt 21:7 *They brought the donkey and the colt, placed their cloaks on them, and Jesus sat on them.*

In both Zechariah and Matthew it says Jesus is "gentle and riding on a donkey." Many Bibles use the words, "meek," "lowly," or "humble," instead of "gentle." So we could say, "Jesus came to us humble and riding on a donkey."

Jesus could have had his disciples bring a horse for him to ride on, but he chose a more common animal. Even though Jesus created the whole universe, he chose to show humility by riding on a donkey.

MAY 18

Copy Cat

Have you ever played the game of "Shadow" or "Copy Cat?" That's when you watch someone else, and everything they do or say, you copy. It can be a fun game.

God wants us to "be a copy cat of Jesus."

If we say we are living for God we should act like Jesus did. John says that if we claim we are living "in God" we should live our lives like Jesus lived his life.

I Jn 2:6 *Whoever claims to live in him must walk as Jesus did.*

What does this mean "to claim to live in Jesus?" It means a person claims to be a Christian. John says that person "must walk as Jesus did." The Bible doesn't mean we should wear sandals like Jesus did when he walked. It doesn't mean we should have twelve disciples following us when we walk. When the Bible says we "must walk as Jesus did," it means we should love God and love other people like Jesus did, even sometimes suffer as Jesus did.

Jesus is the example we follow. Peter says we are called to suffer.

I Pet 2:21 *To this you were called, because Christ suffered for you, leaving you an example, that you should follow in his steps.*

We should be like Jesus not just in our actions but also in our attitudes.

Phil 2:5 *Your attitude should be the same as that of Christ Jesus.*

Jesus said he is gentle and humble in heart.

Mt 11:29 *Take my yoke upon you and learn from me, for I am gentle and humble in heart, and you will find rest for your souls.*

We should have gentle and humble hearts because Jesus did.

God would like us to play the "Copy Cat" game every day and copy how Jesus lived.

HUMBLE YOURSELVES

MAY 19

Born in a Stable

Kings are supposed to live in palaces and have the nicest clothes and the best food. Jesus was the king of the Jews. That is the title they put on the cross when Jesus was crucified.

Mt 27:37 *Above his head they placed the written charge against him:* THIS IS JESUS, THE KING OF THE JEWS.

Jesus was the king of the Jews, but he never lived in a palace. He wasn't even born in a hospital like many babies are. He was born in a stable. The inn that Mary and Joseph wanted to stay in was full, so the innkeeper let them stay in his stable. While they were there the baby Jesus' time to be born came. Luke tells what Mary did.

Lk 2:7 *And she gave birth to her firstborn, a son. She wrapped him in cloths and placed him in a manger,* because there was no room for them in the inn.*

An angel announced to some shepherds that a Savior was born in Bethlehem and that they should go see him. The angel told the shepherds they would know they had found the right one when they found the baby wrapped and lying in a manger. They said,

Lk 2:12 *This will be a sign to you: You will find a baby wrapped in cloths and lying in a manger.*

The shepherds did what the angel told them to.

Lk 2:16 *So they hurried off and found Mary and Joseph, and the baby, who was lying in the manger.*

God could have chosen a rich family to bring Jesus into the world. Instead, he chose humble people in humble circumstances.

Manger—a feeding container for animals

MAY 20

Famous
Bible

Those of us who are not rich or popular sometimes feel like we are not very important. Mary was a young Jewish girl who could have felt that way. She was not rich and her family was not famous. Yet, the angel Gabriel came to her with a message from God.

Lk 1:28 *The angel went to her and said, "Greetings, you who are highly favored! The Lord is with you."*

The angel then told Mary that God had chosen her to be the mother of his son—the Son of God! Mary accepted God's will for her life.

Lk 1:38 *"I am the Lord's servant," Mary answered. "May it be to me as you have said." Then the angel left her.*

Mary praised God because he had chosen her. She said,

Lk 1:48 *For he has been mindful of the humble state of his servant. From now on all generations will call me blessed.*

Lk 1:52 *He has brought down rulers from their thrones but has lifted up the humble.*

Mary is known by many people today because she is the mother of Jesus; Mary said, "all generations will call me blessed." You could say that Mary is famous. She didn't start out that way, though. She said "(God) has been mindful of the humble state of his servant." That means God noticed her even though she wasn't rich or popular.

MAY 21

Blue or White?

People who work are often divided into two groups. They are called "blue-collar workers" or "white-collar workers." The dictionary gives these definitions: Blue-collar workers are "wage earners in jobs performed in rough clothing and often involved in manual labor." White-collar workers are workers, salaried or professional, "whose work does not involve manual labor and who are expected to dress with some degree of formality."

Jesus was a worker. To find out which kind of worker he was, let's look at a story in Matthew 13. The Bible says that Jesus had been telling parables at the lake. Then he came back to preach in his home town of Nazareth.

Mt 13:53 *When Jesus had finished these parables, he moved on from there.* **Mt 13:54** *Coming to his hometown, he began teaching the people in their synagogue, and they were amazed. "Where did this man get this wisdom and these miraculous powers?" they asked.*

The people in Nazareth saw Jesus' miracles and heard his teaching. They had a hard time believing in him, though, because he had grown up among them. The people didn't think he was anyone great. Some people were asking questions. The gospels of Matthew and Mark differ a little about the questions the people asked:

Mt 13:55 *Isn't this the carpenter's son? Isn't his mother's name Mary, and aren't his brothers James, Joseph, Simon and Judas?*

Mk 6:3 *"Isn't this the carpenter? Isn't this Mary's son and the brother of James, Joseph, Judas and Simon? Aren't his sisters here with us?" And they took offense at him.*

In Matthew the people ask if Jesus isn't the son of the carpenter. In Mark they ask if he isn't the carpenter. Jesus probably worked in Joseph's shop and became a carpenter himself. Then both questions could be answered, "Yes." Jesus was the carpenter's son and he was a carpenter. Do you think Jesus was a blue-collar worker or a white-collar worker? A carpenter does manual labor, so Jesus would be considered a blue-collar worker.

MAY 22

Grazing
Bible

Have you ever heard of the word "grazing?" "Grazing" is what animals do when they eat the grass that is growing. What kinds of animals graze? Cows, sheep, horses, rabbits, antelope, buffalo and even elephants are all common grazing animals. Have you ever heard of a *person* grazing? The Bible tells us about one such person. He wasn't just any person; he was King Nebuchadnezzar [neb you cud *nehz* er].

Dan 4:33 *Immediately what had been said about Nebuchadnezzar was fulfilled. He was driven away from people and ate grass like cattle. His body was drenched with the dew of heaven until his hair grew like the feathers of an eagle and his nails like the claws of a bird.*

Why did the king eat grass like the cows and grow shaggy hair like feathers and claws like a bird? The Bible tells us it was because he was proud; he did not give God the credit for the greatness of his kingdom. Instead, he thought Babylon was great because of what he had done.

Dan 4:30 *He said, "Is not this the great Babylon I have built as the royal residence, by my mighty power and for the glory of my majesty?"*

The king should have said that he was able to build Babylon because of the wisdom God had given him. He should have said that he built Babylon for God's glory, not for his own glory. God was not pleased with how proud the king was.

Dan 4:31 *The words were still on his lips when a voice came from heaven, "This is what is decreed for you, King Nebuchadnezzar: Your royal authority has been taken from you."*

For seven years the king acted like a crazy man; he ate grass and grew shaggy hair like feathers and fingernails like claws. When the seven years were over, the king "raised (his) eyes toward heaven, and (his) sanity was restored." He praised God.

Dan 4:37 *Now I, Nebuchadnezzar, praise and exalt and glorify the King of heaven, because everything he does is right and all his ways are just. And those who walk in pride he is able to humble.*

God can humble proud people.

HUMBLE YOURSELVES

MAY 23

Eating Pig Food

There is another story in the Bible about a person eating animal food. It is found in Jesus' parable of the prodigal* son. This young man did not eat pig food, but he was so hungry that he wanted to.

Lk 15:16 *He longed to fill his stomach with the pods that the pigs were eating, but no one gave him anything.*

How did this young man get so hungry that he wanted to eat pig food? Jesus told the story: A father had two sons. The younger son wanted to leave home, so he asked his father for his share of the inheritance.* The father gave it to him and the son left.

Lk 15:13 *Not long after that, the younger son got together all he had, set off for a distant country and there squandered* his wealth in wild living.* **Lk 15:14** *After he had spent everything, there was a severe famine in that whole country, and he began to be in need.*

This young man found work feeding a man's pigs. That's when he wished he could eat some of their food. The young man took some time to think about his life. He decided he would go back to his father and ask for a job there. He would at least have enough to eat.

When the boy met his father he said he was sorry for what he had done.

Lk 15:21 *The son said to him, "Father, I have sinned against heaven and against you. I am no longer worthy to be called your son."*

The young son humbled himself before his father by admitting he had done wrong. When we tell God or people we are sorry for our wrongdoing we are showing humility.

Prodigal—someone who spends their money wastefully and lives for pleasure, not for God
Inheritance—the money or property given by parents to their children
Squandered—spent wastefully

MAY 24

Belshazzar

The day before yesterday we read about King Nebuchadnezzar. He was the king who ate grass. King Nebuchadnezzar had a son. He named his son Belshazzar [bell *shaz* er]. When Nebuchadnezzar died, his son became the next king. King Belshazzar knew the story of how his father had become full of pride and lived like a crazy man for seven years. King Belshazzar knew that after his father admitted God is in control of everything, he was again allowed to rule Babylon. King Belshazzar should have been careful not to let pride rule in his life. Daniel came and talked to King Belshazzar. Daniel reminded the king of all that had happened to his father:

Dan 5:22 *But you his son, O Belshazzar, have not humbled yourself, though you knew all this.*

Daniel said that because the king knew of his father's humbling experience, he should have honored God. Instead, King Belshazzar lived a life of pleasure. The King had taken the sacred vessels out of the temple so he could use them at a party. Daniel told the king he should have humbled himself. Then Daniel said,

Dan 5:23a *"Instead, you have set yourself up against the Lord of heaven. You had the goblets from his temple brought to you, and you and your nobles, your wives and your concubines drank wine from them.* **Dan 5:23b** *You praised the gods of silver and gold, of bronze, iron, wood and stone, which cannot see or hear or understand. But you did not honor the God who holds in his hand your life and all your ways."*

Belshazzar knew the truth about God, but he refused to humble himself. He died the same night that Daniel told him about his wrong choices.

Dan 5:30 *That very night Belshazzar, king of the Babylonians, was slain.**

King Nebuchadnezzar is certainly a better example for us than his son Belshazzar.

Slain—killed violently, as in battle

HUMBLE YOURSELVES

MAY 25

Request of Solomon
Bible

Solomon built a magnificent temple in Jerusalem. Then the people gathered for the dedication of the temple. King Solomon blessed the people. Then he got up on the platform in the center of the outer court. He knelt down and spread his arms toward heaven. He asked God to look with favor on the people who came there to worship and to confess their sins. Solomon prayed a prayer that was two pages long in the Bible.

God was pleased with Solomon for building the temple as a place for worship.

II Chr 7:11 *When Solomon had finished the temple of the Lord and the royal palace, and had succeeded in carrying out all he had in mind to do in the temple of the Lord and in his own palace,* **II Chr 7:12** *the Lord appeared to him at night and said:*

"I have heard your prayer and have chosen this place for myself as a temple for sacrifices. **II Chr 7:13** *When I shut up the heavens so that there is no rain, or command locusts to devour the land or send a plague among my people,* **II Chr 7:14** *if my people, who are called by my name, will humble themselves and pray and seek my face and turn from their wicked ways, then will I hear from heaven and will forgive their sin and will heal their land."*

Solomon asked God to hear whenever his people came to the temple and prayed. God said that he would do what Solomon asked. God said if the people would do four things, then he would hear their prayers and answer them. Do you remember the four things God said he wanted them to do? God said the people should humble themselves, pray, seek his face and turn from their wicked ways. What was the first thing he asked them to do? The first thing God asked them to do was to humble themselves.

MAY 26

Admit You are Wrong
Bible

King Solomon ruled in Israel for forty years. When he died, the kingdom of Israel was divided. Jeroboam [jare oh *boe* um] son of Nebat [*nee* bat] ruled in the north and Solomon's son, Rehoboam [ree hoe *boe* um], ruled in the south. Jeroboam was causing the people to turn away from God. Many people were not happy that Jeroboam was making goat and calf idols. They went south to Jerusalem into rival King Rehoboam's land to worship at the temple there.

II Chr 11:16 *Those from every tribe of Israel who set their hearts on seeking the* LORD, *the God of Israel, followed the Levites to Jerusalem to offer sacrifices to the* LORD, *the God of their fathers.*

Many of God's people knew it was wrong for King Jeroboam to teach the people to worship goats and calves. They knew that they should worship God alone. King Rehoboam knew that he should worship God alone. However, after three years King Rehoboam also started turning away from God.

II Chr 12:1 *After Rehoboam's position as king was established and he had become strong, he and all Israel with him abandoned the law of the* LORD.

God sent a prophet to King Rehoboam and the leaders who ruled with him. The prophet said because they had abandoned God, that God would let them be attacked by the Egyptian army. Rehoboam and the leaders knew they had done wrong. They humbled themselves.

II Chr 12:6 *The leaders of Israel and the king humbled themselves and said, "The* LORD *is just."*

Because the leaders humbled themselves, God's anger turned from them.

II Chr 12:12 *Because Rehoboam humbled himself, the* LORD's *anger turned from him, and he was not totally destroyed. Indeed, there was some good in Judah.*

The leaders humbled themselves by admitting they were wrong and asking God to forgive them.

MAY 27

False Humility

If humility means admitting that all our gifts come from God, what would false humility be? The apostle Paul writes about false humility in the letter to the Colossians.

Col 2:18 *Do not let anyone who delights in false humility and the worship of angels disqualify you for the prize. Such a person goes into great detail about what he has seen, and his unspiritual mind puffs him up with idle notions.*

What is this false humility Paul is talking about? It is when people pretend to be humble. How do you think a person would do that? Paul explains it a little more in the end of Colossians, chapter 2. Paul says that when we became Christians, we were cleansed from our sins by Jesus' sacrifice of himself on the cross. When we accept that sacrifice we become humble before God. Many Christians in Colossae added more rules. They said that in addition to asking Jesus' forgiveness, Christians needed to follow a whole bunch of other rules. Paul tells what some of these rules were:

Col 2:21 *Do not handle! Do not taste! Do not touch!*

Paul tells us that all these extra rules are based merely on faulty human ideas of holiness.

Col 2:22 *These are all destined to perish with use, because they are based on human commands and teachings.*

Paul tells us that when people live strictly according to the rules, they might pride themselves on how "humble" they are.

Col 2:23 *Such regulations indeed have an appearance of wisdom, with their self-imposed worship, their false humility and their harsh treatment of the body, but they lack any value in restraining sensual indulgence.*

Paul is trying to get the people to put their focus back on Jesus Christ. He does not want them to think they are holy because of the things they do. That is false humility. True humility is trusting Jesus Christ to save us and to lead us into holiness.

MAY 28

Grace to the Humble

Many times the writers of books in the New Testament quoted scriptures from the Old Testament. For the writers of the New Testament their Bible was the Old Testament; the New Testament had not been written. James is one of those writers who quoted an Old Testament scripture.

Jas 4:6 *But he gives us more grace. That is why Scripture says: "God opposes the proud but gives grace to the humble."*

James quoted that scripture from the book of Proverbs.

Prov 3:34 *He mocks proud mockers but gives grace to the humble.*

The first half of the verse is a little different but the second half, "gives grace to the humble," is just the same. Both these scriptures say that God gives grace to the humble. Grace from God is his kindness towards us.

The writer of the letter to the Hebrews says that we should come before God's throne. He tells us we can find grace there to help us in our time of need.

Heb 4:16 *Let us then approach the throne of grace with confidence, so that we may receive mercy and find grace to help us in our time of need.*

God shows us grace, or kindness, by answering our prayers.

Peter tells us that we can grow in the grace of Jesus Christ.

II Pet 3:18 *But grow in the grace and knowledge of our Lord and Savior Jesus Christ. To him be glory both now and forever! Amen.*

After we humble ourselves and trust Jesus as our Savior we learn more about God's grace, his kindness, toward us.

MAY 29

God is Close
Marigny

Because Reyne and Rachael were twins, they spent lots of time together. When one of them made the other upset, they usually wanted to "fix it" right away. The one who made the other angry would often go to her and apologize. It takes humility for people to admit they are wrong.

Children don't often like to admit they are wrong. Their parents will sometimes make them tell someone that they are sorry. Once when Gladys apologized to Kerri for being mean, Kerri asked if Mommy had told her to say that.

Have you ever admitted you were wrong without your parents telling you to say you are sorry? God is close to people that are humble.

Ps 25:9 *He guides the humble in what is right and teaches them his way.*

God promises to guide the humble and teach them his way.

Ps 147:6 *The Lord sustains the humble but casts the wicked to the ground.*

God says he will sustain the humble. That means he will support or help them.

Ps 149:4 *For the Lord takes delight in his people; he crowns the humble with salvation.*

God says he will crown the humble with salvation; that means God will give them salvation as a gift.

Close to the end of the Old Testament God tells Micah what it is he wants of man.

Mic 6:8 *He has showed you, O man, what is good. And what does the Lord require of you? To act justly and to love mercy and to walk humbly with your God.*

God wants us to act justly; that means he wants us to do what is right. God wants us to love mercy; that means we act kindly toward others. Finally, God wants us to walk humbly with him. If we are humble, God will be close to us.

MAY 30

Humility Required

If you were going to set up a club, you would probably make some rules about whom you would let in. You would probably say, "Only boys can enter this club," or "Only girls can enter this club." Almost every club has some rules about the people who can be in it. They might have rules that say you have to do this or that to be in the club. Many clubs charge yearly dues that people must pay in order to be members.

In order to be a member of certain honors societies, people need to earn high grades in school. If they earn those grades and want to be a part of the society, they can join.

If you want to be a member of a sports or dance team or a member of a band or choir, there are usually tryouts. At these tryouts the coach or director will choose the most talented people to be members.

In all these groups, there is a requirement for membership. It might be money, or grades or talent. What does God require of people who want to join his club—who want to go to heaven? Does God only let in those who pay a certain amount of money? Does he require that people who want to get into heaven have good grades? Does God require people who want to get into heaven to have athletic or musical talents? God doesn't require any of these things. What are his rules then? God requires that everyone who wants to get into heaven be humble!

Jesus told a story about how a Pharisee and a tax collector went to the temple to pray. The Pharisee stood bragging about how he was better than those "evil people." He said,

Lk 18:12 *"I fast twice a week and give a tenth of all I get."*

Lk 18:13 *But the tax collector stood at a distance. He would not even look up to heaven, but beat his breast and said, "God, have mercy on me, a sinner."*

Lk 18:14a *I tell you that this man, rather than the other, went home justified before God.**

Lk 18:14b *For everyone who exalts himself will be humbled, and he who humbles himself will be exalted.*

Justified before God—at peace with God

HUMBLE YOURSELVES

MAY 31 — The Plan of God

If God is looking for humble people, how does he set up a plan by which he will know people are humble? God made a good plan. Since the beginning of creation he knew that Jesus would come and die for our sins.

I Pet 1:18 *For you know that it was not with perishable things such as silver or gold that you were redeemed from the empty way of life handed down to you from your forefathers,*

I Pet 1:19 *but with the precious blood of Christ, a lamb without blemish or defect.* **I Pet 1:20** *He was chosen before the creation of the world, but was revealed in these last times for your sake.*

God created the world and the people living in it. He knew before he created the world that people would turn away from him. He knew they would need a way to get back to him. He knew he would send Jesus to the earth to die on a cross. God's plan of salvation has been the same since he created the world.

Prophets and other men of God in the Old Testament searched the scriptures to learn of God's plan. They prayed and studied God's Word, but they didn't know exactly how God was going to save people. Since Jesus came to the earth, people have a clear picture of how God saves people.

Paul preached in Athens. He said that people used to think God was like the idols that were made of gold or silver, or carved out of stone. Paul said,

Acts 17:30 *In the past God overlooked such ignorance, but now he commands all people everywhere to repent.*

Paul preached to all people that they needed to trust Jesus for their salvation.

When people trust Jesus for their salvation, they humble themselves before God. This is the humility that is required for people to go to heaven.

JUNE 1

Created for Good Works

Did you know that God created you to do good deeds?

Eph 2:10 *For we are God's workmanship, created in Christ Jesus to do good works, which God prepared in advance for us to do.*

When God made the world, he also made people. He knew that there would be plenty of work to be done on this earth. You can think of your chores as some of the good works God prepared ahead of time for you.

Even though these good works can't earn us a way into heaven—only Jesus can do that—they do earn us rewards in heaven.

In Proverbs God tells us he will repay each person for what he has done.

Prov 24:12 *If you say, "But we knew nothing about this," does not he who weighs the heart perceive it? Does not he who guards your life know it? Will he not repay each person according to what he has done?*

God sees all that we do and he will reward us for all our good deeds.

God often calls his people "the Daughter of Zion." Isaiah says this about our future reward:

Isa 62:11 *The LORD has made proclamation to the ends of the earth: "Say to the Daughter of Zion, 'See, your Savior comes! See, his reward is with him, and his recompense* accompanies him.'"*

In the Book of Revelation Jesus speaks to John:

Rev 22:12 *Behold, I am coming soon! My reward is with me, and I will give to everyone according to what he has done.*

Since God will reward us for our deeds, we should do all the good deeds that we can.

Recompense—reward

JUNE 2

God is Good

Psalm 136 begins by saying that we should give thanks to God because he is good.

Ps 136:1 *Give thanks to the Lord, for he is good. His love endures forever.*

What does it mean when we say God is good? God's goodness is shown in all the good things he does for people. Psalm 136 tells us some of the good things God has done. After every verse, all twenty-six of them, is written these words, "His love endures forever." Let's read about some of the good things God has done for us. (Children may read the ending of each verse, "His love endures forever." I left it out because of lack of space.)

Ps 136:5-9 *. . . who by his understanding made the heavens.*
who spread out the earth upon the waters.
who made the great lights.
the sun to govern the day.
the moon and stars to govern the night.

God made all things. God's goodness is seen in the fact that he created the world for us.

Ps 136:10-15 *. . . to him who struck down the firstborn of Egypt.*
and brought Israel out from among them.
with a mighty hand and outstretched arm.
to him who divided the Red Sea asunder.
and brought Israel through the midst of it.
but swept Pharaoh and his army into the Red Sea.

God delivered his people from Egypt. In the same way, God delivers us from sin. God is good to deliver his people.

Ps 136:21-22 *. . . and gave their land as an inheritance.*
an inheritance to his servant Israel.

God gave his people the Promised Land. God promises to bring us to heaven one day.

God is good to us: he created the earth for us; he delivers us from our sins; and he promises us a future home in heaven.

JUNE 3

What Did Jesus Do?

If someone were to ask you what Jesus did when he lived on the earth, you could quote this scripture:

Acts 10:38 *. . . how God anointed Jesus of Nazareth with the Holy Spirit and power, and how he went around doing good and healing all who were under the power of the devil, because God was with him.*

Jesus came down here to earth to show us what God is like. This scripture in Acts says he went around doing good and healing people. Besides Jesus' healings, what are some good deeds Jesus did?

Mk 10:13-16 *People were bringing little children to Jesus to have him touch them, but the disciples rebuked them. When Jesus saw this, he was indignant. He said to them, "Let the little children come to me, and do not hinder them, for the kingdom of God belongs to such as these. I tell you the truth, anyone who will not receive the kingdom of God like a little child will never enter it." And he took the children in his arms, put his hands on them and blessed them.*

Jesus cared about young children and blessed them.

Mk 1:38 *Jesus replied, "Let us go somewhere else—to the nearby villages—so I can preach there also. That is why I have come."*

Jesus taught people about God.

Jn 14:8-9 *Philip said, "Lord, show us the Father and that will be enough for us."*

Jesus answered: "Don't you know me, Philip, even after I have been among you such a long time? Anyone who has seen me has seen the Father. How can you say, 'Show us the Father'?"

Jesus showed people what God is like.

We can do the same good deeds that Jesus did. He cared about children, he taught people about God and he lived a good life showing others what God is like.

OBEY YOUR PARENTS/BE GOOD

JUNE

4

Clean Up!

Juan always put his things away when he was done using them. Miguel was just the opposite. He would go from playing with one toy to another until his room was just a mess.

The boys' mom had a rule that before they could come to the table to eat, their things needed to be put away. Miguel knew the rule, but he would still wait until his mom reminded him that he needed to put things away. Sometimes, he would even whine, "Why do I have to? It's just going to get messy again."

Being good is sometimes a hard thing to do, but God tells us:

Phil 2:14 *Do everything without complaining or arguing.*

Col 3:20 *Children, obey your parents in everything, for this pleases the Lord.*

Obeying your parents is so important that God put it in the Ten Commandments. He doesn't use the word "obey," but he tells us to honor our parents. If we honor our parents, we will obey them. The Ten Commandments are found in Exodus and Deuteronomy.

Honoring your parents is the fifth commandment.

Ex 20:12 *Honor your father and your mother, so that you may live long in the land the Lord your God is giving you.*

Deut 5:16 *Honor your father and your mother, as the Lord your God has commanded you, so that you may live long and that it may go well with you in the land the Lord your God is giving you.*

If Miguel wants to obey God, he should obey God's commandments. The fifth commandment tells us to obey our parents.

JUNE 5

He Knows It All

Whenever his mom was around Joey was such a good little boy. Madeline, his older sister, was sure it was just because he didn't want to get into trouble and be punished. Madeline couldn't believe he could be so bad when Mom wasn't looking, yet so good when she was.

Maybe if Joey would know that God can see everything he is doing, he would try to be better.

I Jn 3:20b *For God is greater than our hearts, and he knows everything.*

God knows everything. A big word for knowing everything is "omniscient" [om *nih* shunt]. God is omniscient.

What are some of the things God knows?

Lk 12:7a *Indeed, the very hairs of your head are all numbered.*

"Numbered" is another word for "counted." That means God knows how many hairs are on your head.

Ps 139:4 *Before a word is on my tongue you know it completely, O LORD.*

God knows what we are going to say even before we say it.

Ps 139:2 *You know when I sit and when I rise; you perceive my thoughts from afar.*

God knows when we sit down and when we stand up. He even knows what we are thinking.

Do you think if Joey knew that God was seeing how bad he was, that he would still act the same way?

JUNE

6

Caretakers

God is great and he is worthy of praise. In comparison, we human beings are his creation. God shows us his goodness by letting us take care of his creation. When God created Adam and Eve, he wanted them to take care of the world he had created.

Gen 1:28 *God blessed them and said to them, "Be fruitful and increase in number; fill the earth and subdue it. Rule over the fish of the sea and the birds of the air and over every living creature that moves on the ground."*

To "subdue the earth" means to "take charge of it, and to care for it."

Gen 2:15 *The LORD God took the man and put him in the Garden of Eden to work it and take care of it.*

David lived a long time after Adam and Eve. He praised God because God is so great. He said God is good because he allows man to care for what God has made.

Ps 8:6-7 *You made him ruler over the works of your hands; you put everything under his feet: all flocks and herds, and the beasts of the field,*

Ps 8:8-9 *the birds of the air, and the fish of the sea, all that swim the paths of the seas. O LORD, our Lord, how majestic is your name in all the earth!*

We know that God is good because he allows us to take care of his creation.

JUNE 7

Hate Evil

Amos 5:14 *Seek good, not evil, that you may live. Then the Lord God Almighty will be with you, just as you say he is.* **Amos 5:15** *Hate evil, love good; maintain justice in the courts. Perhaps the Lord God Almighty will have mercy on the remnant of Joseph.*

Verse 15 says to hate evil. How can someone hate evil? One way is to become angry when we see something that is not right. This happened to Jesus; he became angry when he saw things that were not right.

Jesus healed many people. He would even heal people on the Sabbath. The Jewish leaders did not like him doing that because their scriptures told them they were not allowed to work on the Sabbath. Jesus told them that God made the Sabbath a day of rest for people.

Mk 2:27 *Then he said to them, "The Sabbath was made for man, not man for the Sabbath."*

Jesus continued to heal on the Sabbath. One time when he went into a synagogue, a Jewish church, a man with a shriveled hand was there. Jesus told him to stand in front of everyone. Then Jesus asked the people if it was against the law to do good or save life on the Sabbath. No one said anything. Jesus knew what they were thinking.

Mk 3:5 *He looked around at them in anger and, deeply distressed at their stubborn hearts, said to the man, "Stretch our your hand." He stretched it out, and his hand was completely restored.*

Why was Jesus angry? It was because the people were stubborn. They did not want him to heal on the Sabbath. He had the power to heal the man of his disability, but the people were more interested in "keeping the law." Jesus didn't let the people stop him. He healed the man right then and there.

If we see people doing mean things to others, we should get angry like Jesus did. If we have the chance to make things right, we should. This will show that we hate evil.

JUNE 8

Jesus Hates Evil

In the Old Testament, God had set up a system of people bringing sacrifices to the temple. People would often need to buy cows, sheep or doves. Sellers of these animals thought they could make more money if they took the animals to the temple where the people who wanted to offer sacrifices would be. The temple had a courtyard around it and the sellers even went inside so they could make more money.

The Bible says there were also people exchanging money. They were there because Jews came from many different countries to offer sacrifices in Jerusalem. They would need to have their money changed into the kind of money that was used in Jerusalem. Jesus became very angry when he saw the people selling animals and exchanging money in the temple.

Jn 2:14 *In the temple courts he found men selling cattle, sheep and doves, and others sitting at tables exchanging money.* **Jn 2:15** *So he made a whip out of cords, and drove all from the temple area, both sheep and cattle; he scattered the coins of the money changers and overturned their tables.* **Jn 2:16** *To those who sold doves he said, "Get these out of here! How dare you turn my father's house into a market!"*

It is hard to picture Jesus getting so angry that he would take a whip and chase the animals out of the courtyard of the temple. Then he turned over the tables where people were sitting exchanging money. Why would Jesus get so angry? The reason is because the temple was the place where people who wanted to get close to God would come. God had always wanted it to be a holy place where people could come and talk to him. But with all the activity, people just thought God's house was like a market place. Jesus hated to see that happen, so he did something about it.

Rom 12:9 *Love must be sincere. Hate what is evil; cling to what is good.*

Jesus hated what was evil. He loved doing good.

JUNE 9

Friends: God's Gift

Susan and Laura are best of friends. They live just down the street from each other. Almost every night after supper they meet at the corner and go for a long walk. They talk to each other about anything and everything. They enjoy their friendship so much that they can even walk comfortably in silence.

Adam and Eve were the first people whom God created. They probably enjoyed going on walks in the evening, too. But one evening was not so much fun.

Gen 3:8 *Then the man and his wife heard the sound of the Lord God as he was walking in the garden in the cool of the day, and they hid from the Lord God among the trees of the garden.*

Why did Adam and Eve hide from God? It was because they had disobeyed God. God had told Adam and Eve not to eat the fruit from a certain tree.

Gen 3:3 *But God did say, "You must not eat fruit from the tree that is in the middle of the garden, and you must not touch it, or you will die."*

Adam and Eve did just the thing God told them not to do.

Gen 3:6 *When the woman saw that the fruit of the tree was good for food and pleasing to the eye, and also desirable for gaining wisdom, she took some and ate it. She also gave some to her husband, who was with her, and he ate it.*

Because Adam and Eve disobeyed God, God said he would punish them. The evening did not end well. God wants to give us good things, even great friendships, but we need to obey his commands.

Deut 28:2 *All these blessings will come upon you and accompany you if you obey the Lord your God.*

JUNE 10

Three Monkeys

Rom 12:9 *Love must be sincere. Hate what is evil; cling to what is good.*

Have you ever seen the three monkeys where one has his hands over his eyes, one over his ears, and one has his hands over his mouth? The caption reads, "See no evil, hear no evil, speak no evil." If your eyes are covered you can't see evil; in fact, if your eyes are closed you can't see anything. If your ears are covered you can't hear evil; in fact, if your ears are covered tightly you can only hear very loud noises. If your mouth is covered you won't say anything evil; in fact, it's hard to talk at all if your mouth is covered.

Does God want us to cover our eyes, ears and mouths so that we won't see, hear, or speak evil? No, but God does want us to avoid evil. This is what God says his people should be like:

Isa 33:15a *He who walks righteously and speaks what is right,*
We should try to do right and speak truth.

Isa 33:15b *. . . who rejects gain from extortion and keeps his hand from accepting bribes,*
Extortion is like stealing; we should not steal. Bribing is like when someone tells you they'll be your friend if you don't tell the teacher what a bad thing they did. We shouldn't accept those bribes.

Isa 33:15c *. . . who stops his ears against plots of murder and shuts his eyes against contemplating evil.*
In this part of the scripture, God talks about stopping our ears. That means that we will not listen to plots of murder. Your friends probably don't talk of murdering, but they may make plans to do mean things. God says we should "stop our ears;" we should not be a part of those plans. God says we should "shut our eyes" to evil—we should not look at evil things on TV or in books.

God wants us to hate evil. We should be careful that our eyes and our ears are not taking in evil. We should be careful that our mouths are not speaking evil. We would do well to be like the three monkeys that see no evil, hear no evil and speak no evil.

Three Pigs

JUNE 11

How many of you know the story of the three little pigs? It's the story of three pigs who built their homes out of different materials. The first pig built his out of straw, the second built his of wood, and the third built his out of brick.

Then the big, bad wolf came along. He huffed and he puffed and he blew the first little pig's house of straw down. When he came to the second little pig's house he huffed and he puffed again. He blew down the little pig's house that was built of wood. The third little pig's house was built of brick but the wolf had strong lungs, so he huffed and he puffed. He huffed and he puffed some more, but he couldn't blow the house down.

The apostle Paul also talks about different kinds of building materials.

I Cor 3:12 *If any man builds on this foundation using gold, silver, costly stones, wood, hay or straw, . . .*

Paul didn't mention bricks, but he did say costly stones, which is probably like marble or granite. He talked about wood and straw, just like the pigs' houses. He also mentioned gold and silver as building materials. Let's read I Cor 3:12 again:

I Cor 3:12 *(see above)*   **I Cor 3:13a** *his work will be shown for what it is, because the Day will bring it to light.* **I Cor 3:13b** *It will be revealed with fire, and the fire will test the quality of each man's work.*

When Paul says "the Day" he is talking about the Day of Judgment when we will all stand before God. God won't huff and puff and blow away all our deeds that weren't done with a right heart, but Paul says that fire will test the quality of each person's works.

We can think of our good works that are done because we love Jesus as the gold, silver, or precious stones. They do not burn in a fire. Those good works will last.

We can think of our good works that are done because we want others to notice or because they will benefit us in some way as the wood, hay and straw. Wood, hay and straw do burn. These good works done for the wrong reasons will not last.

JUNE 12

On the Move

Dustin and Bruce's mom, Mrs. Archer, took an interest in an elderly man in their church. Mr. Wells was old enough to be Mrs. Archer's grandfather. He was an independent sort of man. He left his daughter's home in Washington and bought a bus ticket to North Dakota. He was getting older and he wanted to be buried beside his mother, who had died when he was only six. But Mr. Wells couldn't live in one place for too long. He moved to Arkansas to be with a friend. When he was 100 years old, he made plans to move back from Arkansas to North Dakota. He decided he would drive his van straight through. He made most of the trip but then got pulled over for weaving on the highway in South Dakota. Mr. and Mrs. Archer drove down to pick him up and bring him "home." The Archer boys didn't understand why their mom cared about this very old man, who could hardly hear, even *with* his hearing aid.

Mrs. Archer explained to her sons that they, as a family, had each other. Mr. Wells lived alone and might be very lonely. Mrs. Archer knew this man needed encouragement in his faith as he got closer to the day he would see Jesus.

Heb 3:13 *But encourage one another daily, as long as it is called Today, so that none of you may be hardened by sin's deceitfulness.* **Heb 3:14** *We have come to share in Christ if we hold firmly till the end the confidence we had at first.*

Mrs. Archer planned a party for Mr. Wells' 103rd birthday. It was celebrated in the church with about twenty friends. Mr. Wells got the itch to move again. The Archers arranged for his flight to Arkansas. They showed respect and love for their "adopted grandfather." Their good deeds were an encouragement to those in their church.

Heb 10:24 *And let us consider how we may spur one another on toward love and good deeds.* **Heb 10:25** *Let us not give up meeting together, as some are in the habit of doing, but let us encourage one another—and all the more as you see the Day approaching.*

JUNE 13

A Seamstress
Bible

Dorcas was a seamstress; she sewed clothes. The Bible says she "was always doing good and helping the poor." Let's read her story:

Acts 9:36-37 *In Joppa there was a disciple named Tabitha (which, when translated, is Dorcas), who was always doing good and helping the poor. About that time she became sick and died, and her body was washed and placed in an upstairs room.*

Acts 9:38-39 *Lydda was near Joppa; so when the disciples heard that Peter was in Lydda, they sent two men to him and urged him, "Please come at once!"*

Peter went with them, and when he arrived he was taken upstairs to the room. All the widows stood around him, crying and showing him the robes and other clothing that Dorcas had made while she was still with them.

Acts 9:40-41 *Peter sent them all out of the room; then he got down on his knees and prayed. Turning toward the dead woman, he said, "Tabitha, get up." She opened her eyes, and seeing Peter she sat up. He took her by the hand and helped her to her feet. Then he called the believers and the widows and presented her to them alive.* **Acts 9:42-43** *This became known all over Joppa, and many people believed in the Lord. Peter stayed in Joppa for some time with a tanner named Simon.*

God wants all his people to be like Dorcas. He wants us to do good and to help the poor.

JUNE 14 — Blessed to Bless Others

Seven-year-old Christy had received a beading kit for Christmas. She decided to make bracelets for her three best friends. Some of the beads had letters so she could even put their names on them. Christy's mom asked her, "What about Claire?"

Christy explained that Claire was not friends with her and the other three girls. Mom knew that Claire often felt left out when the other four girls were playing.

Mom told Christy that God had given her those three friends, but God also wanted to give Claire a friend and she might be that person. Mom explained to Christy how God had blessed Abraham.

Gen 15:5 *He took him outside and said, "Look up at the heavens and count the stars—if indeed you can count them." Then he said to him, "So shall your offspring be."*

God promised Abraham many offspring—that means children, grandchildren, great grandchildren, etc.—more offspring than there were stars in the sky! God also promised Abraham land.

Gen 15:7 *He also said to him, "I am the Lord, who brought you out of Ur of the Chaldeans to give you this land to take possession of it."*

God gave Abraham many offspring and the land of Canaan. The reason God blessed Abraham was so he could pass that blessing on to others.

Gen 12:2 *I will make you into a great nation and I will bless you; I will make your name great, and you will be a blessing.* **Gen 12:3** *I will bless those who bless you, and whoever curses you I will curse; and all peoples on earth will be blessed through you."*

God blessed Abraham so that he would be a blessing, and so that others would be blessed through him.

If Christy would make a bracelet for Claire like she did for her other friends, she would be a blessing to Claire.

JUNE 15

Sliced
Warren Marigny

Terry was about fourteen years old when his godmother did something extra special for him. Every year at Mardi Gras* [*mar* dee grah] she bought him a new plaid shirt and a pair of jeans. This year, however, she had purchased an outfit not just for him but for several of his brothers and sisters. Terry couldn't wait for the big day! But when Terry came home from school one day, he found the clothes were ruined.

A neighbor girl, who was envious of Terry's family having these nice clothes, had taken a razor blade and sliced through all the jeans.

The Bible says we should not covet, or be envious of other people's things. God felt so strongly about this that he made it one of the Ten Commandments.

Ex 20:17a *You shall not covet your neighbor's house.* **Ex 20:17b** *You shall not covet your neighbor's wife, or his manservant or maidservant, his ox or donkey, or anything that belongs to your neighbor.*

Deu 5:21a *You shall not covet your neighbor's wife.* **Deu 5:21b** *You shall not set your desire on your neighbor's house or land, his manservant or maidservant, his ox or donkey, or anything that belongs to your neighbor.*

When we are envious, or covetous, of what other people have, we might be tempted to steal or destroy their things. God says we "shall not covet."

Mardi Gras—a carnival in New Orleans celebrated with parades and festivities on the Tuesday before Ash Wednesday; some people begin celebrating Mardi Gras as early as two weeks before the actual day of Mardi Gras

OBEY YOUR PARENTS/BE GOOD

JUNE 16

Apple War
Warren Marigny

Terry and Raymond were spending the summer in Atlanta with their Aunt Elise. They slept in the bedroom at one end of the upstairs hall and their cousin Lisa slept at the other end. When Terry and Raymond's sister, Gail, came for a visit, she slept with Lisa in her room. One day they had picked some crab apples from a neighbor's tree.

Terry and Raymond were awakened from their sleep that night; they heard a thud, then another, and another. When they heard some giggling they knew the girls were up to something. Those thuds were crab apples landing in their room. Terry and Raymond couldn't let the volleys go unchallenged, so they joined in what became a full-blown apple fight. Crab apples sailed up and down the hall. When someone got hit hard with an apple, the children stopped their throwing and went to sleep.

Fortunately no one had been hurt in the fight, but Aunt Elise was "madder than a wet hen." There was a lot of scrubbing that needed to be done to get all the apple stains off the floors and walls. The children were punished for throwing those apples.

Everything we do has consequences. That means what we do causes other things to happen. The apple fight caused messy walls and punishment for the children.

If we sin by doing bad things or deciding not to do good things, we will see the consequences. If we do good we will be rewarded for it.

Rom 2:6 *God "will give to each person according to what he has done."* **Rom 2:7** *To those who by persistence in doing good seek glory, honor and immortality, he will give eternal life.*

Rom 2:9 *There will be trouble and distress for every human being who does evil: first for the Jew, then for the Gentile;* **Rom 2:10** *but glory, honor and peace for everyone who does good: first for the Jew, then for the Gentile.*

JUNE 17

Farmer in the Dell
Marigny

Kerri was in a group of children. The adult watching the children decided they would play "The Farmer in the Dell." In case you've never played the game, I'll explain it. The children stand in a circle. A farmer is chosen and he stands in the middle of the circle. As the first verse of the song is sung, a "farmer" chooses someone to join him in the center. The farmer takes a wife, the wife takes the child, the child takes a nurse, and the nurse takes the cow. It continues through dog, cat, mouse, and cheese. Each child chooses another child to join them in the center. But when the cheese is chosen, the song goes, "the cheese stands alone."

As Kerri's game progressed, she began feeling worse and worse as all the other children were being chosen and she wasn't. When they finally chose her to be the cheese she burst into tears; it was bad enough to be chosen last, but to be "eaten by the mouse" was unbearable.

Maybe if the adult had said before the game started that the cheese gets to be the farmer in the next game, Kerri wouldn't have felt so badly. She would have known that even though she was last, she would have the chance to be first in the next game.

Jesus said something like that:

Mt 19:30 *But many who are first will be last, and many who are last will be first.*

Mk 10:31 *But many who are first will be last, and the last first.*

Mt 20:16 *So the last will be first, and the first will be last.*

Lk 13:30 *Indeed there are those who are last who will be first, and first who will be last.*

What did Jesus mean by that? He means that in this world, some people who are very important now, will not be very important in eternity. Some very poor people who don't seem important on this earth will have a special place in heaven.

JUNE 18

Church Discipline
Warren Marigny

Terry went to church with his godmother. When a young person would misbehave during church—this could mean they were just looking around or they were talking—a nun would come. She would reach across the child's parents, take the child by the ear and twist it so the child would stand up to relieve the pain. The nun then escorted, by the way of the ear, the offender to the back of the church. The child would have to stand at the back for the remainder of the service.

Terry got removed from his pew like this a time or two. It is hard for young people, especially boys, to sit still. Terry tried hard to be good so that he wouldn't get taken to the back of the church. He didn't want to have his ear twisted.

Another reason people might have for trying to be good is because God is pleased when we are good.

Heb 13:16 *And do not forget to do good and to share with others, for with such sacrifices God is pleased.*

When God is pleased with us, we have made him happy.

Jesus is the example that we should follow. He did good things.

Acts 10:38 *. . . how God anointed Jesus of Nazareth with the Holy Spirit and power, and how he went around doing good and healing all who were under the power of the devil, because God was with him.*

Jesus "went around doing good." Jesus said that he always pleased God.

Jn 8:29 *The one who sent me is with me; he has not left me alone, for I always do what pleases him.*

God himself said he was pleased with Jesus. A voice from heaven came and said,

Mt 17:5b *This is my Son, whom I love; with him I am well pleased. Listen to him!*

JUNE 19

Thumb Sucker

Alicia was eight years old, but she still sucked her thumb. No, she didn't do it all the time. She would never suck her thumb in school because her classmates would call her a baby. She did suck her thumb at home and even sometimes at church, because her church friends wouldn't tease her.

Alicia's mom had told her to stop many times. She even threatened to tape Alicia's thumb with duct tape if she didn't stop.

Many babies like to suck their thumb or their fingers. They do this instead of using a pacifier. It helps to comfort them. Babies should stop doing this eventually; they should "grow out of it." Most children have stopped sucking their thumb by the time they begin kindergarten.

The Bible says:

Eccl 3:1 *There is a time for everything, and a season for every activity under heaven:*

Eccl 3:2 *a time to be born and a time to die, a time to plant and a time to uproot,*

Eccl 3:6 *a time to search and a time to give up, a time to keep and a time to throw away.*

There is also a time to suck thumbs and fingers and a time to stop doing those things.

The apostle Paul said:

I Cor 13:11 *When I was a child, I talked like a child, I thought like a child, I reasoned like a child. When I became a man, I put childish ways behind me.*

As we grow up we should show that we are doing so by our actions. We should act like a baby only when we are a baby.

OBEY YOUR PARENTS/BE GOOD

JUNE
20

Glass Eye
Warren Marigny

Terry had a great uncle who people called Yay-Yay. He had a glass eye. One time Yay-Yay had taken Terry fishing and his glass eye fell out. Terry remembers his uncle almost tipped their boat over, but fortunately he was able to catch the eye before it sank to the bottom of the lake. The glass eye was important to Yay-Yay.

Jesus tells us about a "Pearl of Great Price" that was important to another man.

Mt 13:45 *Again, the kingdom of heaven is like a merchant looking for fine pearls.* **Mt 13:46** *When he found one of great value, he went away and sold everything he had and bought it.*

All of us are looking for something in life. We want to have a reason for living. We are like the merchant. He was looking for a fine pearl and we are looking for God. When the man found his pearl, he did all he could to be able to buy it so it would be his.

When we find God by trusting Jesus as our Savior, we should do all we can to get ready to go to heaven. Jesus gives us this advice:

Mt 6:19 *Do not store up for yourselves treasures on earth, where moth and rust destroy, and where thieves break in and steal.* **Mt 6:20** *But store up for yourselves treasures in heaven, where moth and rust do not destroy, and where thieves do not break in and steal.*

We should be doing good deeds to store up treasure in heaven. If we do that, we will be valuing something that is important—even more important than Yay-Yay's glass eye was to him.

JUNE 21

A Good Man

After Paul's three missionary trips he sailed to Rome. While he was in Rome he preached the gospel to those who came to hear him. He also wrote letters to churches from Rome. One of the letters he wrote was to the Philippians or "to the Christians in the town of Philippi [fih *lip eye*]." In this letter Paul tells his readers that he is sending back to them Epaphroditus [ee paff roe *dye* tuss].

The Philippian church had heard how Paul was in prison in Rome. They wanted to send him a gift. They chose Epaphroditus as the one who would take the gift to Paul.

Phil 4:18 *I have received full payment and even more; I am amply supplied, now that I have received from Epaphroditus the gifts you sent. They are a fragrant offering, an acceptable sacrifice, pleasing to God.*

The Philippian church members sent Epaphroditus to take Paul their gift, but they also sent him as a personal servant for Paul. They intended him to stay as long as Paul needed him. However, Epaphroditus got sick—so sick that he almost died. Paul decided it would be best if Epaphroditus went back to Philippi.

Phil 2:25 *But I think it is necessary to send back to you Epaphroditus, my brother, fellow worker and fellow soldier, who is also your messenger, whom you sent to take care of my needs.* **Phil 2:26** *For he longs for all of you and is distressed because you heard he was ill.*

Because some people in Philippi might think Epaphroditus was a quitter for not staying on with Paul, Paul encouraged the people to accept him back.

Phil 2:29-30 *Welcome him in the Lord with great joy, and honor men like him, because he almost died for the work of Christ, risking his life to make up for the help you could not give me.*

Epaphroditus almost lost his life performing a good work for the church of Philippi. He probably was willing to stay on with Paul, but Paul sent him back. Epaphroditus was a good man.

JUNE
22

Good King, Bad King
Bible

Do you think Solomon was a good king or a bad king? Let's look at what the Bible says about him.

When King David died, Solomon was crowned as king. He did not know how to be a king so he prayed that God would help him rule the people. He prayed that God would help him be able to tell the difference between right and wrong.

I Ki 3:10 *The Lord was pleased that Solomon had asked for this.*

Solomon built a magnificent temple for God's people to worship in. He prayed a prayer of dedication. He asked God to answer the prayers of the people who came there.

It seems, with all of this, that King Solomon was a good king. But the Bible also says some other things about King Solomon.

I Ki 11:1-2 *King Solomon, however, loved many foreign women besides Pharaoh's daughter—Moabites, Ammonites, Edomites, Sidonians and Hittites. They were from nations about which the Lord had told the Israelites, "You must not intermarry with them, because they will surely turn your hearts after their gods." Nevertheless, Solomon held fast to them in love.*

I Ki 11:3-4 *He had seven hundred wives of royal birth and three hundred concubines, and his wives led him astray. As Solomon grew old, his wives turned his heart after other gods, and his heart was not fully devoted to the Lord his God, as the heart of David his father had been.*

I Ki 11:5-6 *He followed Ashtoreth the goddess of the Sidonians, and Molech the detestable god of the Ammonites. So Solomon did evil in the eyes of the Lord; he did not follow the Lord completely, as David his father had done.*

Solomon was a good king, but later he became a bad king.

We might be good people loving God with all our hearts. We need to be careful that we don't let our hearts stray away from God. A good person can become a bad person.

JUNE 23

Bad Man, Good Man
Bible

Last night we learned that a good person can become a bad person. It is also true that a bad person can become a good person. The Apostle Paul is a good example.

Paul was a Pharisee, a Jewish religious leader. He thought that Christians were bad. Paul traveled from town to town. He arrested Christians and sometimes killed them. Paul is telling his story to a crowd when he talks about Christians belonging to "the Way."

Acts 22:4 *I persecuted* the followers of this Way to their death, arresting both men and women and throwing them into prison,* **Acts 22:5** *as also the high priest and all the council can testify. I even obtained letters from them to their brothers in Damascus, and went there to bring these people as prisoners to Jerusalem to be punished.*

When Paul was on that trip to Damascus he had a strange experience.

Acts 9:3 *As he neared Damascus on his journey, suddenly a light from heaven flashed around him.*

Jesus appeared to Paul. He said that Paul was persecuting *him* when he was persecuting Christians. Paul was converted because of this experience; he became a Christian. Jesus chose him to take the message of salvation to the Gentiles. From that day on, Paul stopped persecuting Christians. Instead, he started telling people about salvation through Jesus. Paul tells of the many places where he preached:

Acts 26:20 *"First to those in Damascus, then to those in Jerusalem and in all Judea, and to the Gentiles also, I preached that they should repent and turn to God and prove their repentance by their deeds."*

Paul was once a man who did bad things. He became a man who did good things. A bad person can become a good person.

Persecuted—hurt or did bad things to

JUNE 24

Son of Nebat
Bible

Joshua led the Israelites into the land of Canaan about the year 1400 B.C. He divided the land among the twelve tribes. For almost 500 years, the Israelites were one country divided into twelve tribes.

When Solomon died around 925 B.C. the kingdom was divided in two. Jeroboam son of Nebat ruled the northern ten tribes; these tribes as a unit kept the name of "Israel." Rehoboam, Solomon's son, ruled the southern two tribes, which together became known as "Judah."

Jeroboam was not a good king. A prophet named Ahijah [uh *hie* juh] gave Jeroboam a message from God:

I Ki 14:8 *I tore the kingdom away from the house of David and gave it to you, but you have not been like my servant David, who kept my commands and followed me with all his heart, doing only what was right in my eyes.* **I Ki 14:9** *You have done more evil than all who lived before you. You have made for yourself other gods, idols made of metal; you have provoked me to anger and thrust me behind your back.*

I Ki 14:10 *Because of this, I am going to bring disaster on the house of Jeroboam. I will cut off from Jeroboam every last male in Israel—slave or free. I will burn up the house of Jeroboam as one burns dung, until it is all gone.* **I Ki 14:11** *Dogs will eat those belonging to Jeroboam who die in the city, and the birds of the air will feed on those who die in the country. The L*ORD *has spoken!*

God gave a harsh message to Jeroboam: He would be punished for his evil ways.

OBEY YOUR PARENTS/BE GOOD

Good or Bad Example?

JUNE 25

Jeroboam was an evil king. He did not live the way he should. He worshipped gods other than the true God in heaven. Jeroboam had a bad effect not only on himself and on his family; his behavior was the cause of much sin even long after he had died.

The books of I and II Kings say more than twenty times that the kings who ruled after Jeroboam continued to commit sins like those of Jeroboam son of Nebat. Let's read about some of them. Baasha [*bay a sha*] was one of them.

I Ki 15:34 *He did evil in the eyes of the Lord, walking in the ways of Jeroboam and in his sin, which he had caused Israel to commit.*

Ahaziah is another king who followed Jeroboam's bad example.

I Ki 22:52 *He did evil in the eyes of the Lord, because he walked in the ways of his father and mother and in the ways of Jeroboam son of Nebat, who caused Israel to sin.*

Joram was another king who sinned like Jeroboam.

II Ki 3:3 *Nevertheless he clung to the sins of Jeroboam son of Nebat, which he had caused Israel to commit; he did not turn away from them.*

Jeroboam II was given his title because Jeroboam son of Nebat would have been Jeroboam the first. Do you think this Jeroboam was evil also? The Bible says he was.

II Ki 14:24 *He did evil in the eyes of the Lord and did not turn away from any of the sins of Jeroboam son of Nebat, which he had caused Israel to commit.*

Jeroboam son of Nebat set a bad example for the kings that followed him. Are you setting a good example or a bad example? Do you encourage others to be good or to be bad?

JUNE 26

Free Will

From the time Jeroboam son of Nebat ruled until Israel was taken captive to Babylon was about 200 years. About 15 evil kings ruled during that time. Why would God let all those rulers do evil?

God gives to every person free will. He wants us to choose to be good and live according to his Word. But he will never force us to choose good. He gives us a choice to be good and serve him or to be bad and worship other gods.

When the Israelites were entering the Promised Land, Moses told them:

Deu 30:15 *See, I set before you today life and prosperity, death and destruction.* **Deu 30:16** *For I command you today to love the LORD your God, to walk in his ways, and to keep his commands, decrees and laws; then you will live and increase, and the LORD your God will bless you in the land you are entering to possess.*

Deu 30:17 *But if your heart turns away and you are not obedient, and if you are drawn away to bow down to other gods and worship them,* **Deu 30:18** *I declare to you this day that you will certainly be destroyed. You will not live long in the land you are crossing the Jordan to enter and possess.*

God commands his people to love him and to walk in his ways and keep his laws. Still, he gives us the free will to choose. All those evil kings in the kingdom of Israel chose to turn away from God. Let us choose always to serve God each day.

JUNE 27

Turn From Evil

God warned the Israelites that if they did not obey him, they could not live long in the land he was giving them. Many evil kings led Israel. The people followed the example of those rulers. God sent prophets to warn them that they needed to turn back to him.

II Ki 17:13 *The LORD warned Israel and Judah through all his prophets and seers: "Turn from your evil ways. Observe my commands and decrees, in accordance with the entire Law that I commanded your fathers to obey and that I delivered to you through my servants the prophets."*

The people did not obey God. They chose to worship other gods. Hoshea was the last king of Israel and he "did evil in the eyes of the Lord."

Finally God had enough. He allowed Assyria to invade Israel and take the capital city of Samaria.

II Ki 17:5 *The king of Assyria invaded the entire land, marched against Samaria and laid siege [seej] to* it for three years.* **II Ki 17:6** *In the ninth year of Hoshea, the king of Assyria captured Samaria and deported the Israelites to Assyria. He settled them in Halah, in Gozan on the Habor River and in the towns of the Medes.*

II Ki 17:18 *So the LORD was very angry with Israel and removed them from his presence. Only the tribe of Judah was left.*

God commands us to obey his laws. We have the choice to obey or disobey. If we disobey and choose to do bad things, God will not protect us.

Laid siege to—attacked or surrounded the city with their army trying to get the people to surrender

JUNE

28

For Our Protection

Kendra's mom had told her she could ride her Hot Wheels around in their driveway. Kendra was also allowed to ride up and down the sidewalk on their block. She was not allowed to turn the corners at the end of the block and she was not allowed to cross the street. Kendra played within those rules for a while. The neighbor kids would come over sometimes and ride with her. Erica even came to her house and they played together in the back yard.

One day Erica asked Kendra to come to her house; it was just around the corner. Kendra went to Erica's house and they played for a while. When Kendra got home, her mom was very angry. Mom had not known where she was, and had been very worried about her safety. She asked where Kendra had been. Kendra told her. Mom punished Kendra for disobeying the rules. The rules that were given to her were for Kendra's protection.

God's rules for us are for our protection and for our good. Let's look at some of God's commandments. The first commandment is,

Ex 20:3 *You shall have no other gods before me.*

God knows that when we worship other gods we fail to live to our full potential on earth. He also knows that we give up our life in heaven. God wants the best for us, so he commands us to worship only him.

Ex 20:12 *Honor your father and your mother, so that you may live long in the land the LORD your God is giving you.*

God is the one who invented families. He wants families to be strong and happy. If children honor their parents, then families will be stronger and happier than they would be otherwise.

Ex 20:13 *You shall not murder.*

Ex 20:15 *You shall not steal.*

God knows that if we respect other people's lives and their property that the world will be a better place for us to live. God's rules are for our protection.

JUNE 29

Caught

Vincent had a toy box in his room and he had a book shelf. Mom had taught him that every time he was done playing with something he needed to put it back in its place; he should put it in the toy box or on his bookshelf. One day Vincent got a little carried away. He took several different toys out without putting the other ones away. When mom called him down for breakfast he quickly shoved everything under his bed. He thought he would put everything away when he came back to his room. But Vincent got busy with other things that day. He didn't get the toys put away.

The next day Vincent pulled a few things out from under his bed. He also took some other toys out. Yesterday it was so easy to just push things under his bed, so he did the same thing today.

After a week Vincent was having a hard time finding things he wanted to play with. He had to crawl under the bed to get his toys. One morning Mom came into the room and two legs were sticking out from under the bed. Mom got down on the floor beside Vincent and saw the mess under his bed. Vincent had been caught.

Num 32:23b *And you may be sure that your sin will find you out.*

Vincent didn't put his toys away after he was done playing with them. He disobeyed his parents' rule. His sin found him out.

Often in the Bible people who do what is right are called "upright." Let's look at some scriptures that talk about being upright.

Ps 125:4 *Do good, O LORD, to those who are good, to those who are upright in heart.*

Ps 140:13 *Surely the righteous will praise your name and the upright will live before you.*

Prov 2:21 *For the upright will live in the land, and the blameless will remain in it.*

JUNE 30

Bath Towels
Marigny

After bath time Mommy often found wet towels on the floor. Each of the girls said that it wasn't her towel. Mommy finally had a solution. She embroidered the girls' initials on their towels. When towels were on the floor after that, Mommy could find the girl who did it.

Some people are naturally neater than others. The ones of us who are less neat need to work at putting things where they belong. For big families this can be very important. If children do not pick up after themselves, moms can spend most of their day putting things where they belong. The fifth commandment tells us to honor our parents.

Deut 5:16 *Honor your father and your mother, as the Lord your God has commanded you, so that you may live long and that it may go well with you in the land the Lord your God is giving you.*

One way children can honor their mothers—and their fathers, if they have stay-at-home dads—is to pick up after themselves. When you pick up things you are being good.

Ps 34:14 *Turn from evil and do good; seek peace and pursue it.*

Ps 37:3 *Trust in the Lord and do good; dwell in the land and enjoy safe pasture.*

Ps 37:27 *Turn from evil and do good; then you will dwell in the land forever.*

All these scriptures tell us to do good. We can do good even in simple matters like keeping our things picked up and out of the way of other people.

JULY 1

The Fifth Commandment

Darryl and his brother Andre shared a bedroom. The room often got messy, but Darryl didn't do his share of putting things away. One day Darryl told Andre that he couldn't make him clean the room, and then he left with his basketball. He was planning on playing in the driveway where the basketball hoop was set up.

On his way out the front door, Darryl's dad stopped him and asked if the room was clean. Darryl didn't say the same thing to his dad that he had said to his brother. He didn't say, "I don't have to clean our room. You can't make me." Darryl knew better than that. He knew that he could not talk to his parents the same way he talked to his brother or to his friends. Darryl knew that his father would punish him if he did.

God commands that we honor our parents.

Ex 20:12 *Honor your father and your mother, so that you may live long in the land the LORD your God is giving you.*

Deut 5:16 *Honor your father and your mother, as the LORD your God has commanded you, so that you may live long and that it may go well with you in the land the LORD your God is giving you.*

When we honor our parents, we are careful not to say things that are disrespectful.

Lev 19:3 *Each of you must respect his mother and father, and you must observe my Sabbaths. I am the LORD your God.*

When God's people were entering the Promised Land, Moses told the Levites to warn the people about doing certain things. One of the things the Levites warned people about was dishonoring their parents.

Deut 27:16 *"Cursed is the man who dishonors his father or his mother." Then all the people shall say, "Amen!"*

Darryl did the right thing when he showed respect for, when he honored, his father.

JULY 2

Respect Your Parents

Jenny's mom had told Jenny that she couldn't watch a certain TV program. Jenny's mom didn't like the show because the children in it spoke disrespectfully to their parents.

Jenny knew that all her friends watched this show; they talked about it whenever they were together. It made Jenny feel left out because she didn't know what the girls were talking about. Jenny knew her mom wasn't going to change her mind. She would just have to make the best of it. Jenny's mom knows how important it is for children to show respect for their parents.

Eph 6:1 *Children, obey your parents in the Lord, for this is right.* **Eph 6:2** *"Honor your father and mother"—which is the first commandment with a promise—***Eph 6:3** *"that it may go well with you and that you may enjoy long life on the earth."*

The apostle Paul is saying that obeying our parents is part of honoring our parents. He is saying if children obey their parents they are keeping the fifth commandment. The fifth commandment says, "Honor your mother and father."

Jesus told people that God says we should honor our parents.

Mt 15:4 *For God said, "Honor your father and mother" and "Anyone who curses his father or mother must be put to death."*

Jenny's mom does not want her daughter to watch programs that show children disrespecting their parents. She knows how watching programs can influence children to become disrespectful. God wants all children to honor their parents.

JULY 3

Addressing Adults
Marigny

The Marignys had a house rule about showing respect. It said that any adult who is old enough to be your parent will be addressed as "Mr." or "Mrs." An older lady may be called by their first name but the title Miss should be attached, for example, Miss Linda. People in other positions of authority would be addressed with the proper title in front of their name, for example, Pastor Dave or Sheriff Olson.

God tells us that we are to respect those who are in authority.

Rom 13:1 *Everyone must submit himself to the governing authorities, for there is no authority except that which God has established. The authorities that exist have been established by God.*

The Bible says all authority is established by God. Pastors, sheriffs and teachers all have different types of authority. However, the Bible tells us that all their authority comes from God.

Rom 13:2 *Consequently, he who rebels against the authority is rebelling against what God has instituted, and those who do so will bring judgment on themselves.*

If we disrespect our church, law enforcement or educational leaders, we are disrespecting the institutions that God has established.

Rom 13:3 *For rulers hold no terror for those who do right, but for those who do wrong. Do you want to be free from fear of the one in authority? Then do what is right and he will commend you.*

If we obey people in positions of authority, we should have nothing to fear from them. They will tell us, "Good job."

Rom 13:7 *Give everyone what you owe him: If you owe taxes, pay taxes; if revenue, then revenue; if respect, then respect; if honor, then honor.*

We should respect those in authority over us.

JULY 4

Holy, Holy, Holy

When the Marignys were stationed in Italy they had a chance to go swimming in the Mediterranean Sea. There was a certain place where Americans could go; it was called "the American Beach." Every Fourth of July a huge fireworks display was held there. Soldiers on the pier and in boats lit up the sky with sprays of color and filled the air with pops and bangs. You could hear the "Ooos" and "Ahhs" from the audience.

No matter how great fireworks displays may be, they cannot compare to what God looks like. Because we are physical our eyes cannot see God, who is spiritual. However, sometimes people have seen part of how glorious God is. Isaiah said he saw the Lord.

Isa 6:1 *In the year that King Uzziah died, I saw the Lord seated on a throne, high and exalted, and the train of his robe filled the temple.* **Isa 6:2-3** *Above him were seraphs* [sare ufs], each with six wings: With two wings they covered their faces, with two they covered their feet, and with two they were flying. And they were calling to one another, "Holy, holy, holy is the Lord Almighty; the whole earth is full of his glory."*

If we were able to see God's glory we would probably say "Ooo" and "Ahh." When Isaiah saw God's glory, what did he do? First he realized how sinful he was, so he confessed his sin.

Isa 6:5 *"Woe to me!" I cried. "I am ruined! For I am a man of unclean lips, and I live among a people of unclean lips, and my eyes have seen the King, the Lord Almighty."*

After Isaiah confessed his sin, he said he would do what God asked of him.

Isa 6:8 *Then I heard the voice of the Lord saying, "Whom shall I send? And who will go for us?"*

And I said, "Here am I. Send me!"

Reverence for God caused Isaiah to confess his sins and obey God; we should do the same.

Seraphs—special angels

SHOW PROPER RESPECT/REVERENCE

JULY 5

Respect Policemen
Marigny

Mr. Marigny served as the Hettinger County Sheriff for almost six years. As a law enforcement officer, one of his duties was writing tickets for motorists who exceeded the speed limit. When people were respectful Sheriff Marigny would sometimes give them a break. (Depending on their department's policies, law enforcement officers can choose simply to give people warnings rather than writing them a ticket.) However, when people were disrespectful, the sheriff would usually write them a ticket.

When Sheriff Marigny stopped a speeding motorist, he approached the person and said, "I stopped you for exceeding the posted speed limit. Is there an emergency?"

If the person responded respectfully they might say, "No officer, I just wasn't paying attention," or "No sir. I just had my radio turned up loud. I didn't realize I was going that fast."

One night after a basketball game several motorists exceeded the speed limit as they left town. Sheriff Marigny stopped one of them. The wife of the motorist said, "What about all the other people that were speeding?" She wanted to argue that her husband should not get a ticket.

Sheriff Marigny asked the lady if she liked to fish. When the lady said that indeed she did, the sheriff asked her if she ever caught all the fish.

The lady understood the sheriff's point. If she had been driving, she would have received a ticket because she did not show proper respect.

Tit 3:1 *Remind the people to be subject to rulers and authorities, to be obedient, to be ready to do whatever is good.*

God wants us to respect those in authority.

I Pet 2:13 *Submit yourselves for the Lord's sake to every authority instituted among men: whether to the king, as the supreme authority,* **I Pet 2:14** *or to governors, who are sent by him to punish those who do wrong and to commend those who do right.*

I Pet 2:17 *Show proper respect to everyone: Love the brotherhood of believers, fear God, honor the king.*

JULY 6

Respect the Elderly

Many people who live in nursing homes are old. They cannot take care of themselves so others have to help them. They may need help getting dressed, or bathing, or even eating. Old people are still special to God, even though they are old. God does not want people to be forgotten or unloved when they are old. He tells us we should respect those who are old.

Prov 23:22 *Listen to your father, who gave you life, and do not despise your mother when she is old.*

Lev 19:32 *Rise in the presence of the aged, show respect for the elderly and revere your God. I am the L*ORD*.*

This scripture says to "rise in the presence of the aged." In the Army, when a senior ranking officer enters the room it is military courtesy for someone to call the room to attention. Everyone stands until the officer tells them otherwise. Another example of people standing to show respect is when a judge enters the courtroom and the clerk says, "All rise." Standing when an old person enters a room is not how we customarily show respect for them today.

One way we *can* show respect for old people is to take time to talk to them and to listen to them. Because many old people can't hear well, it is a little harder to have a conversation with them. You show respect for them when you make the effort. Another way you might respect old people is to watch out for them. If they live in your neighborhood you might stop by their house once a week and see how they are doing. You might ask if they need anything. Because old people have a hard time getting around, you might watch to see if they need help carrying something or if you could make room for them to get by when a place is crowded.

God says he will take care of us even when we are old.

Isa 46:4a *Even to your old age and gray hairs I am he, I am he who will sustain you.*

Isa 46:4b *I have made you and I will carry you; I will sustain you and I will rescue you.*

God cares about old people and we should, too.

JULY 7

Good Manners

Holly noticed that Amy was a smart aleck. She would say things that were funny and made people laugh. But those same things would be mean to someone. Amy wasn't only a smart aleck on the playground; she talked the same way to her teacher. Holly even noticed that Amy talked this same way to her mom. Amy had not been taught that respecting her parents and respecting those in places of authority are the right things to do. Amy was not a very happy girl.

Holly *was* happy. Her parents had taught her to be respectful. Part of being respectful is having good manners. When someone asks Holly if she wants something, she says, "Yes, please." When they give it to her she says, "Thank you."

Holly shows respect to adults who speak to her. She looks at them and then speaks loudly and clearly enough for them to hear her.

When Holly needs to get by someone she says, "Excuse me, please."

Holly has good table manners. By having good table manners, for example, not talking with food in her mouth, she shows respect for the other people at the table.

Daniel was a young man in the Bible who showed respect. He had been taught some very strict eating habits at home. When he was taken captive to Babylon he could have said, "I won't eat your food." Instead he asked for permission.

Dan 1:8a *But Daniel resolved not to defile himself with the royal food and wine,* **Dan 1:8b** *and he asked the chief official for permission not to defile himself this way.*

The official was afraid that Daniel and his friends would look unhealthy if they ate only vegetables. Daniel respectfully asked if they could try it for ten days:

Dan 1:12a *Please test your servants for ten days:* **Dan 1:12b** *Give us nothing but vegetables to eat and water to drink.*

Daniel showed respect by asking permission. He showed he had manners when he asked with a "please."

SHOW PROPER RESPECT/REVERENCE

JULY 8

Respect Worshippers

The temple in Jerusalem and the synagogues in each town were the Jewish "churches" in Jesus' time. The temple and the synagogues were places where people came to get close to God. When Jesus lived on the earth, he often went to a synagogue or to the temple courtyard to teach people about God.

Mt 12:9 *Going on from that place, he went into their synagogue.*

Lk 4:15 *He taught in their synagogues, and everyone praised him.*

Lk 4:16 *He went to Nazareth, where he had been brought up, and on the Sabbath day he went into the synagogue, as was his custom. And he stood up to read.*

When Jesus was being questioned by the high priest, he said he had taught openly in the synagogues and at the temple.

Jn 18:20 *"I have spoken openly to the world," Jesus replied. "I always taught in synagogues or at the temple, where all the Jews come together. I said nothing in secret."*

Jesus said he was sent to the lost sheep of Israel. Even though the people were going to church they did not understand the things of God. Jesus came to tell them about God. He knew he would find people who were searching for God if he went to the "churches," that is, their synagogues and the temple.

When we go to church, we see people there who are still searching for God. The people who have trusted Christ as Savior, are coming to worship him. We should be careful when we are in church to respect the other people that are there searching for and worshipping God. If we make a lot of noise we might keep them from doing that.

God speaks to many people in churches. We should be quiet when we are in church so people are able to pray and listen to God.

JULY 9

Don't Make Fun

Willie knew that his parents loved each other. But sometimes Willie felt badly for his dad. His dad would be so embarrassed when Mom would laugh at him for using the wrong word. Dad would laugh along with her and the other people. But Willie saw how red his dad's face was. Willie knew his dad didn't really think it was funny.

Yes, children should respect their parents, but God also wants wives to respect their husbands.

Eph 5:22 *Wives, submit to your husbands as to the Lord.*

Eph 5:23 *For the husband is the head of the wife as Christ is the head of the church, his body, of which he is the Savior.*

Eph 5:24 *Now as the church submits to Christ, so also wives should submit to their husbands in everything.*

Paul says wives should submit to their husbands. That means wives should respect their husbands and help them become all that God made them to be.

Husbands should also help their wives to become all that God wants them to be. Paul tells husbands to love their wives like Christ loved the church. How much did Christ love the church? He gave his very life for the church. If husbands loved their wives like that, then they would be willing to give their lives for their wives. Paul says husbands should love like that, and then he says that wives in return must respect their husbands.

Eph 5:33 *However, each one of you also must love his wife as he loves himself, and the wife must respect her husband.*

If Willie's mom knew that God wanted her to respect his dad, she wouldn't make fun of him any more. She might, instead, correct him privately so as not to embarrass him, and to help him learn.

JULY 10
Respect Other's Property

Garrett raced into the bank in front of his Dad. There were balloons there that the bank was giving away. He grabbed two of the ribbons hanging from a couple of balloons that were bumping up against the ceiling. Dad quickly corrected his son. He told Garrett to let the balloons go. He needed to ask the teller if he could please have one. Garrett was a little bit embarrassed, but he did as his father asked.

Garrett failed to show respect for the bank's property. Even though the bank was giving the balloons away they belonged to the bank.

I Pet 2:17 *Show proper respect to everyone: Love the brotherhood of believers, fear God, honor the king.*

Peter says we should show proper respect to all people. If we show proper respect to people we will also respect their property—that means we will not take or damage other people's things. God thought the rule about not stealing was so important that he made it one of the Ten Commandments. "You shall not steal" is the eighth commandment.

Ex 20:15 *You shall not steal.*

Deu 5:19 *(same as Ex 20:15)*

Paul told the Ephesians that if someone has been stealing they should stop.

Eph 4:28 *He who has been stealing must steal no longer, but must work, doing something useful with his own hands, that he may have something to share with those in need.*

When you respect other people, you respect what belongs to them. You do not steal other people's things. The things you borrow from others should be returned in good condition.

JULY 11

Don't Litter

When Kiara finished swimming at the pool, she liked to stop and buy a treat. Today she got a fudgesicle. She took the wrapper off the top but wrapped it around the stick to keep the treat from making her hands sticky. She and her friends headed toward home with their treats. On the way, Kiara dropped her wrapper in the street, because there was no garbage can close by.

The next morning, some ladies who walked every weekday came by. One of them picked up the fudgesicle wrapper and put it in a bag she carried just for this purpose. These ladies had decided that by picking up trash on their walks they could keep their town looking much nicer. The neighborhood did look better, because these ladies picked up after the town litterbugs.

God wants us to take care of the world he has given us. When he made Adam and Eve he wanted them to take care of the garden he gave them.

Gen 2:15 *The LORD God took the man and put him in the Garden of Eden to work it and take care of it.*

The apostle Paul talks about how God had entrusted him with the preaching of the gospel. He said,

I Cor 4:2 *Now it is required that those who have been given a trust must prove faithful.*

Paul said he needed to be faithful in his preaching because God trusted him to do it.

We have been given this world to live in. Since God placed the world in our care, we should take good care of it. We should not litter.

God made the world, and everything he created was good.

Gen 1:1 *In the beginning God created the heavens and the earth.*
I Tim 4:4a *For everything God created is good.*

We have the privilege of taking care of God's good earth. If we respect our world we will not litter.

JULY 12

Fear God

Nero was an emperor in Roman times. He did many bad things; he especially delighted in hurting and killing Christians. Many people who lived during his time believed that he was the one who started the fire that burned much of the city of Rome. Nero blamed the fire on the Christians. Many people were afraid of Nero. He would kill people for no reason.

This is the way some people feel about God; they are afraid of him. They think God is just waiting for them to do something wrong so he can punish them. God is not someone we should be afraid of, but the Bible says we should "fear him." "To fear God" means "to be in awe of him" or "to revere him."

Deu 6:13 *Fear the* LORD *your God, serve him only and take your oaths in his name.*

We should be in awe of and revere God because he is all-powerful. One of the greatest examples of God's power is when he opened the Red Sea to save his people from the Egyptians. Moses had led a million of God's people out of Egypt. They came to the edge of the water with nowhere to go.

Ex 14:10 *As Pharaoh approached, the Israelites looked up, and there were the Egyptians, marching after them. They were terrified and cried out to the* LORD.

Ex 14:21 *Then Moses stretched out his hand over the sea, and all that night the* LORD *drove the sea back with a strong east wind and turned it into dry land. The waters were divided,* **Ex 14:22** *and the Israelites went through the sea on dry ground, with a wall of water on their right and on their left.*

Can you imagine that huge body of water dividing so God's people could walk through on dry ground? After the Israelites arrived safely on the opposite shore, God caused the Red Sea to go back in its place.

God is very powerful. Yet, he does not want us to be afraid of him; he wants us to be in awe of him, to revere him.

JULY 13

Offering Incense
Bible

Moses, with God's help, led God's people out of Egypt. God told Moses how he wanted the people's place of worship, the tabernacle, to be built:

Ex 25:9 *Make this tabernacle and all its furnishings exactly like the pattern I will show you.*

Moses built the tabernacle just like God told him to. God also told Moses that Moses' brother, Aaron, and Aaron's sons were to be the priests:

Ex 28:1 *Have Aaron your brother brought to you from among the Israelites, along with his sons Nadab [nay dab] and Abihu [uh bie hue], Eleazar [el ee ay zer] and Ithamar [ith uh mar], so they may serve me as priests.*

Moses did exactly what God told him to do. God then instructed Moses how these priests should sacrifice the people's offerings. Even though Moses was careful to do just as God told him, two of Aaron's sons were not so careful. God had told the priests exactly how he wanted the sacrifices made. Nadab and Abihu did not fear, they did not reverence, God. They decided to do things their own way.

Lev 10:1 *Aaron's sons Nadab and Abihu took their censers, put fire in them and added incense; and they offered unauthorized fire before the LORD, contrary to his command.* **Lev 10:2** *So fire came out from the presence of the LORD and consumed them, and they died before the LORD.*

Nadab and Abihu knew the rules for serving in the tabernacle. They were not showing reverence when they offered the sacrifice in a different way.

God desires that his people show him reverence. His priests especially are required to show reverence.

JULY 14

Shining Face
Bible

Moses was a very reverent man. That means he had a great respect and love for God. Moses spent a lot of time praying and he asked God to teach him his ways. He also asked God if he could see God's glory. God told Moses he would show him his goodness and proclaim his name in Moses' presence. He also told Moses that no one was allowed to see God's face.

Ex 33:20 *"But," he said, "you cannot see my face, for no one may see me and live."*

Moses then went up the mountain. He spent forty days and nights there without eating or drinking. God showed Moses his glory. When Moses came down from the mountain his face was shining.

Ex 34:29-30 *When Moses came down from Mount Sinai with the two tablets of the Testimony in his hands, he was not aware that his face was radiant because he had spoken with the Lord. When Aaron and all the Israelites saw Moses, his face was radiant, and they were afraid to come near him.* **Ex 34:31 & 33** *But Moses called to them; so Aaron and all the leaders of the community came back to him, and he spoke to them.*

(vs 33) When Moses finished speaking to them, he put a veil over his face. **Ex 34:34-35** *But whenever he entered the Lord's presence to speak with him, he removed the veil until he came out. And when he came out and told the Israelites what he had been commanded, they saw that his face was radiant. Then Moses would put the veil back over his face until he went in to speak with the Lord.*

Moses walked closely with God and Moses showed God reverence. Because of Moses' reverence, God showed Moses some of his glory.

Date with Dad

JULY 15

Alexis loved her daddy very much. On Thursdays she would get up a little earlier than usual. She and her daddy would go to the gas station for breakfast. They would eat doughnuts and have something to drink. Then Alexis was off to school, and Daddy to work. Alexis looked forward to this time. What made it extra special was that Alexis's younger brother and sister were not yet old enough to "go on dates" with Daddy.

One Thursday morning Daddy explained to Alexis that her excitement about getting to spend time with him is the same way Alexis should look forward every day to her prayer time with God. Daddy showed Alexis a scripture verse.

Ex 34:14 *Do not worship any other god, for the Lord, whose name is Jealous, is a jealous God.*

When we trust Jesus as our Savior, God adopts us as his children. Because he is our father, he wants us to make him the most important person in our lives.

David was a man who loved God. This is what he says in Psalm 5:

Ps 5:1 *Give ear to my words, O Lord, consider my sighing.*

David must have had a bad day. He continues his prayer:

Ps 5:2 *Listen to my cry for help, my King and my God, for to you I pray.*

David reminds God that he is praying:

Ps 5:3 *In the morning, O Lord, you hear my voice; in the morning I lay my requests before you and wait in expectation.*

In this psalm David says he prays in the morning. Then he waits to see how God will answer.

Are you excited about being able to talk to God every morning? He wants us to be.

JULY
16

Hannah's Prayer

When God chose David to be the next king of Israel he said:

I Sam 16:7b *The LORD does not look at the things man looks at. Man looks at the outward appearance, but the LORD looks at the heart.*

We, as people, cannot see other people's hearts, like God can. He knows not only everything that people do, but he knows *why* people do things. God knows everyone who is serving him and everyone who is not.

God knew that Hannah was someone who was serving him. Hannah's story is found in I Samuel. She and her husband went to the temple in Shiloh [*shy* low] every year to worship and sacrifice.

I Sam 1:9-11 *Once when they had finished eating and drinking in Shiloh, Hannah stood up. Now Eli the priest was sitting on a chair by the doorpost of the LORD's temple. In bitterness of soul Hannah wept much and prayed to the LORD. And she made a vow, saying, "O LORD Almighty, if you will only look upon your servant's misery and remember me, and not forget your servant but give her a son, then I will give him to the LORD for all the days of his life, and no razor will ever be used on his head."*

I Sam 1:12-14 *As she kept on praying to the LORD, Eli observed her mouth. Hannah was praying in her heart, and her lips were moving but her voice was not heard. Eli thought she was drunk and said to her, "How long will you keep on getting drunk? Get rid of your wine."*

I Sam 1:15-17 *"Not so, my lord," Hannah replied, "I am a woman who is deeply troubled. I have not been drinking wine or beer; I was pouring out my soul to the LORD. Do not take your servant for a wicked woman; I have been praying here out of my great anguish and grief."*

Eli answered, *"Go in peace, and may the God of Israel grant you what you have asked of him."*

God answered the prayer of reverent Hannah. Hannah gave birth to a son, Samuel.

JULY

Hand it Over

17

Bible

Aaron's two sons, Nadab and Abihu, were killed by fire for not being reverent. That should have been a warning for other priests' sons. In I Samuel we find out that Hophni [*hof* nee] and Phinehas [*fin* ee us], two sons of the priest Eli, were not reverent either.

I Sam 2:12 *Eli's sons were wicked men; they had no regard for the LORD.*

It was the job of the priests to take care of the tabernacle and assist the people in offering their sacrifices. The priests did not have land to raise food or livestock. They were allowed to eat some of the meat brought as sacrifices. God had instructed the Israelites how to make offerings, but Hophni and Phinehas didn't follow those rules. They sent servants to deal with the people. The servants demanded that the people give raw meat to the priests. This is what would happen if a man making an offering disagreed with the servant.

I Sam 2:16 *If the man said to him, "Let the fat be burned up first, and then take whatever you want," the servant would then answer, "No, hand it over now; if you don't, I'll take it by force."* **I Sam 2:17** *This sin of the young men was very great in the LORD's sight, for they were treating the LORD's offering with contempt.*

Eli knew Hophni and Phinehas were doing wicked things. God told the prophet Samuel he would bring judgment on Eli's family. This is how it happened: The Israelites went to fight the Philistines. About 4000 Israelites were killed. That night the elders wondered why they were losing; God was supposed to be on their side. They decided to bring the ark from Shiloh. Hophni and Phinehas came to the battlefield with the ark. But the ark did not help them win. In fact, 30,000 more Israelite soldiers were killed.

I Sam 4:11 *The ark of God was captured, and Eli's two sons, Hophni and Phinehas, died.*

Let us not behave like Hophni and Phinehas did! Let us revere and obey God!

JULY 18

Here I Am

Let's read a story about Samuel.

I Sam 3:1-3 *The boy Samuel ministered before the Lord under Eli. In those days the word of the Lord was rare; there were not many visions.*

One night Eli, whose eyes were becoming so weak that he could barely see, was lying down in his usual place. The lamp of God had not yet gone out, and Samuel was lying down in the temple of the Lord, where the ark of God was.

I Sam 3:4-6 *Then the Lord called Samuel.*

Samuel answered, "Here I am." And he ran to Eli and said, "Here I am; you called me."

But Eli said, "I did not call; go back and lie down." So he went and lay down.

Again the Lord called, "Samuel!" And Samuel got up and went to Eli and said, "Here I am; you called me."

"My son," Eli said, "I did not call; go back and lie down."

I Sam 3:7-8 *Now Samuel did not yet know the Lord: The word of the Lord had not yet been revealed to him.*

The Lord called Samuel a third time, and Samuel got up and went to Eli and said, "Here I am; you called me."

Then Eli realized that the Lord was calling the boy.

I Sam 3:9-10 *So Eli told Samuel, "Go and lie down, and if he calls you, say, 'Speak, Lord, for your servant is listening.'" So Samuel went and lay down in his place.*

The Lord came and stood there, calling as at the other times, "Samuel! Samuel!"

Then Samuel said, "Speak, for your servant is listening."

God may have chosen to speak to Samuel because Samuel had a reverence for God.

JULY 19

God Reveals Himself

In the Old Testament God revealed, he showed, what he was like to certain individuals. Abraham was a man of faith. God came and told him about how he would bless him. Jacob had dreams in which God spoke to him. God showed himself to Moses by appearing to him and telling him what he was like. But even in Bible times, there were periods when God's people did not hear much from God.

Ps 74:9 *We are given no miraculous signs; no prophets are left, and none of us knows how long this will be.*

I Sam 3:1 *The boy Samuel ministered before the Lord under Eli. In those days the word of the Lord was rare; there were not many visions.*

Even though not many people were hearing from God, God chose to reveal himself to Samuel.

I Sam 3:20-21 *And all Israel from Dan to Beersheba [beer she buh] recognized that Samuel was attested as a prophet of the Lord. The Lord continued to appear at Shiloh, and there he revealed himself to Samuel through his word.*

Why did God choose to reveal himself to Samuel? It was probably because Samuel's parents had taught him reverence for God.

God wants to make himself known to his people. He promises he will make himself known to a certain type of people. He promises to reveal himself to people that fear him. When God says "people that fear him" he does not mean "people who are afraid of him." To "fear God" means to "respect God" or to "be in awe of God" because he is so great. God wants to make himself known to people who fear, who revere, him.

Ps 25:14 *The Lord confides in those who fear him; he makes his covenant known to them.*

SHOW PROPER RESPECT/REVERENCE

JULY 20

Irreverent Priests
Bible

Samuel showed reverence for God when, awakened in the night, he responded, "Speak for your servant is listening." Let's read what God told Samuel that night.

I Sam 3:11 *And the LORD said to Samuel: "See, I am about to do something in Israel that will make the ears of everyone who hears of it tingle.* **I Sam 3:12** *At that time I will carry out against Eli everything I spoke against his family—from beginning to end.* **I Sam 3:13** *For I told him that I would judge his family forever because of the sin he knew about; his sons made themselves contemptible,* and he failed to restrain* them.* **I Sam 3:14** *Therefore, I swore to the house of Eli, 'The guilt of Eli's house will never be atoned for by sacrifice or offering.'"*

In Israel God had set apart the family of Levi for service in his temple. Because Eli was a Levite, he was a priest in God's temple. His sons Hophni and Phinehas were also priests.

Eli should have corrected his sons when they did things that were not reverent. Eli should have remembered the story of Nadab and Abihu and how God had taken their lives because they were not reverent.

Because Eli failed to correct his sons' bad behavior, God would send judgment on them. Eli had been warned before, but didn't make the necessary corrections. God told Samuel what he was going to do. God said he would judge Eli's family.

God wants his people, especially leaders in the church, to be reverent. He will judge those who are not. God sent judgment on Eli's sons.

(to be cont.)

Made themselves contemptible—they said and did bad things
Failed to restrain—did not control

JULY 21

Samuel Feared God
Bible (cont.)

It probably looked pretty hopeless for God's people when the ark was captured and Hophni and Phinehas were killed. But that's not all that happened. A messenger from the battlefield came back to Shiloh and told Eli the bad news.

I Sam 4:18 *When he mentioned the ark of God, Eli fell backward off his chair by the side of the gate. His neck was broken and he died, for he was an old man and heavy. He had led Israel forty years.*

The Israelites could have felt like they had no hope. The ark was captured and their three priests were dead. But God did not leave them without a leader. Hannah had promised her son, Samuel, would be given to the Lord.

I Sam 1:11 *And she made a vow, saying, "O Lord Almighty, if you will only look upon your servant's misery and remember me, and not forget your servant but give her a son, then I will give him to the Lord for all the days of his life, and no razor will ever be used on his head."*

Samuel was faithful to God his entire life. He served God's people as a judge.

I Sam 7:15 *Samuel continued as judge over Israel all the days of his life.*

When God's people did things that were not pleasing to God, they would ask Samuel to pray for them. Samuel would pray for them. One time after he prayed for them, he gave them some advice:

I Sam 12:24 *But be sure to fear the Lord and serve him faithfully with all your heart; consider what great things he has done for you.*

Samuel feared God all his days. He told God's people to do the same.

JULY 22

Not Embarrassed
Bible

As a young king, Solomon had a great reverence for God. His father, King David, had taught him that he needed to honor God.

Sometimes young people are embarrassed to let people know that they love God and his Son, Jesus. Solomon was not embarrassed. After he built God's very large and beautiful temple, he wanted to thank God. This is what Solomon did in front of all the people of Israel:

II Chr 6:12 *Then Solomon stood before the altar of the Lord in front of the whole assembly of Israel and spread out his hands.* **II Chr 6:13** *Now he had made a bronze platform, five cubits long, five cubits wide and three cubits high, and had placed it in the center of the outer court. He stood on the platform and then knelt down before the whole assembly of Israel and spread out his hands toward heaven.*

King Solomon prayed a very long prayer to God. He showed his reverence for God by praying in front of all the people. He knelt down with his hands raised toward heaven.

Jesus doesn't want us to be embarrassed that we believe in him. He tells us this in the gospels of Mark and Luke.

Mk 8:38 *If anyone is ashamed of me and my words in this adulterous and sinful generation,* the Son of Man will be ashamed of him when he comes in his Father's glory with the holy angels.*

Lk 9:26 *If anyone is ashamed of me and my words, the Son of Man will be ashamed of him when he comes in his glory and in the glory of the Father and of the holy angels.*

Adulterous generation—people serving other gods rather than the one true God

God is Jealous

JULY 23

Ever since Troy came to town, Martin felt left out. He and Craig had been best friends since kindergarten. When Troy's family moved into the neighborhood, Craig always played with him instead. Martin was jealous. He wanted to still be Craig's best friend.

Martin was jealous of Craig's friendship. Did you know that God can be jealous of our friendship? God wants to be our best friend. He wants to be the most important person in our lives.

Deu 6:14-15 *Do not follow other gods, the gods of the peoples around you; for the Lord your God, who is among you, is a jealous God and his anger will burn against you, and he will destroy you from the face of the land.*

Ex 20:3 *You shall have no other gods before me.*

Ex 20:4 *You shall not make for yourself an idol in the form of anything in heaven above or on the earth beneath or in the waters below.* **Ex 20:5a** *You shall not bow down to them or worship them; for I, the Lord your God, am a jealous God.*

What are some things we might do that would make God jealous?
- If we never pray, never talk to God, God might become jealous.
- If we decide we just want to be bad, instead of being good like God wants us to, God might become jealous.
- If we spend all our time thinking about the sport or hobby that we enjoy the most, God might become jealous.

In all these ways we might make God jealous. God doesn't want us to shut him out of our lives. He doesn't want us doing bad things. He doesn't want other things or activities to be more important to us than he is.

JULY 24

Great Salvation

What is the greatest thing God has ever done? His salvation of mankind is probably the biggest. The writer of the letter to the Hebrews called it "a great salvation."

Heb 2:3 *How shall we escape if we ignore such a great salvation? This salvation, which was first announced by the Lord, was confirmed to us by those who heard him.*

The salvation of mankind was won by Jesus' suffering and death on the cross. Jesus' resurrection shows us that God has power over death. Every other religious leader has died and their bodies have decayed. But Jesus rose from the dead. When the women went to Jesus' tomb, the stone was rolled away and the body was gone. Mary, one of Jesus' disciples, ran to tell Peter and John.

Jn 20:3-4 *So Peter and the other disciple started for the tomb. Both were running, but the other disciple outran Peter and reached the tomb first.* **Jn 20:5-6** *He bent over and looked in at the strips of linen lying there but did not go in. Then Simon Peter, who was behind him, arrived and went into the tomb. He saw the strips of linen lying there,* **Jn 20:7-8** *as well as the burial cloth that had been around Jesus' head. The cloth was folded up by itself, separate from the linen. Finally the other disciple, who had reached the tomb first, also went inside. He saw and believed.*

If Jesus had not risen from the dead, people could say that he was just a good man. Because Jesus rose from the dead, he proved that all he said about himself is true. He is our risen Savior!

JULY 25

The Transfiguration
Bible

Moses' face shone with the radiance of God's glory. Can you picture someone's face actually shining?

There are other times in the Bible when people saw some of God's glory. Peter, James and John were Jesus' closest friends and disciples. They saw Jesus transfigured—that means changed in a really big way. When Jesus was transfigured it is called "The Transfiguration." This is the story:

Mt 17:1 *After six days Jesus took with him Peter, James and John the brother of James, and led them up a high mountain by themselves.* **Mt 17:2** *There he was transfigured before them. His face shone like the sun, and his clothes became as white as the light.*

Jesus' face was like the sun—probably brighter than Moses' face was—and his clothes were like light. What happened next at Jesus' transfiguration?

Lk 9:30-31a *Two men, Moses and Elijah, appeared in glorious splendor, talking with Jesus.*

Moses and Elijah were glorious also. These men had lived and died hundreds of years before Jesus was even born. They were talking there with Jesus. Peter started talking and then God interrupted him.

Mt 17:5 *While he was still speaking, a bright cloud enveloped them, and a voice from the cloud said, "This is my Son, whom I love; with him I am well pleased. Listen to him!"*

Peter, James and John saw some of God's glory. The story of The Transfiguration is told by Matthew, Mark and Luke. These different accounts say the disciples were "afraid," "frightened," and "terrified." If we were to see God's glory we would probably also be afraid.

God is a great God. We should not be afraid of him, but we should reverence him.

JULY 26

Too Holy to Say

In Old Testament times the Israelites had many different names for God. They called him "adon" which is a title of respect meaning, "sir," "master" or "lord." When they called him adonai they meant "God is my master."

The Israelites also called God "El" which means "mighty one." Sometimes they called God "Elah" or "Eloah," which means "an object of worship." "Elohim" is plural for Elah or Eloah.

The people in many countries near Israel had gods that they also called by these names, "Master," "the mighty one," or "the one to be worshipped." The Israelites had another name for God that no one else used for their god. It was Yahweh [*Yah* way]. It was written YHWH in their Scriptures and it was so holy that no one was allowed to say it.

It may seem strange to us that people thought God so holy that they would not even say his name. But God is holy and we should reverence him.

Ps 97:9 *For you, O Lord, are the Most High over all the earth; you are exalted far above all gods.*

This scripture says the God who is Yahweh is above all gods that are worshipped, above all other "elohim."

Ps 47:2 *How awesome is the Lord Most High, the great King over all the earth!*

Ps 48:1 *Great is the Lord, and most worthy of praise, in the city of our God, his holy mountain.*

Ps 29:2 *Ascribe* [uh *skribe*] *to the Lord* the glory due his name; worship the Lord in the splendor of his holiness.*

In the Psalms we find words we can use to praise God. We can also think of our own words to praise and reverence God.

Ascribe to the Lord—give God the credit for—praise God for

JULY 27

Names of God

Adon, Adonai, El and Elohim are all names that the Hebrew people used to talk about God. We find these names in the Hebrew Old Testament. But in English Bibles that we use today there are just two words for God—they are God and Lord. Adon and Adonai are translated Lord.

Like we said yesterday, Adon is a title of respect meaning "sir, lord, or master."

Ps 147:5 *Great is our Lord and mighty in power; his understanding has no limit.*

Adonai means "my master." David called God "his master" in Psalm 51.

Ps 51:15 *O Lord, open my lips, and my mouth will declare your praise.*

Both "Adon" and "Adonai" are translated into the English word "Lord." In the two scriptures we just read, we saw the word Lord. Adon and Adonai are translated as Lord, but "El" and "Elohim" are translated "God." El is a name that means mighty one. Here is a scripture that in Hebrew has the word "El," but in English, "God."

Ps 16:1 *Keep me safe, O God, for in you I take refuge.*

"Elohim" means "objects of worship." God is the one who deserves our worship. Ps 108:1, written in Hebrew, uses the word Elohim. As this scripture is read from our Bible listen for the word "God."

Ps 108:1 *My heart is steadfast, O God; I will sing and make music with all my soul.*

The Hebrews had many names for God that they could say. All of these names show respect or reverence for God. He is master; and he is *our* master if we ask him to be. He is the mighty one and should be the one whom we worship.

SHOW PROPER RESPECT/REVERENCE

JULY 28

Small Caps

In several versions of the Bible you can look in the Old Testament and find the words Lord or God written in small capital letters. That means the words look like this: Lord and God. When you see Lord or God written in small capital letters, in small caps, you know that they were translated from the word YHWH. Yahweh was the name so respected by the Israelites that they never spoke it. It was only to be written. Let's look at some scriptures in which "Lord" is written in small caps.

Gen 2:4 *This is the account of the heavens and the earth when they were created. When the Lord God made the earth and the heavens,*

We see the words Lord and God beside each other. They are taken from the words YHWH and Elohim in the Hebrew.

Josh 24:31 *Israel served the Lord throughout the lifetime of Joshua and of the elders who outlived him and who had experienced everything the Lord had done for Israel.*

Because the word Lord is written in small caps you know it was translated from the Hebrew YHWH. Ezekiel often used the word YHWH. In his book you see Lord in small caps many times. This is one time:

Eze 22:1 *The word of the Lord came to me.*

Another small cap Lord, translated from the word YHWH can be found in Exodus.

Ex 20:7 *You shall not misuse the name of the Lord your God, for the Lord will not hold anyone guiltless who misuses his name.*

On almost every page in the New International Version of the Old Testament you can find Lord in small caps. I want each of you to page through your Old Testament and see if you can find the word "Lord" in small caps. (Give children a few minutes to find examples.)

The Hebrew people reverenced God's name because God is holy. We also should reverence God's name.

God's Name

JULY 29

Ex 20:7 *You shall not misuse the name of the LORD your God, for the LORD will not hold anyone guiltless who misuses his name.*

Deut 5:11 *(same as Ex 20:7)*

You may have memorized the third commandment: "You shall not take the name of the Lord your God in vain."

What is the name of the Lord our God? We serve a triune God. That means there are three persons in one God: God the Father, God the Son, and God the Holy Spirit. God the Father is usually called God or Lord. God the Son is called Jesus or Christ; he may also be called God or Lord. God the Holy Spirit is called the Holy Spirit or the Holy Ghost. That means our God has quite a few different names.

I have never heard people take the Holy Spirit's name in vain, but I have often heard people use the names God, Jesus and Christ in vain. When people take God's name in vain, they might say things like, "O, Lord," or "O, Jesus." It is just an expression they use when they talk. This is treating God's name without proper respect; it is taking God's name in vain.

Another way people take God's name in vain is by using God's name like a curse word. When people get angry or frustrated they might yell out, "God," and then put a curse word behind it. They might say "Jesus Christ" with a snarl in their voice. These examples are other ways that people use God's name in vain.

God's name should be given reverence because God is holy, God is great, and God is glorious.

Ps 29:2 *Ascribe to the LORD the glory due his name; worship the LORD in the splendor of his holiness.*

Ps 96:8 *Ascribe to the LORD the glory due his name; bring an offering and come into his courts.*

SHOW PROPER RESPECT/REVERENCE

JULY 30 — Respect God's Word

Have you seen how some people treat our national flag with a lot of respect? Our military personnel are taught that the flag should never touch the ground. Those who raise the flag on the flagpole hold it carefully so that it won't touch the ground. On military bases, when the flag is taken down, it is folded carefully by several people and then put away. When a flag is flown at night, people who respect it put a light on it. People who show respect for our flag are really showing respect for the thing it represents. Our flag represents our nation, the United States of America.

The Word of God, the Bible, is something that we should respect. It is God's revelation of himself to us. It is a holy book. David, in Psalm 138, said that God has exalted his name and his Word.

Ps 138:2a *I will bow down toward your holy temple and will praise your name for your love and your faithfulness,* **Ps 138:2b** *for you have exalted above all things your name and your word.*

Just like we should respect God's name, we should also respect his Word. Sometimes people use books for different things. They might use them to stand on so they can reach something. They might use them as a booster seat for a child. Some people might even use a book to swat a fly. Because the Bible is God's Holy Book we should not use it like we would an ordinary book. We should treat it respectfully.

David had great respect for God's Word. He said he praised God's Word.

Ps 56:10 *In God, whose word I praise, in the LORD, whose word I praise.*

Ps 56:4 *In God, whose word I praise, in God I trust; I will not be afraid. What can mortal man do to me?*

JULY 31

Glorious God

After Jesus died on the cross he rose from the dead. The Bible tells us that he ascended into heaven. Because Jesus won salvation for every person, God exalted him to a high place.

Phil 2:9 *Therefore God exalted him to the highest place and gave him the name that is above every name.*

Some people believe this new name was "Lord." God gave Jesus the name of Lord. Lord means master. Jesus is the master and ruler of all living things. He is especially the Lord of us human beings whom he came to save. God exalted Jesus and gave him a new name so **Phil 2:10** *that at the name of Jesus every knee should bow, in heaven and on earth and under the earth,* **Phil 2:11** *and every tongue confess that Jesus Christ is Lord, to the glory of God the Father.*

The Bible says every person will confess that Jesus is Lord. Many people who are living right now confess that Jesus is Lord, but others refuse to let Jesus be their Lord. Even those who refuse to call Jesus Lord in this life will call him Lord when they see how great he really is. We can't see him now, but we will one day. John tells us that Jesus will come in the clouds.

Rev 1:7 *Look, he is coming with the clouds, and every eye will see him, even those who pierced him; and all the peoples of the earth will mourn because of him. So shall it be! Amen.*

God has revealed himself to us in the person of Jesus Christ and in his Word. We know some things about God, but when Jesus returns we will know a lot more. We will understand just how great and how glorious our God is. All people will reverence him when they see him.

AUGUST 1

Dirty Dishes

Mom called downstairs, "Who left the dirty dishes on the table?" No one confessed, so Mom waited until Dad came home. She told him the story about the dirty dishes being left on the table "and not a soul knew how they got there." Even Cole, who had left them there, insisted that he hadn't.

In most homes children have told lies. It might seem that because most children lie, that lying is normal, but God takes the sin of lying very seriously. He puts liars in a group with other serious sinners.

Rev 21:8 *But the cowardly, the unbelieving, the vile, the murderers, the sexually immoral, those who practice magic arts, the idolaters and all liars—their place will be in the fiery lake of burning sulfur. This is the second death.*

Do you think because Cole told a lie that God will send him to hell? No, telling a lie does not cause God to send someone to hell.

If Cole repents and asks God to forgive him, he will receive God's forgiveness. If Cole doesn't confess his lie, that can lead him to more and more lies. Paul encouraged the Colossians in a letter:

Col 3:9 *Do not lie to each other, since you have taken off your old self with its practices.*

In another scripture Jesus reprimanded some people who claimed God was their father. He said:

Jn 8:44a *You belong to your father, the devil, and you want to carry out your father's desire. He was a murderer from the beginning, not holding to the truth, for there is no truth in him.* **Jn 8:44b** *When he lies, he speaks his native language, for he is a liar and the father of lies.*

Jesus said that the devil is a liar and the father of lies. Cole would do the right thing if he confessed his lies. He should decide that from now on he will tell the truth.

AUGUST 2

Garage Cleaning

The consequences for lying in Jake's home were that anyone caught lying would be grounded for a weekend.

Jake had told his dad that he couldn't help clean the garage on Saturday because he had soccer practice. Jake didn't really have soccer practice; he just didn't want to help clean the garage.

Jake thought about his lie. He knew if he said that he had lied he would be grounded for the weekend. He would have to clean the garage with his dad. Then Jake thought maybe he could get away with his lie. He could go over to a friend's house and spend the afternoon there. Mom and Dad would probably never find out. Wouldn't that be the best thing for him to do?

If Jake chooses to do the right thing, he will tell the truth.

Eph 4:25 *Therefore each of you must put off falsehood and speak truthfully to his neighbor, for we are all members of one body.*

When the Bible says we must speak truthfully to our neighbor that means to other people. In I Corinthians 13 we read about truth.

I Cor 13:6 *Love does not delight in evil but rejoices with the truth.*

Truth is a good thing, something we can rejoice in.

The writer of Proverbs 30 prayed that God would keep him from lying.

Prov 30:8a *Keep falsehood and lies far from me.*

Zephaniah tells of how things will be for God's people in the future. He says,

Zeph 3:13a *The remnant of Israel will do no wrong; they will speak no lies, nor will deceit be found in their mouths.*

The best thing for Jake to do is to tell the truth, even if it means suffering the consequences.

DO NOT LIE

AUGUST 3

Nothing False
Bible

Nathanael was sitting under a fig tree one day. Philip found him and was very excited to tell him who he and his friends had found. Philip told Nathanael they had found "the one to come" written about in the Old Testament; they had found the Messiah. Philip took Nathanael to Jesus. Jesus saw Nathanael coming.

Jn 1:47 *When Jesus saw Nathanael approaching, he said of him, "Here is a true Israelite, in whom there is nothing false."*

Jesus was telling everyone that Nathanael was an honest man. Jesus said Nathanael was a man who told the truth.

There is a long sentence in the Bible that has the word truth in it four times.

II Jn 1:1 *The elder,*

*To the chosen lady and her children, whom I love in the truth—and not I only, but also all who know the truth—***II Jn 1:2** *because of the truth, which lives in us and will be with us forever:*

II Jn 1:3 *Grace, mercy and peace from God the Father and from Jesus Christ, the Father's Son, will be with us in truth and love.*

When "the truth" is used here, the apostle John is talking about the truth of the gospel, the truth that Jesus is the Savior of all people.

God wants us to be honest like Nathanael and speak the truth. God also wants us to tell people about "the truth" that Jesus is the Savior of all people.

On God's Holy Hill

AUGUST 4

Li and Chen were playing with a ball. They would throw it on the roof of the garage and it would come rolling back to them. One time Li threw the ball just a little too hard and it broke the second story window. The crash was loud, but the boys' parents weren't home. They could lie and say they hadn't done it, but they decided they would tell their parents the truth.

Ps 15:1 *Lord, who may dwell in your sanctuary? Who may live on your holy hill?*

Ps 15:2 *He whose walk is blameless and who does what is righteous, who speaks the truth from his heart.*

Li and Chen chose to be honest and tell the truth. God says that people who tell the truth will live in his sanctuary, on his holy hill.

Psalm 15, from which we just read, and Psalm 24 are similar. They are both written by David.

Ps 24:3 *Who may ascend the hill of the Lord? Who may stand in his holy place?*

Ps 24:4 *He who has clean hands and a pure heart, who does not lift up his soul to an idol or swear by what is false.*

The last thing in this list says a person does not swear by what is false. What does it mean to "swear by what is false?" It could mean that you tell someone a lie and then you say, "I swear."

God wants us always to speak the truth. He does not want us swearing that what is false is true.

AUGUST 5

Tax Man

In Jesus' time the Jews did not like paying taxes. Their tax money was collected by the Romans and often sent to Rome. Many of the tax collectors were unfair and took more money from people than they should have. Dishonest tax collectors would often keep this money for themselves. Zacchaeus [zak *key* us] was one of these tax collectors. When Zacchaeus heard about Jesus he had a change of heart. Let's read the story.

Lk 19:1-4 *Jesus entered Jericho and was passing through. A man was there by the name of Zacchaeus; he was a chief tax collector and was wealthy. He wanted to see who Jesus was, but being a short man he could not, because of the crowd. So he ran ahead and climbed a sycamore-fig tree to see him, since Jesus was coming that way.*

Lk 19:5-6 *When Jesus reached the spot, he looked up and said to him, "Zacchaeus, come down immediately. I must stay at your house today." So he came down at once and welcomed him gladly.*

Lk 19:7-8 *All the people saw this and began to mutter, "He has gone to be the guest of a 'sinner.'"*

But Zacchaeus stood up and said to the Lord, "Look, Lord! Here and now I give half of my possessions to the poor, and if I have cheated anybody out of anything, I will pay back four times the amount."

Lk 19:9-10 *Jesus said to him, "Today salvation has come to this house, because this man, too, is a son of Abraham. For the Son of Man came to seek and to save what was lost."*

Zacchaeus realized that he was not living like he should. He promised to pay back the people from whom he had taken too much money. Zacchaeus repented of cheating the people; he became an honest man and a disciple of Jesus.

AUGUST 6

False Prophets

Prophets are people who speak for God. Some of the great prophets in the Old Testament are Isaiah, Jeremiah and Ezekiel. These men would often say, "This is what the Lord says." Then they would speak a message to the people that was given to them by God.

Sometimes people who were not listening to, or hearing from, God would stand up and say, "this is what the Lord says." Then they would make something up, or say things that they thought God might say. God was not happy with these false prophets. God told Ezekiel what to say to these false prophets—these people that were lying:

Eze 13:8 *Therefore this is what the Sovereign Lord says: Because of your false words and lying visions, I am against you, declares the Sovereign Lord.*

God said he would be against the lying prophets. He is also against us if we are lying. A scripture in Proverbs tells us that God detests, or hates, lying.

Prov 12:22 *The Lord detests lying lips, but he delights in men who are truthful.*

Two scripture passages call God, "the God of truth."

Ps 31:5 *Into your hands I commit my spirit; redeem me, O Lord, the God of truth.*

Isa 65:16 *Whoever invokes a blessing in the land will do so by the God of truth; he who takes an oath in the land will swear by the God of truth. For the past troubles will be forgotten and hidden from my eyes.*

God is the God of truth and we are his people. We should be people of truth.

AUGUST 7

Truth

The Bible is God's Word to us. Through his Word, God reveals to us, or shows us, what he is like.

Ps 119:142 *Your righteousness is everlasting and your law is true.*

The Bible says that God's law is true. That means that we can believe what the Bible says. When someone tells us something that is the opposite of what the Bible says, we know that what they are saying is not the truth. Opposite things cannot both be true.

We can be sure that the Bible is true because of this scripture,

II Tim 3:16 *All Scripture is God-breathed and is useful for teaching, rebuking, correcting and training in righteousness.*

All Scripture is inspired by God. Because God is the God of truth, the book he inspired men to write is truth.

Jesus said that God's Word is Truth.

Jn 17:17 *Sanctify them by the truth; your word is truth.*

Besides saying that God's Word is the Truth, Jesus also said that he is the Truth. Thomas asked Jesus how the disciples could know the way to go.

Jn 14:6 *Jesus answered, "I am the way and the truth and the life. No one comes to the Father except through me."*

We find truth in the Bible, which is God's Word. We also find truth in Jesus Christ.

AUGUST 8

Pay Your Taxes

Working people in our country are required to pay taxes. Why is that? It is so governments can pay for things like public roads, public libraries, public schools and public parks. By using our tax dollars, agencies provide us with things that communities need and want.

Some taxing is important and necessary. It wouldn't make sense for each family to take care of the roads around their homes. Each person pays taxes and then road crews are hired to care for the roads. When people give a portion of their money, then parks and libraries can be built for everyone's use.

Some people cheat on their taxes. That means they do not pay to the government the taxes that the government says they owe. They can cheat by saying that they did not make as much money as they really did. Some very wealthy people cheat by putting their money in foreign bank accounts. What does God's Word say about paying taxes? One time the religious leaders tried to trap Jesus. They thought that he didn't want people to pay their taxes, so they sent spies who tried to get Jesus in trouble with the rulers.

Lk 20:21 *So the spies questioned him: "Teacher, we know that you speak and teach what is right, and that you do not show partiality but teach the way of God in accordance with the truth.* **Lk 20:22** *Is it right for us to pay taxes to Caesar or not?"*

Lk 20:23-24 *He saw through their duplicity* and said to them, "Show me a denarius.* Whose portrait and inscription are on it?"*

Lk 20:25 *"Caesar's," they replied.*

He said to them, "Then give to Caesar what is Caesar's, and to God what is God's."

Jesus said it is right to pay our taxes. We should not cheat on our taxes.

Saw through their duplicity—knew they were trying to trick him
Denarius [dih *nare* ee us]—an ancient Roman silver coin

DO NOT LIE

AUGUST 9

Lying Jerusalem

In some places, children are in the habit of telling lies. They know that their friends are doing it, and so it seems to them everyone tells lies.

Jeremiah lived in Jerusalem, the city where God's temple stood. You would think most people in that city would be honest, but that wasn't the case. God told Jeremiah:

Jer 5:1 *Go up and down the streets of Jerusalem, look around and consider, search through her squares. If you can find but one person who deals honestly and seeks the truth, I will forgive this city.*

God says the same thing a few chapters later:

Jer 9:5 *Friend deceives friend, and no one speaks the truth. They have taught their tongues to lie; they weary themselves with sinning.*

It is sad to think that God's people no longer were living the way God wanted them to. God said not one person was honest; no one was speaking the truth.

Jer 9:8 *Their tongue is a deadly arrow; it speaks with deceit. With his mouth each speaks cordially to his neighbor, but in his heart he sets a trap for him.*

God wants us to be truthful with others. God does not want us to say nice things to a person and then talk about her behind her back.

God told Jeremiah he would punish the people.

Jer 9:9 *"Should I not punish them for this?" declares the LORD. "Should I not avenge* myself on such a nation as this?"*

We should be truthful in all our dealings because God loves truth.

Avenge—punish them like they deserve to be punished

AUGUST 10

Abraham Lies

Abraham, in the Bible, is called the friend of God. A prayer in the Old Testament reads:

II Chr 20:7 *O our God, did you not drive out the inhabitants of this land before your people Israel and give it forever to the descendants of Abraham your friend?*

Abraham is also called the father of us all.

Rom 4:16 *Therefore, the promise comes by faith, so that it may be by grace and may be guaranteed to all Abraham's offspring—not only to those who are of the law but also to those who are of the faith of Abraham. He is the father of us all.*

Why do you think Abraham is called the father of us all? It is because of his faith in God. Abraham believed and trusted in God. When we believe and trust in Jesus Christ as Savior then we are doing what Abraham did; we are believing and trusting in God. When we do that, we become Abraham's children, not physically, but spiritually.

Since Abraham is called a friend of God and the spiritual father of all of us, you would think he was a perfect person. Abraham was not perfect; he asked his wife to tell a lie. (Remember that Abraham's name was Abram before God changed it to Abraham.)

Gen 12:10-11 *Now there was a famine in the land, and Abram went down to Egypt to live there for a while because the famine was severe. As he was about to enter Egypt, he said to his wife Sarai, "I know what a beautiful woman you are.* **Gen 12:12-13** *When the Egyptians see you, they will say, 'This is his wife.' Then they will kill me but will let you live. Say you are my sister, so that I will be treated well for your sake and my life will be spared because of you."*

Abraham was afraid the Egyptians would kill him so that they could take his beautiful wife. He forgot he should trust that God would take care of him. If Abraham had trusted God completely he would not have asked his wife to lie.

DO NOT LIE

AUGUST
11
Isaac Lies
Bible

Abraham thought that Pharaoh would kill him so he asked Sarah to say she was his sister. Do you know that Abraham's son, Isaac, did almost the same thing?

Isaac married Rebekah. When another famine struck the land of Israel, Isaac didn't go to Egypt; he went to live in the land of the Philistines.

Gen 26:1 & 7 *Now there was a famine in the land—besides the earlier famine of Abraham's time—and Isaac went to Abimelech* [uh bim uh lek] *king of the Philistines in Gerar.*

(vs 7) When the men of that place asked him about his wife, he said, "She is my sister," because he was afraid to say, "She is my wife." He thought, "The men of this place might kill me on account of Rebekah, because she is beautiful."

Gen 26:8-9 *When Isaac had been there a long time, Abimelech king of the Philistines looked down from a window and saw Isaac caressing his wife Rebekah. So Abimelech summoned Isaac and said, "She is really your wife! Why did you say, 'She is my sister'?"*

Isaac answered him, "Because I thought I might lose my life on account of her."

Isaac lied because he feared the same thing that his father Abraham had feared. He thought the king would kill him and then take his beautiful wife.

Do you think God was angry at Isaac for lying? God was probably sad that Isaac did not put his full trust in him. However, God must have forgiven Isaac because God then blessed him.

Gen 26:12 *Isaac planted crops in that land and the same year reaped a hundredfold, because the* Lord *blessed him.*

God blessed Isaac with great wealth. Then Isaac moved to a new place.

Gen 26:24 *That night the* Lord *appeared to him and said, "I am the God of your father Abraham. Do not be afraid, for I am with you; I will bless you and will increase the number of your descendants for the sake of my servant Abraham."*

God forgave and blessed Isaac. God will forgive us, but he is not happy when we lie.

AUGUST 12

Rebekah Deceives
Bible

Rebekah was Isaac's wife. She more than likely knew that Isaac had lied to the king. Isaac had told the king that she was his sister.

When Isaac grew old it was time for him to give his blessing to his firstborn son. Esau was Isaac and Rebekah's firstborn. The firstborn son usually got double the inheritance of the other children.

Gen 27:1 *When Isaac was old and his eyes were so weak that he could no longer see, he called for Esau his older son and said to him, "My son."*

"Here I am," he answered.

Isaac told his firstborn son, Esau, to hunt some wild game, fix a good-tasting meal for him, and then receive his blessing.

Isaac's wife Rebekah favored their younger son Jacob.

Gen 25:28 *Isaac, who had a taste for wild game, loved Esau, but Rebekah loved Jacob.*

Rebekah wanted Jacob to get the bigger inheritance. She schemed with Jacob to make it happen.

Gen 27:6 *Rebekah said to her son Jacob, "Look, I overheard your father say to your brother Esau,* **Gen 27:7** *'Bring me some game and prepare me some tasty food to eat, so that I may give you my blessing in the presence of the LORD before I die.'"*

Rebekah told Jacob to go kill two goats and she would make a good meal for Isaac. Then Jacob would take the food to his father. If Isaac thought that Jacob was Esau, then Isaac would bless Jacob instead of Esau. Jacob would get the blessing that rightfully belonged to his brother.

Rebekah was not telling a lie, but she was trying to deceive Isaac. She was trying to make Isaac think something that was not true. She was being dishonest, or deceptive.

AUGUST 13

Jacob Lies

Abraham, Jacob's grandfather, Isaac and Rebekah, Jacob's parents, and even Jacob himself did things that were dishonest. Abraham and Isaac said their wives were their sisters. Rebekah plotted with Jacob so he could take his brother's blessing.

Jacob was involved in deceiving his father. He had two chances to tell the truth, but he lied instead. Yesterday we talked about how Rebekah and Jacob planned to get the blessing for Jacob.

Esau was hairy and Jacob had smooth skin. Rebekah told Jacob to wear Esau's clothes and cover his bare skin with goatskins so he would feel hairy like his brother. Jacob would try to fool his dad so that Isaac would think he was really Esau.

It must have been scary for Jacob when his dad asked him, "Who is it?"

Gen 27:19 *Jacob said to his father, "I am Esau your firstborn. I have done as you told me. Please sit up and eat some of my game so that you may give me your blessing."*

Jacob was probably even more worried when his dad asked him to come close to him.

Gen 27:21 *Then Isaac said to Jacob, "Come near so I can touch you, my son, to know whether you really are my son Esau or not."*

Gen 27:22 *Jacob went close to his father Isaac, who touched him and said, "The voice is the voice of Jacob, but the hands are the hands of Esau."* **Gen 27:23-24** *He did not recognize him, for his hands were hairy like those of his brother Esau; so he blessed him. "Are you really my son Esau?" He asked.*

"I am," he replied.

Jacob lied three times. He said, "I am Esau." When his dad asked him, "Are you really my son, Esau?" Jacob replied, "I am." Jacob also told his father to eat some of his hunted game when it was really goat from the flock that he brought.

God did not want Jacob to lie. God doesn't want us to lie, either.

AUGUST 14

He Believed a Lie
Bible

Jacob had twelve sons. These twelve sons had four different mothers. Rachel was the mother of Joseph and Benjamin. Because Jacob loved Rachel more than the other mothers, he favored her sons Joseph and Benjamin over the other ten sons.

Jacob's grandfather and father, Abraham and Isaac, had lied to keep from getting killed. Jacob lied in order to get Esau's blessing. Now Jacob's sons will lead their father to believe a lie about Joseph, their brother.

Joseph's brothers were envious of him. They sold him to the Midianites as a slave. They didn't want to tell their father Jacob what they had done. They decided to deceive their father.

Gen 37:31 *Then they got Joseph's robe, slaughtered a goat and dipped the robe in the blood.* **Gen 37:32** *They took the ornamented robe back to their father and said, "We found this. Examine it to see whether it is your son's robe."*

Gen 37:33 *He recognized it and said, "It is my son's robe! Some ferocious animal has devoured him. Joseph has surely been torn to pieces."*

Gen 37:34 *Then Jacob tore his clothes, put on sackcloth and mourned for his son many days.*

Joseph's brothers wanted their dad to think that Joseph had been killed by a wild animal. It worked; Jacob thought Joseph was dead. Joseph's brothers deceived their father.

If we cause someone to believe something that isn't true, we are deceiving them. Deception is just like the sin of lying.

DO NOT LIE

AUGUST 15

God is Honest

We have just read five stories in the Bible that say God's people told lies. If you were God and your people were telling lies, wouldn't you leave that part out of your holy book? Why did God, who inspired the writers of the Bible, not leave out the stories of lying and deception? He could have chosen not to inspire men to write the stories of how Abraham, Isaac, Rebekah, Jacob and Jacob's sons all lied or deceived other people. Perhaps God wanted those stories in the Bible because children often imitate the behavior of their parents or older brothers and sisters. This record of the same family committing the same sin for four generations could be a warning for us. If we are doing something that isn't right, our family members might think they can do the same thing.

Another reason God might have told us this about his people is because God is honest. God knew when he created people that they would be sinful. He loves us even though we continue to sin. The Bible says God is the one who makes us holy and that Jesus is not ashamed to call us his brothers.

Heb 2:11 *Both the one who makes men holy and those who are made holy are of the same family. So Jesus is not ashamed to call them brothers.*

In another chapter of Hebrews the author says that many people of faith in the past were looking forward to heaven.

Heb 11:16 *Instead, they were longing for a better country—a heavenly one. Therefore God is not ashamed to be called their God, for he has prepared a city for them.*

God is not ashamed to be called our God, even though we sometimes do wrong things.

The apostle Paul said when he was weak, that's when he was strong. Paul knew he could be strong if he trusted Jesus for strength, instead of trying to be strong all by himself.

II Cor 12:10a *That is why, for Christ's sake, I delight in weaknesses, in insults, in hardships, in persecutions, in difficulties.* **II Cor 12:10b** *For when I am weak, then I am strong.*

AUGUST 16

Carrots or Dirt
Kilzer

Mom sent Rich, Paul and Roger down to the carrot patch. The boys were supposed to fill the bucket with carrots and bring them back so Mom could scrub them and put them in the refrigerator. Rich started digging and realized the ground was as hard as a rock. The boys had brought only screwdrivers to dig up the carrots. They knew in order to fill that bucket, they would be there for most of the morning.

Rich had an idea. He filled the bottom of the pail with dirt and then set a few layers of carrots on top. The boys took the bucket home and then went back to playing.

Mom didn't know the boys had taken the easy way out. She came in the kitchen and dumped the bucket upside down into a sink filled with water. All the dirt turned into thick carrot-filled mud. What a mess Mom had to clean up!

The apostle Peter says,

I Pet 2:1 *Therefore, rid yourselves of all malice and all deceit, hypocrisy, envy, and slander of every kind.*

We should rid ourselves of all deceit. That means we should always be honest.

Prov 14:5a *A truthful witness does not deceive,*
Prov 14:5b *but a false witness pours out lies.*

Truthful people do not deceive others.

Prov 24:28 *Do not testify against your neighbor without cause, or use your lips to deceive.*

We should not use our lips or our actions to deceive others. When Rich, Paul and Roger filled the bucket with dirt they were being deceitful; they caused Mom to think they had dug a bucketful of carrots. They should have been honest and told Mom they were having a problem.

AUGUST 17

Vegetable Thief
Kilzer

The Kilzer family was a big one; there were fourteen children in all. Mom had a garden, which was one of her favorite pastimes. Every time people came to visit during the summer she took them for a tour of her garden.

Lauretta liked the kohlrabi* that Mom grew. She would pull one up and then run and hide in the chaff wagon, where she could eat it without anyone knowing. This snitching of kohlrabi may have been just a thrill to see if she could get away with the "theft."

Solomon, in the book of Proverbs, says that the woman Folly tries to get us to do things we shouldn't. Folly would tell us:

Prov 9:17 *Stolen water is sweet; food eaten in secret is delicious!*
God commands us not to steal.
Ex 20:15 *You shall not steal.*
Deut 5:19 *(same as Ex 20:15)*
Eph 4:28 *He who has been stealing must steal no longer, but must work, doing something useful with his own hands, that he may have something to share with those in need.*

If Lauretta had volunteered to regularly help with the garden, Mom may have been willing to let her eat some of its fruit.

Kohlrabi [call *ra* bee]—a vegetable in the cabbage family that grows
    above the ground; it is peeled and usually eaten raw

AUGUST 18

Honest Abe

Have you ever heard about Abraham Lincoln being called "Honest Abe?" One incident that showed he was honest was when he worked in a store. A man had overpaid him four cents. After work he walked four miles to repay the man his money before he went home—four miles for four cents!

In Bible times, sellers of goods often weighed what they were selling. Scales back in those times had weights on one side and then the item to be weighed would be placed in a container on the other side. When the product was as heavy as the weight, the scales would balance across from each other. The buyer and seller could see how heavy the product was.

If sellers wanted to cheat people, they could say the weights were heavier than they really were. Each person who bought something would be cheated out of a small amount and the seller would get away with cheating.

God told his people that this cheating was wrong.

Lev 19:36 *Use honest scales and honest weights, an honest ephah and an honest hin. I am the* L<small>ORD</small> *your God, who brought you out of Egypt.*

An ephah was a measurement of dry things. It is a little more than a bushel. A hin was how they measured wet things. It was about one and a half gallons. God wanted all measuring to be done honestly.

Deut 25:13-14 *Do not have two differing weights in your bag—one heavy, one light. Do not have two differing measures in your house—one large, one small.*

Deut 25:15 *You must have accurate and honest weights and measures, so that you may live long in the land the* L<small>ORD</small> *your God is giving you.*

Deut 25:16 *For the* L<small>ORD</small> *your God detests anyone who does these things, anyone who deals dishonestly.*

God must have been pleased with Abraham Lincoln's honesty.

AUGUST 19 — No False Testimony

Brian ran home to ask his mom a question. His sister Kayla told him that "you shall not lie" was one of the Ten Commandments. Brian said it wasn't. He was so sure it wasn't one of the commandments that he made a bet with Kayla. He told Kayla that if it was one of the Ten Commandments he would do Kayla's chore of washing the dishes after dinner. Kayla smiled and agreed; she knew she was right.

Is "You shall not lie" one of the Ten Commandments?

The Bible says God spoke the law to Moses. We can find the law that God gave to Moses in 12 chapters of Exodus—Exodus 20-31. The first part of that law is what we call the Ten Commandments. Men have added chapter and paragraph headings in the Bibles we have today. Look at the headings of Chapter 20 in Exodus and Chapter 5 of Deuteronomy.

Heading for Ex 20 *The Ten Commandments*
Heading for Deut 5 *(same as Heading for Ex 20)*

These are God's Ten Commandments to his people.

Exodus 20 and Deuteronomy 5 are where you can find the Ten Commandments in the Bible. Let's read the ninth commandment.

Ex 20:16 *You shall not give false testimony against your neighbor.*

Deut 5:20 *(same as Ex 20:16)*

In the Ten Commandments written in most Bibles you do not find the words, "You shall not lie." However, the command not to give false testimony against your neighbor is like saying "you shall not lie."

Mom told her children that they were both right. Brian was right because the ninth commandment does not explicitly say "you shall not lie." Kayla was right because those two statements mean the same thing. Brian agreed to help Kayla with the dishes.

AUGUST 20

Children are Honest
Marigny

The Marignys invited their pastor and his wife over for dinner. Rachael enjoyed their company so much that she asked, "When are you going to have us over for dinner?"

Mr. Marigny quickly corrected Rachael. He told her that she should tell the pastor and his wife how much she enjoyed their company, but she should not ask for an invitation to their home. Rachael learned about good manners and the guests felt complimented. Rachael was honest in telling her guests how she felt.

David, in the Bible, also told how he felt. He wrote almost half of all the Psalms. In them he talks to God. He tells God when he is happy and when he is sad. He talks to God by praising him, and also by telling him how bad things are. David even comes to talk to God after he commits a big sin.

Sometimes when people sin they don't want to admit it. They might even lie and say they didn't do it. David was not like that; he admitted that he was wrong. He wrote Psalm 51 as a confession to God of his sin.

Ps 51:4 *Against you, you only, have I sinned and done what is evil in your sight, so that you are proved right when you speak and justified when you judge.*

Then David asks God to forgive him.

Ps 51:9 *Hide your face from my sins and blot out all my iniquity.*

David asks God if they can still be friends.

Ps 51:11 *Do not cast me from your presence or take your Holy Spirit from me.*

God wants us to be honest about sin like David was.

Ps 51:6 *Surely you desire truth in the inner parts; you teach me wisdom in the inmost place.*

God appreciates when we are honest, when we tell him how we feel. David was honest with God, just like Rachael was honest with the pastor's family.

DO NOT LIE

AUGUST 21

Tempted to Steal

Sometimes we are tempted to be mean to our brothers and sisters and not even because they were mean to us. We just feel naughty. We should be careful not to give in to these temptations.

I Pet 5:8 *Be self-controlled and alert. Your enemy the devil prowls around like a roaring lion looking for someone to devour.* **I Pet 5:9** *Resist him, standing firm in the faith, because you know that your brothers throughout the world are undergoing the same kind of sufferings.*

Every Christian is tempted to do bad things.

One time, a very rich man fell into temptation. He repeatedly cheated store owners out of small amounts of money. Eventually the man was caught. He resigned from his job and had to appear in court. The judge said the man had to pay a fine, return money to the store, and do several hours of community service. The man also was put on probation for a year.

This man didn't need the money; he was a rich man. However, he was tempted to steal and he gave in to that temptation.

Jas 1:13 *When tempted, no one should say, "God is tempting me." For God cannot be tempted by evil, nor does he tempt anyone;* **Jas 1:14** *but each one is tempted when, by his own evil desire, he is dragged away and enticed.*

We should be careful not to give in to the temptation to steal.

AUGUST 22

A Baggy Fit
Warren Marigny

When Terry was about fifteen years old he bought his first pair of dress pants. He was so proud to show them to his godmother. When he had tried them on in the store they looked great and fit perfectly.

When Terry tried them on at home, though, they were so big they would not stay up. His godmother explained what must have happened. The salesman in the store must have pulled them tight in the back when Terry looked in the mirror to see how they fit in the front. When Terry had turned around and looked over his shoulder to see how they fit in the back, the salesperson must have pulled them tight in the front.

The person in the store probably didn't have Terry's size available, so he made Terry believe the pants he did have available fit Terry. The man was being dishonest.

God wants us to be honest.

Eph 4:15 *Instead, speaking the truth in love, we will in all things grow up into him who is the Head, that is, Christ.*

We should speak the truth.

Ps 26:3 *For your love is ever before me, and I walk continually in your truth.*

We should live truthfully.

Ps 25:5 *Guide me in your truth and teach me, for you are God my Savior, and my hope is in you all day long.*

Ps 86:11 *Teach me your way, O Lord, and I will walk in your truth; give me an undivided heart, that I may fear your name.*

The man who sold Terry his pants was dishonest. God wants us to be honest.

AUGUST 23

Wallet Found
Warren Marigny

When Terry was about ten, he walked with his godmother to Dooky [the oo sounds like those in took] Chase. It was a bar and a restaurant. They sold *the best* shrimp and oyster Po-boy sandwiches. Because Terry was too young to go inside, he sat on the steps and listened to Fats Domino play the piano.

Terry found a wallet someone must have dropped. He put the wallet on the steps and then sat on it to keep it safe. When he gave it to his godmother she took it inside and gave it to the restaurant manager. That way if the owner of the wallet came back, he would be able to find it.

Terry's godmother taught him to be honest, to be truthful.

The Bible says that Jesus was full of truth, and that truth came through Jesus Christ. When John talks about Jesus in the first chapter of his gospel, he calls Jesus "the Word."

Jn 1:14 *The Word became flesh and made his dwelling among us. We have seen his glory, the glory of the One and Only, who came from the Father, full of grace and truth.*

Jn 1:17 *For the law was given through Moses; grace and truth came through Jesus Christ.*

Jesus also said he *is* the truth.

Jn 14:6 *Jesus answered, "I am the way and the truth and the life. No one comes to the Father except through me."*

The Pharisees often tried to catch Jesus saying something that was wrong. Once when they were doing this, they said they knew that Jesus taught the way of God according to the truth.

Mk 12:14 *They came to him and said, "Teacher, we know you are a man of integrity. You aren't swayed by men, because you pay no attention to who they are; but you teach the way of God in accordance with the truth. (Is it right to pay taxes to Caesar or not?)"*

Jesus is full of truth; he is the channel through which truth came; he is the truth; and he taught the way of God according to the truth.

When Terry's godmother taught him to be honest, she was teaching him the way of God.

AUGUST 24

Keep Your Word

Leon had told his T-ball coach that he would be able to make it to an extra practice on Saturday morning, but then he slept in and missed Saturday morning practice completely.

Leon's mother noticed that Leon also promised his friends that he would do things. Often Leon did not do what he said he was going to do. Leon's mom explained to him the importance of keeping his word. She told him that if he said he was going to do something, then he needed to make sure that he followed through on what he had promised.

If Leon does what he promises he will do, then he will be a person of integrity. A person with integrity is honest and upright; he does what he says he will do.

Job was a man of integrity. The Bible says that Satan and God were discussing God's servant Job. This was after Job had lost his flocks and his children to theft and storms.

Job 2:3 *Then the LORD said to Satan, "Have you considered my servant Job? There is no one on earth like him; he is blameless and upright, a man who fears God and shuns evil. And he still maintains his integrity, though you incited me against him to ruin him without any reason."*

Even though Job had lost his possessions and most of his family, he still believed that God was good. He still lived an upright life; he maintained his integrity.

Job's friends came and tried to get him to confess his sins. Job said he didn't have any unconfessed sins in his life. Job told his friends they were wrong:

Job 27:5 *I will never admit you are in the right; till I die, I will not deny my integrity.*

Job 27:6a *I will maintain my righteousness and never let go of it.*

Job said that God knows he is upright:

Job 31:6 *Let God weigh me in honest scales and he will know that I am blameless.*

Job walked in integrity. Leon should do the same, fulfilling what he promises to do.

AUGUST 25

Do What You Promise

Some people in the Bible promised Moses that they would do something. The Israelites were going to enter the Promised Land. Before the Israelites had crossed the Jordan River into the land God intended for his people, two of the tribes, Gad and Reuben, had found land that was good for their livestock to graze on. They went to Moses and asked if they could just live there, instead of crossing the Jordan River to find a place to settle.

At first Moses was angry with these people from the tribes of Gad and Reuben. He said they were sinning against God by not going in to take the Promised Land from the people who lived there. But then the people of Gad and Reuben promised they would be willing to help conquer the land if they could come back and live on the east side of the Jordan River.

Moses agreed that would be alright.

Num 32:20 *Then Moses said to them, "If you will do this—if you will arm yourselves before the Lord for battle,* **Num 32:21** *and if all of you will go armed over the Jordan before the Lord until he has driven his enemies out before him—* **Num 32:22** *then when the land is subdued before the Lord, you may return and be free from your obligation to the Lord and to Israel. And this land will be your possession before the Lord."*

The people of Gad and Reuben promised they would go and conquer the land with the rest of the Israelites. Moses agreed that if they did so, they could come back and live east of the Jordan. Moses gave them a warning:

Num 32:23 *But if you fail to do this, you will be sinning against the Lord; and you may be sure that your sin will find you out.*

God wants his people to keep their word. If they promise to do something they should do it. Moses warned the tribes of Gad and Reuben. He said if they didn't carry through on what they said—if they failed to be people of integrity—their sin would find them out.

AUGUST 26

Stolen
Marigny

Gladys was about six years old when she took a five-cent piece of Bazooka bubble gum from the store. The family got in the van and began their trip home. Kerri could see something in Gladys' pocket, so she asked what it was. Gladys said it was an eraser. Kerri said, "No, it's not." Gladys showed her what it was. Kerri told Daddy that Gladys had stolen a piece of gum.

Daddy turned the van around and drove right back to the store. He made Gladys give the gum back and apologize to a gentleman in Customer Service. Gladys did so with tears streaming down her face. The man was kind and accepted her apology. Gladys said she never stole anything after that.

If children steal and don't get caught, they may begin to steal bigger things. God tells us that thieves will not get into heaven:

I Cor 6:9 *Do you not know that the wicked will not inherit the kingdom of God?*

Do not be deceived: Neither the sexually immoral nor idolaters nor adulterers nor male prostitutes nor homosexual offenders **I Cor 6:10** *nor thieves nor the greedy nor drunkards nor slanderers nor swindlers will inherit the kingdom of God.*

God clearly tells us that thieves will not get into heaven—that is, unless they repent. The Bible tells us that two thieves were crucified with Jesus.

Mt 27:38 *Two robbers were crucified with him, one on his right and one on his left.*

One of these thieves was sorry for what he had done. He asked Jesus to remember him when he came into his kingdom. Jesus forgave him and told him he could go to heaven.

Lk 23:43 *Jesus answered him, "I tell you the truth, today you will be with me in paradise."*

DO NOT LIE

AUGUST

27

No Bribes

What is a bribe? The dictionary says it is "anything, such as money, property, or a favor, offered or given to someone in a position of trust to induce him to act dishonestly." The following is an example of a bribe:

A police officer pulls you over. You know that if you get a ticket your insurance will go up. You say to the officer, "I'll give you $50.00 if you do not give me a ticket." You are offering the police officer a bribe. You are offering money to someone in a position of trust so that he will act dishonestly. The police officer, if he accepts the bribe, would be acting dishonestly. Even though he may be allowed to simply give people a warning rather than a ticket, he should not accept money for doing that.

An example of a small bribe might be like this:

Terrell was supposed to watch his little brother, Dwayne, while his mom went out to do some errands. Terrell knew his mom would be gone a couple of hours, so he put a video on for Dwayne to watch. Then Terrell went down the street to play with his friends. When Terrell came home Dwayne was still watching the video. Terrell told Dwayne he would give him two candy bars if he didn't tell Mom that he had left for a while. Terrell was offering Dwayne a bribe. Should Dwayne take the candy bars and not tell Mom? If he did that, he would be accepting a bribe.

God told his people not to accept bribes:

Ex 23:8 *Do not accept a bribe, for a bribe blinds those who see and twists the words of the righteous.*

Even though God told his people not to accept bribes, some people still did.

I Sam 8:1 *When Samuel grew old, he appointed his sons as judges for Israel.* **I Sam 8:2** *The name of his firstborn was Joel and the name of his second was Abijah* [uh *bye* juh]*, and they served at Beersheba.* **I Sam 8:3** *But his sons did not walk in his ways. They turned aside after dishonest gain and accepted bribes and perverted justice.*

We should neither offer nor accept bribes. We should act with integrity.

Chronic Liar

AUGUST 28

George knew that telling lies was wrong, but he just couldn't seem to stop. What was he going to do? George told his Dad about the problem he was having. George's dad told him that all people are tempted to do bad things, all people are weak. If they don't have a lying problem, they have a problem with something else.

George's dad explained that our weaknesses are ways that we can show we love God. George should get up every morning and pray that God will help him not to lie that day. If he makes it to lunch time without lying, he should thank God for helping him. If he makes it to dinner that day without lying, he should thank God for helping him. If George slips up and tells a lie, he should confess the lie both to the person to whom he lied and to God.

George's dad said he would be willing to help him. He would ask him every evening how the day went. George's dad gave him the following scriptures and asked him to memorize one of them.

Ps 119:163 *I hate and abhor falsehood but I love your law.*

Prov 13:5 *The righteous hate what is false, but the wicked bring shame and disgrace.*

Prov 14:5 *A truthful witness does not deceive, but a false witness pours out lies.*

Lev 19:11 *Do not steal. Do not lie. Do not deceive one another.*

When George made up his mind that he wanted to stop lying, the temptation to lie was very strong. As the days went by, George still struggled and still found himself lying. Over time, however, George noticed that it wasn't as hard as it used to be. He thanked God for helping him with his weakness.

AUGUST 29

Truth Tellers
Bible

Aaron and his sons were the first people that God appointed to be priests in his tabernacle. They were given the tasks of offering sacrifices and blessing the people. They were also to teach the Israelites the way of God.

Lev 10:11 *And you must teach the Israelites all the decrees the Lord has given them through Moses.*

God told Moses to present the tribe of Levi to Aaron so they could assist him.

Num 3:7 *They are to perform duties for him and for the whole community at the Tent of Meeting by doing the work of the tabernacle.*

The Levites were God's priests all through the Old Testament. In the last book of the Old Testament, the book of Malachi, God talks to the priests. He says that, in years past, the tribe of Levi used to revere him and stand in awe of his name.

Mal 2:6 *True instruction was in his mouth and nothing false was found on his lips. He walked with me in peace and uprightness, and turned many from sin.*

God at one time was pleased with the work his priests were doing. They were teaching the people; they were speaking the truth; they were upright; and they were turning many people from sin. However, the Levites stopped speaking the truth. God said to them,

Mal 2:8 *"But you have turned from the way and by your teaching have caused many to stumble; you have violated the covenant with Levi," says the Lord Almighty.*

God wanted his priests to teach truth to the people. When they stopped doing the job God gave them, he was not pleased with them.

AUGUST 30

Cheating

Jenna was very busy the night before her math test. She had a volleyball game, and by the time she got home she was very tired. She pulled out her book and saw there were several formulas that she was supposed to memorize. She thought, "There is no way I will be able to memorize these by tomorrow." Jenna decided she would write them on a small piece of paper. She would put the paper in her pocket. She hoped that the seating arrangement for the class would not have her in the front row of the classroom. Jenna planned on cheating on her test.

God wants us to be honest people, not cheaters. Honest people are people of integrity. David asked that integrity would protect him.

Ps 25:21 *May integrity and uprightness protect me, because my hope is in you.*

David says God will uphold us if we have integrity.

Ps 41:12 *In my integrity you uphold me and set me in your presence forever.*

Asaph wrote Psalm 78. In that psalm he tells how God took David from being a shepherd and made him the king of Israel. Asaph said that David ruled God's people with integrity of heart.

Ps 78:72 *And David shepherded them with integrity of heart; with skillful hands he led them.*

David lived a life of integrity. He prayed that God would judge him accordingly.

Ps 7:8 *Let the LORD judge the peoples. Judge me, O LORD, according to my righteousness, according to my integrity, O Most High.*

Because Jenna cheated on her test, she did not act as a person of integrity; she acted dishonestly. Jenna should not pray that God judge her "according to her integrity." Instead, she should ask for God's mercy.

AUGUST 31

Why Not Lie?

Why do children tell lies? The most common reason is because they did something they weren't supposed to do. Their mom or dad might ask them, "Did *you* do this?" The first thing that comes out of their mouth is, "No." A lie happens before they even have a chance to think about it. Sometimes children might lie and say they did something that they haven't done yet, like clean their room. Sometimes children lie to avoid being punished. Sometimes children lie just because they have gotten into the habit of lying.

These are all reasons children might lie. The Bible gives us some reasons why people *shouldn't* lie. The first reason we shouldn't lie is because God says he hates lying tongues.

Prov 6:16-17 *There are six things the LORD hates, seven that are detestable* to him: haughty eyes, a lying tongue, hands that shed innocent blood . . .*

God says he hates a lying tongue.

Prov 12:22 *The LORD detests lying lips, but he delights in men who are truthful.*

If you want to make God happy, you tell the truth.

The writer of Psalm 120 asks God to deliver him from lying lips.

Ps 120:2-3 *Save me, O LORD, from lying lips and from deceitful tongues. What will he do to you, and what more besides, O deceitful tongue?*

The psalm writer asks what God will do with the deceitful tongue, the lying tongue. Then he answers his own question.

Ps 120:4 *He will punish you with a warrior's sharp arrows, with burning coals of the broom tree.*

God hates lying and will punish liars, but he delights in people that tell the truth.

Detestable to—hated by

SEPTEMBER 1

Self-control

Dylan got mad at his brother, Colin, and they had a big fight. When Dylan got sent to his room he was even angrier because he said Colin started the fight. He was so angry he slammed the door behind him.

Anger is an emotion that God has given us, but God does not want us to be controlled by our anger. He wants us to have control of it. That is called self-control. Self-control is one of the fruits of the Spirit.

Gal 5:22-23 *But the fruit of the Spirit is love, joy, peace, patience, kindness, goodness, faithfulness, gentleness and self-control. Against such things there is no law.*

There are other scriptures that tell us to be self-controlled. Paul has this advice for God's people.

I Thes 5:8 *But since we belong to the day, let us be self-controlled, putting on faith and love as a breastplate, and the hope of salvation as a helmet.*

Peter says we should be self-controlled because we have received the good news of the gospel.

I Pet 1:13 *Therefore, prepare your minds for action; be self-controlled; set your hope fully on the grace to be given you when Jesus Christ is revealed.*

Peter also says we should be self-controlled so that we can pray.

I Pet 4:7 *The end of all things is near. Therefore be clear minded and self-controlled so that you can pray.*

Self-control is a good thing to have. Dylan could have used some when he got mad at Colin.

SEPTEMBER 2

A Gentle Answer

Jas 1:19a *My dear brothers, take note of this: Everyone should be quick to listen,* **Jas 1:19b** *slow to speak and slow to become angry.*

    Joey thought it just wasn't right. His mom had dropped him off in the nursery and he wanted to play with the other children. Eric and Mariah were playing together and leaving him out. Sure, they had given him some building blocks to make a tower, but then they built their tower together and left him out. He built his tower and knocked it over just like they were building their tower and knocking it over. It wasn't as much fun playing by himself, though.

    Then Eric told Mariah, "Don't let Joey have any of our blocks." Joey wanted to crash their tower down, and then go sit with his mom in church.

    Joey knew he should not be so angry.

    Jas 1:19 *My dear brothers, take note of this: Everyone should be quick to listen, slow to speak and slow to become angry.*

    Joey had listened to what the other children were saying. He didn't lash out and say mean things, but he was boiling over inside. How could he keep that anger from spilling out of him?

    Proverbs 15:1 says:

    Prov 15:1 *A gentle answer turns away wrath, but a harsh word stirs up anger.*

    Joey could offer his blocks to Eric and Mariah. If they still wanted to leave him out he could play a game with the nursery worker.

SEPTEMBER 3

Control Your Temper
Bible

David was a great king who loved God, but his life was filled with trouble. One time he had to leave Jerusalem because someone else wanted to be king.

He and his men were passing by a small town when a man named Shimei [*shim* ee eye] saw them. Shimei came toward David and his men and started cursing—he said really mean things to King David. Then he started throwing rocks.

II Sam 16:6 *He pelted* David and all the king's officials with stones, though all the troops and the special guard were on David's right and left.*

One of the king's soldiers wanted to do something.

II Sam 16:9 *Then Abishai [uh bish uh eye] son of Zeruiah [zer you eye uh] said to the king, "Why should this dead dog curse my lord the king? Let me go over and cut off his head."*

David told Abishai that maybe God had told Shimei to curse him. David thought that if this was God's doing, he would not fight back. David said:

II Sam 16:12 *It may be that the LORD will see my distress and repay me with good for the cursing I am receiving today.*

King David may have wanted to yell back at Shimei; he may even have wanted to throw rocks back at him. King David didn't do those things; instead David exercised self-control.

Peter tells us that self-control is something we should strive for.

II Pet 1:5-6 *For this very reason, make every effort to add to your faith goodness; and to goodness, knowledge; and to knowledge, self-control; and to self-control, perseverance; and to perseverance, godliness.*

Self-control is a character quality that God wants his people to possess.

Pelted—threw things at

EXERCISE SELF-CONTROL

SEPTEMBER 4

Slow to Anger

Did you know that God gets angry? Most of the time in the Old Testament when God got angry, it was because his people were sinning. They were disobeying God and not following his laws.

Eze 5:5 *This is what the Sovereign* [sahv er un] Lord says: This is Jerusalem, which I have set in the center of the nations, with countries all around her.*

Eze 5:6 *Yet in her wickedness she has rebelled against my laws and decrees more than the nations and countries around her. She has rejected my laws and has not followed my decrees.*

God is angry when his people turn away from him.

However, God is not always angry and he is not a mean God. In Psalm 103 David tells us what God is like:

Ps 103:8 *The Lord is compassionate and gracious, slow to anger, abounding in love.*

David writes that God is slow to anger. You could say that God is "self-controlled." God's people have to do a lot of bad things—they have to be very stubborn—before God gets angry with them.

One time God's people were being just that bad! They kept complaining and complaining. They even complained about their leaders, Moses and Aaron. God became very angry; he wanted to destroy the people. Moses "reminded" God that he was slow to anger. He said this in his prayer to God:

Num 14:18a *The Lord is slow to anger, abounding in love and forgiving sin and rebellion.*

Then Moses prayed that God would forgive the people for their complaining, and God forgave them.

Sovereign—ruling over all

SEPTEMBER 5

Excuses, Excuses

God's people had been slaves in Egypt for four hundred years. God heard their prayers and wanted to set them free. He chose Moses as the man he would use to bring his people out of Egypt. God said to Moses:

Ex 3:10 *So now, go. I am sending you to Pharaoh to bring my people the Israelites out of Egypt.*

Moses didn't think he could do it.

Ex 3:11 *But Moses said to God, "Who am I, that I should go to Pharaoh and bring the Israelites out of Egypt?"*

God told Moses that He would help him, but Moses was worried about what the people would think. He asked what to say when the people asked who had sent him. God told Moses to say that the God of Abraham, Isaac and Jacob had sent him.

Moses complained to God, "What if they still don't believe me?"

God showed Moses a couple of miracles. He turned Moses' staff into a snake and then back into a staff. He turned Moses' hand leprous* and then he cleared it up. God said if the people didn't believe these signs, they would believe when they saw water from the Nile River turned to blood. Moses still made an excuse.

Ex 4:10 *Moses said to the LORD, "O Lord, I have never been eloquent,* neither in the past nor since you have spoken to your servant. I am slow of speech and tongue."*

God knew all about Moses. God said he would be there to help him.

Ex 4:13 *But Moses said, "O Lord, please send someone else to do it."*

The next verse says that the Lord's anger burned against Moses. God could have been angry when Moses first refused to accept his call, but God is slow to anger. Moses made excuses four times before God became angry.

Leprous—having leprosy, a disease of the skin
Eloquent—able to speak well

EXERCISE SELF-CONTROL

SEPTEMBER

6

An Angry King
Bible

King Saul knew that he would one day have to give up his throne to another man. The king really liked being king and he wanted his son, Jonathan, to rule after him.

David, the son of Jesse, was becoming more and more famous as a soldier. Samuel had anointed David to be the next king of Israel. For these reasons, Saul wanted to kill David. However, he knew that Jonathan and David were best friends.

One day Saul became very angry with Jonathan.

I Sam 20:30 *Saul's anger flared up at Jonathan and he said to him, "You son of a perverse and rebellious woman! Don't I know that you have sided with the son of Jesse to your own shame and to the shame of the mother who bore you.* **I Sam 20:31** *As long as the son of Jesse lives on this earth, neither you nor your kingdom will be established. Now send and bring him to me, for he must die!"*

I Sam 20:32-33 *"Why should he be put to death? What has he done?" Jonathan asked his father. But Saul hurled his spear at him to kill him. Then Jonathan knew that his father intended to kill David.*

I Sam 20:34 *Jonathan got up from the table in fierce anger; on that second day of the month he did not eat, because he was grieved at his father's shameful treatment of David.*

It was a bad day at the king's house! King Saul, the dad, was angry with his son; and Jonathan, his son, was angry with his dad.

Saul was angry because his son was befriending the person who would take his throne. Jonathan was angry that his father wanted to kill his best friend.

Saul and Jonathan would have had a much better chance of working out their differences if both of them were trying to serve God. Saul was more interested in keeping the throne in the family than in accepting God's will for his life. If Saul would have put God first, then his anger would not have gotten out of control.

SEPTEMBER 7

Always Angry

Mike was getting angry a lot lately. His big brother, Chad, treated him like a baby. Mom acted as if she liked Chad more than him. Mike's little sister was constantly asking him questions. Mike thought maybe there was something wrong with him because it seemed he was always angry.

Mike asked his dad if they could talk about something on Saturday when Dad would have time to listen. Dad could see something was really bothering Mike, so he invited him to go to town with him that evening to pick up some things he needed.

Dad listened to Mike and then explained that anger is not a bad thing. However, when anything controls you, including anger, then there is a problem. Proverbs talks about controlling your temper.

Prov 16:32 *Better a patient man than a warrior, a man who controls his temper than one who takes a city.*

A person who could capture a whole city, even in Old Testament times, was pretty famous. God says a person who controls his temper is greater than that. Mike's dad told him how proud he was of him for having not lost his temper yet. He said that exercising self-control is hard. Then Dad shared these scriptures:

Ps 46:1 *God is our refuge and strength, an ever-present help in trouble.*

Heb 4:16a *Let us then approach the throne of grace with confidence,* **Heb 4:16b** *so that we may receive mercy and find grace to help us in our time of need.*

When they pulled up at the store Dad prayed with Mike that he might have God's help in controlling his anger.

EXERCISE SELF-CONTROL

SEPTEMBER 8

The Idol of Food

From the time of our birth until the day we leave this earth, our bodies need nourishment. We get hungry several times during the day. God made us that way. If we are not careful though, food can become an idol in our life.

How can food become an idol? An idol is anything that we give more attention to than we should. If the first thing we think about when we wake up is food, then food is probably an idol to us. If all through the day we think about what we will eat at the next meal or snack, then food is probably an idol to us.

God wants to have first place in our lives. We should keep our minds on God, not on food.

In Psalm 1 we read about the thoughts of a person who is blessed by God.

Ps 1:2 *But his delight is in the law of the LORD, and on his law he meditates day and night.*

In Deuteronomy, God told his people to carefully follow his commands so that he could bless them. He said he had tested them in the desert so they would learn to live according to his Word.

Deut 8:3 *He humbled you, causing you to hunger and then feeding you with manna, which neither you nor your fathers had known, to teach you that man does not live on bread alone but on every word that comes from the mouth of the LORD.*

Jesus quoted this scripture when he was tempted by the devil.

Mt 4:4 *Jesus answered, "It is written: 'Man does not live on bread alone, but on every word that comes from the mouth of God.'"*

God would like our minds to be on him and his Word. If we do that, then "food thoughts" will not be central in our lives—God will. David said that he wanted to find rest in God alone.

Ps 62:5 *Find rest, O my soul, in God alone; my hope comes from him.*

If God is at the center of our lives, then thoughts of food will not control us.

SEPTEMBER 9

Food & Exercise

After God created the world he created Adam, the first man.

Gen 2:7 *The LORD God formed the man from the dust of the ground and breathed into his nostrils the breath of life, and the man became a living being.*

Then God caused Adam to fall into a deep sleep. He took a rib from Adam and made the first woman.

Gen 2:22 *Then the LORD God made a woman from the rib he had taken out of the man, and he brought her to the man.*

From Adam and Eve came all the people who live on the earth today. Adam and Eve were the only two people created by God who did not come into the world as children. But that does not mean that we are not created by God. When Isaiah spoke to the Israelites, it was a long time after the creation of the world. He said that God's people were created by God. He called God's people Jacob, or Israel.

Isa 43:1a *But now, this is what the LORD says—he who created you, O Jacob, he who formed you, O Israel.*

Every person that has ever lived was created by God. Paul said that it is because of God that we exist, that we live and can breathe.

Acts 17:28 *"For in him we live and move and have our being." As some of your own poets have said, "We are his offspring."*

God created us; he has given us a body that we will have until we leave this earth. That is why we should take care of our bodies; we should eat right and exercise.

In taking care of our bodies we need to use self-control. It takes self-control to eat right. We should not eat too much, nor should we eat too much of foods that are not good for us.

Some people don't exercise enough and some people exercise more than they should. People need to have self-control in how much they exercise and in how much they eat.

EXERCISE SELF-CONTROL

SEPTEMBER

10

Kept Safe
Marigny

The Marigny family had invited their children's pastor and his wife, the Nunleys, over for dinner. It was a fun time because the girls all played piano. Mrs. Nunley played some duets with Kerri, but that wasn't what Kerri remembered most about the evening. When Mrs. Nunley sat on the couch, there was a squeaking noise. Kerri knew what had happened. Mrs. Nunley had sat on one of their guinea pigs. After the pastor's wife jumped quickly back to her feet, Kerri retrieved the "flat pig." It wasn't flat, only a little frightened. Kerri put the guinea pig back in his cage.

The guinea pig was safe when it was in its cage. It could run and play and not have to worry about getting hurt.

Some people think that God has rules that keep people from having fun. That is not true. The rules God gives us are like that guinea pig's cage. If we choose to live within God's rules we will be kept safe. We can enjoy the life he has given us.

When Moses was reminding God's people about God's law he said:

Deut 4:8 *And what other nation is so great as to have such righteous decrees and laws as this body of laws I am setting before you today?*

God's laws are right and good for us. The apostle Paul said this about God's law:

Rom 7:12 *So then, the law is holy, and the commandment is holy, righteous and good.*

Paul says the same thing in I Timothy:

I Tim 1:8 *We know that the law is good if one uses it properly.*

David said that God's law is perfect.

Ps 19:7 *The law of the LORD is perfect, reviving the soul. The statutes of the LORD are trustworthy, making wise the simple.*

God's law is not meant to keep us from having fun. It protects us, like the guinea pig cage protected the guinea pig. If we obey God's law, we can enjoy life.

SEPTEMBER 11

Because We Love God

What are some things that God tells us not to do? He tells us not to steal, lie or deceive others.

Lev 19:11 *Do not steal. Do not lie. Do not deceive one another.*

God says we should not be immoral, impure or greedy.

Eph 5:3 *But among you there must not be even a hint of sexual immorality, or of any kind of impurity, or of greed, because these are improper for God's holy people.*

Jesus taught that we should not judge others.

Mt 7:1-2 *Do not judge, or you too will be judged. For in the same way you judge others, you will be judged, and with the measure you use, it will be measured to you.*

This is just a small list of things that we should not do. We should not steal, lie or deceive others. We should not be immoral, impure or greedy. We should not judge others. If you look through the Bible for things God says not to do, you will probably have a list that is a page long.

God's law sets boundaries for us so that we can prosper in this life, but our focus should not be on the "do's and don'ts." When someone came and asked Jesus what the most important commandment was he said it was to love God as much as you could and then to love your neighbor as yourself. Jesus said:

Mt 22:40 *All the Law and the Prophets hang on these two commandments.*

If we love God like we should, he will give us the self-control we need to obey all his other commands.

EXERCISE SELF-CONTROL

SEPTEMBER
12

Accidents
Marigny

Mr. Marigny had to drive about twenty miles to work every day. His wife did not work outside their home; she took care of the four girls and the house. Mr. Marigny always made sure his wife had a vehicle at the house in case she needed to go somewhere. For several years they had a Volkswagen van. The van served the family well, but it did get a few bumps.

Mrs. Marigny was backing out of the fenced yard in Italy. This was a heavy duty fence. Although the gate was a light metal, across the front of the yard was a three-foot-high brick wall. Mrs. Marigny backed the van into the brick and put a dent in the van. Another time Kerri was playing with the passenger side mirror. It fell out and broke on the concrete drive.

Because Mr. Marigny had a high stress job, Mommy thought he would be angry about the van mishaps. But Mr. Marigny, Daddy, didn't get angry either time. He knew both were accidents. In fact, he had fun telling the story of Mommy hitting the fence. Daddy could have gotten angry; instead he exercised self-control.

Prov 14:17 *A quick-tempered man does foolish things, and a crafty man is hated.*

Prov 15:18 *A hot-tempered man stirs up dissension, but a patient man calms a quarrel.*

God tells us to get rid of anger in our lives.

Eph 4:31 *Get rid of all bitterness, rage and anger, brawling and slander, along with every form of malice.*

Paul told the Colossians that before they became Christians they did many things. Now that they were Christians they should get rid of certain types of behavior.

Col 3:8 *But now you must rid yourselves of all such things as these: anger, rage, malice, slander, and filthy language from your lips.*

SEPTEMBER 13

Good for All

The apostle Paul wrote a letter to Titus. In it he told three different groups of people to be self-controlled. Listen and see if you can say who they are.

Tit 2:2 *Teach the older men to be temperate, worthy of respect, self-controlled, and sound in faith, in love and in endurance.*

In that verse who did Paul tell to be self-controlled? (See if your children can answer this question.) Paul told Titus to teach the older men to be self-controlled.

Verses four and five tell older women to teach others how they should live.

Tit 2:4 *Then they can train the younger women to love their husbands and children,* **Tit 2:5** *to be self-controlled and pure, to be busy at home, to be kind, and to be subject to their husbands, so that no one will malign the word of God.*

In these two verses Paul doesn't tell Titus to teach about self-control. He says that the older women should teach a certain group of people to be self-controlled. What group of people should the older women teach to be self-controlled? (Have children respond.) Older women should teach the younger women.

Tit 2:6 *Similarly, encourage the young men to be self-controlled.*

In verse two Paul told Titus to teach the older men to be self-controlled. Here in verse six he says Titus should encourage another group of people to be self-controlled. Who is it? (Have children respond.) Titus should encourage the young men to be self-controlled.

Self-control is a good character trait for all people.

EXERCISE SELF-CONTROL

SEPTEMBER
14

Sprinter
Warren Marigny

Terry's brother, Warren, received a scholarship to Doane College in Crete, Nebraska. He was a runner in track. He ran the 50 meter sprints. He competed against great runners. One of them was Olympic Gold-medalist Charlie Green. Warren was a very competitive runner.

Did you know that God tells us to be competitive in the way we live our faith?

I Cor 9:24 *Do you not know that in a race all the runners run, but only one gets the prize? Run in such a way as to get the prize.*

In Rome they had sports events that might have been like our Olympics. Paul says only one runner wins the race. He says the athletes have done strict training to be able to compete.

I Cor 9:25 *Everyone who competes in the games goes into strict training. They do it to get a crown that will not last; but we do it to get a crown that will last forever.*

Paul says that all the athletes get for their hard work is a crown of leaves. Christians get much more for their hard work; they are promised heaven one day. Paul goes on to say how we should train ourselves.

I Cor 9:26 *Therefore I do not run like a man running aimlessly; I do not fight like a man beating the air.* **I Cor 9:27** *No, I beat my body and make it my slave so that after I have preached to others, I myself will not be disqualified for the prize.*

When Paul says he "beats his body" he means that he does not give it everything it wants. Paul exercised self-control by denying himself.

If we do not exercise self-control, then our bodies might control us. We might eat only those things that we thought tasted good. We would probably eat just sweets and things that are not good for us.

If we do not exercise self-control, then our eyes might control us. We might want to read books and watch movies that are bad. Self-control helps us to make wise choices, to "train" for God's race.

SEPTEMBER 15

Can I Hit Her?

Isabel had taken Tae Kwon Do lessons since she was six. She was a very strong little girl. One of her classmates, Sharon, continually picked on her; it was the same thing day after day. Sharon was trying to make Isabel mad. On the night before the last day of school, Isabel asked her mom if she could fight Sharon—just "knock her lights out."

Isabel's mom knew how much trouble Sharon had been to Isabel. She figured that the school officials wouldn't do much because it was the last day of school. Isabel was a little surprised when her mother said that it would be alright to stand up to Sharon. Isabel went to school the next day, but she didn't fight. Isabel exercised self-control.

There are bullies in many schools. Sometimes those bullies can even be girls.

David, in the Bible, was a soldier. He fought many enemies, but King Saul turned out to be his worst enemy. Saul wanted to kill David. David wrote many psalms about how he turned to God for protection.

Ps 9:9 *The LORD is a refuge for the oppressed, a stronghold in times of trouble.*

David trusted that God would help him. David wrote Psalm 59 when King Saul sent men to kill him.

Ps 59:1 *Deliver me from my enemies, O God; protect me from those who rise up against me.*

Ps 59:4 *I have done no wrong, yet they are ready to attack me. Arise to help me; look on my plight!*

Ps 59:9 *O my Strength, I watch for you; you, O God, are my fortress.*

David could have tried to kill those who were trying to kill him. Instead he exercised self-control and he trusted that God would keep him safe. Just like God protected David, he will protect Isabel when she puts her trust in him.

EXERCISE SELF-CONTROL

SEPTEMBER

16

Red Beans
Warren Marigny

Terry's Aunt Coreen liked to fix red beans for her family. She would make a large pot because there were eleven children in her family. This meal worked well because the beans were cooked with meat and then served over rice. Nothing else was required.

One day Terry watched as Uncle Minot came in the house. He looked in the pot and then he said, "Beans, beans, beans! That's all I get around here." Uncle Minot took the pot over to the garbage can and dumped it.

Aunt Coreen wasn't one to get too excited. She was playing cards and just kept playing. Terry couldn't believe it. He knew his aunt had worked hard to make the beans. Aunt Coreen could have become very angry, but instead she showed self-control.

King Solomon wrote the book of Ecclesiastes. He tells us that we should not be quickly provoked. When he says that, he means that we should not be a person "with a short fuse"—someone who becomes angry quickly.

Eccl 7:9 *Do not be quickly provoked in your spirit, for anger resides in the lap of fools.*

David tells us to refrain from anger.

Ps 37:8 *Refrain from anger and turn from wrath; do not fret—it leads only to evil.*

Another way to say "refrain from anger" is "don't be angry."

Prov 27:4a *Anger is cruel and fury overwhelming.*

When people become angry, they sometimes do terrible things.

Prov 19:11 *A man's wisdom gives him patience; it is to his glory to overlook an offense.*

Aunt Coreen overlooked an offense. Can you?

SEPTEMBER 17

Control Your Attitude

God wants us to use self-control. He wants us to control our anger and our appetites. He also wants us to control our attitudes.

If we didn't control our attitudes we might say things like:
- "Why do I have to fill the dishwasher? Whitney never has to."
- "I don't *like* vegetables!"
- "I'm not tired; I don't *want* to go to bed."

Moms and dads make most of the decisions in homes. They decide about chores, bedtimes, meals, and how the family will spend its time. Parents establish house rules. God gives parents the responsibility of raising children.

Eph 6:4 *Fathers, do not exasperate your children; instead, bring them up in the training and instruction of the Lord.*

Prov 22:6 *Train a child in the way he should go, and when he is old he will not turn from it.*

God told the Israelites to teach their children his commandments.

Deu 6:7 *Impress them on your children. Talk about them when you sit at home and when you walk along the road, when you lie down and when you get up.*

Children can rebel against every rule their parents have, or they can decide to obey the rules. When children obey the house rules, there is usually more peace in the home.

Obeying with a bad attitude is sometimes just as bad as disobeying.

If Frank stomps off to do what he has been asked to do, or if he slams the door behind himself, he is obeying with a bad attitude. Frank might be doing what he has been asked, but he makes a lot of people—himself, his family and God—unhappy in the process.

Prov 17:22 *A cheerful heart is good medicine, but a crushed spirit dries up the bones.*

SEPTEMBER
18
Whining

Theodore was a whiner. Whenever he asked his mother for something, he said it in a whining voice. Theodore's mother told him that her ears could not hear whining voices. Theodore's mother would ignore him whenever he whined. When Theodore would ask with a normal voice his mom was happy to get whatever he needed.

When Theodore stopped whining to get things, it seemed his attitude changed. Mom and Dad were certainly glad that the whining stopped.

Many children learn that they can get what they want by whining. If whining works, then children will continue to do it. If it doesn't work, they will probably try something else.

When we pray, do you think God wants us to whine when we ask for things? No, God says we should come with confidence.*

Heb 4:16 *Let us then approach the throne of grace with confidence, so that we may receive mercy and find grace to help us in our time of need.*

When the writer in Hebrews says, "Let us then approach the throne of grace," he is talking about when we come to God in prayer.

Heb 10:22 *Let us draw near to God with a sincere heart in full assurance of faith, having our hearts sprinkled to cleanse us from a guilty conscience and having our bodies washed with pure water.*
Heb 10:23 *Let us hold unswervingly to the hope we profess, for he who promised is faithful.*

When we pray we should believe that God is faithful and will answer our prayers.

Heb 10:35 *So do not throw away your confidence; it will be richly rewarded.*

Theodore will do well to know that his parents want what is best for him. When he asks for things, he should do it without whining.

With confidence—knowing that God wants our best

SEPTEMBER 19

Muttering

Have you heard the expression, "He muttered something under his breath?" How does a person do that? Well, it usually happens when a person is unhappy about something. They don't want to say something that everyone can hear, but they do want people to know they are upset. They say something, but they don't say it loudly or distinctly enough for people to understand. That is called "muttering under your breath."

The Bible doesn't talk about muttering under our breath, but it does say some people muttered. It says the Pharisees and teachers of the law muttered when Jesus ate with "sinners."

Lk 15:2 *But the Pharisees and the teachers of the law muttered, "This man welcomes sinners and eats with them."*

The Bible also tells us that people muttered about Jesus when he said he would visit Zacchaeus' house.

Lk 19:7 *All the people saw this and began to mutter, "He has gone to be the guest of a 'sinner.'"*

The Jews knew they were God's chosen people. They looked down on those in their community who did not live according to God's law. They considered those people "sinners." Jews who worked as tax collectors for the occupying Roman government were also considered sinners. Jesus told the people that the reason he came was to save sinners.

Lk 19:10 *For the Son of Man came to seek and to save what was lost.*

Lk 5:32 *I have not come to call the righteous, but sinners to repentance.*

The Pharisees and Jews didn't need to mutter about Jesus. They could have just asked him why he talked to sinners and ate at their homes. Jesus would have told them.

We don't need to mutter things, either. If we disagree with what our parents ask us to do, we should obey them for now. At a later time when we are not upset, we should talk to them about it. We might not convince them to see things our way, but talking about things is better than muttering. Muttering under our breath won't make things better.

EXERCISE SELF-CONTROL

SEPTEMBER

20

Rolling the Eyes

At the dinner table Dad said, "I heard that Rodney and Raven are going steady." Jasmin rolled her eyes and said, "They are 'going out,' Dad. It's not called 'going steady.'" When Jasmin rolled her eyes she was being disrespectful of her father. By rolling her eyes, she is saying to everyone at the table, "Dad, you are so stupid!"

Sometimes generations use different words or expressions, but Jasmin could teach her father the new expressions without rolling her eyes. Jasmin's Dad would never roll his eyes at her if she said a word or expression wrong. Instead, he would take the time to teach her the correct word or expression.

Prov 23:22 *Listen to your father, who gave you life, and do not despise your mother when she is old.*

Several times in the Book of Proverbs, Solomon tells his son to listen to his instruction.

Prov 3:1 *My son, do not forget my teaching, but keep my commands in your heart.*

Prov 5:1 *My son, pay attention to my wisdom, listen well to my words of insight.*

Prov 6:20 *My son, keep your father's commands and do not forsake your mother's teaching.*

Children do the right thing when they listen to their parents' instructions.

Parents might seem "old-fashioned" sometimes, but they are the people God has given to take care of children. When children think their parents say something "corny" they should teach them the right way. Children should never roll their eyes at their parents.

SEPTEMBER 21

Smart Remarks

I don't think I've ever seen a little boy roll his eyes. Rolling of the eyes is mostly done by girls. Both boys and girls make smart remarks, though. We talked about muttering under our breath earlier. Smart remarks usually are said out loud for everyone to hear. Let's read an example:

Mom calls up the stairs and says, "Bradley, will you please come here?"

Bradley doesn't hear his mom, so he continues reading his book. The next time Mom calls Bradley, she calls a little louder. Bradley opens his door and says very disrespectfully, "I'm not deaf, Mom." Then he comes down the stairs.

Bradley made a smart remark. Bradley's mom knows she will have to punish him.

Prov 13:24 *He who spares the rod hates his son, but he who loves him is careful to discipline him.*

Bradley's mom loves her son, so she is careful to discipline him.

Prov 19:18 *Discipline your son, for in that there is hope; do not be a willing party to his death.*

If parents don't discipline their children, the children often grow up and get in trouble with the law.

Prov 22:15 *Folly is bound up in the heart of a child, but the rod of discipline will drive it far from him.*

Children do foolish things. If parents are careful to discipline them, children learn to be wise.

Prov 29:15 *The rod of correction imparts wisdom, but a child left to himself disgraces his mother.*

If Bradley's mom doesn't discipline him, he will talk to her like that in public. She will be embarrassed by his behavior.

EXERCISE SELF-CONTROL

SEPTEMBER

22

God Will Help

In the last five devotions we learned about behaviors that come from a bad attitude. Those behaviors were whining, muttering under your breath, stomping or slamming doors, rolling of the eyes, and smart remarks.

If someone is in the habit of doing these things, that habit may be hard to break. Say Theodore has been whining for six months, or Jasmin has been rolling her eyes for over a year. If they realize these behaviors are not pleasing to God and they decide they want to change, what should they do? First, they confess that they have sinned.

When David was made aware of his sin, he confessed it to God.

Ps 51:4 *Against you, you only, have I sinned and done what is evil in your sight, so that you are proved right when you speak and justified when you judge.*

After confessing our sins we should promise to try to do better. If we are in the habit of acting a certain way, it will take dependence on God and self-control for us to change. God is faithful if we are determined that we want to change.

Lam 3:22 *Because of the LORD's great love we are not consumed, for his compassions never fail.* **Lam 3:23** *They are new every morning; great is your faithfulness.*

God forgives us and is faithful to help us.

Ps 89:8 *O LORD God Almighty, who is like you? You are mighty, O LORD, and your faithfulness surrounds you.*

SEPTEMBER 23

It's Important

The apostle Paul was called by God to preach the gospel. Everywhere Paul went he told people that Jesus was the way to be saved. When Paul was a prisoner and was brought before the governor Felix, Paul even told Felix about Jesus!

The Bible says Paul talked about faith in Christ Jesus. He also talked about righteousness, self-control and the judgment to come.

Acts 24:25 *As Paul discoursed on righteousness, self-control and the judgment to come, Felix was afraid and said, "That's enough for now! You may leave. When I find it convenient, I will send for you."*

Paul tells how important self-control is in a Christian's life. He puts self-control between righteousness and the judgment to come. We need to get right with God and then use self-control for the rest of our lives until the time we are judged by God.

Proverbs says that a person who lacks self-control is like a city with broken-down walls.

Prov 25:28 *Like a city whose walls are broken down is a man who lacks self-control.*

Peter tells Christians to stay away from sinful desires. Bad behaviors, like whining, stomping, smart remarks, etc., can be considered sinful desires.

I Pet 2:11 *Dear friends, I urge you, as aliens and strangers in the world, to abstain from sinful desires, which war against your soul.*

Self-control is a fruit of the spirit. Because we have the Holy Spirit we should have the fruit of the Spirit.

Gal 5:22-23 *But the fruit of the Spirit is love, joy, peace, patience, kindness, goodness, faithfulness, gentleness and self-control. Against such things there is no law.*

EXERCISE SELF-CONTROL

SEPTEMBER 24

Tongue Control
Marigny

When Gladys was in school she noticed that many people spent their time talking about other people. Gladys tried not to gossip. Once someone made the comment, "Gladys never says anything bad about anyone." She took that as a compliment. Can people say that you never say anything bad about anyone? Are you careful about the things you say?

The letter of James compares our tongues to some little things that cause big effects. It compares our tongue to a bit in a horse's mouth.

Jas 3:3 *When we put bits into the mouths of horses to make them obey us, we can turn the whole animal.*

The letter of James also compares our tongue to a ship's rudder.

Jas 3:4 *Or take ships as an example. Although they are so large and are driven by strong winds, they are steered by a very small rudder wherever the pilot wants to go.*

Finally, the letter of James compares our tongue to a spark.

Jas 3:5 *Likewise the tongue is a small part of the body, but it makes great boasts. Consider what a great forest is set on fire by a small spark.*

Even though our tongues are small they can cause big effects. If a person talks about someone behind her back or even tells lies, he can cause people to hate each other. People might not speak to each other, or they might get into fights. All that could happen because of someone's tongue.

James tells us that if a person can control what he says, he is able to control his whole body.

Jas 3:2 *We all stumble in many ways. If anyone is never at fault in what he says, he is a perfect man, able to keep his whole body in check.*

Are we being careful to control our tongues?

SEPTEMBER 25

Watch What You Say

The Bible tells us to watch what we say.

David writes in Psalm 39 that he will be careful what he says, especially when he is around people who don't believe in God.

Ps 39:1 *I said, "I will watch my ways and keep my tongue from sin; I will put a muzzle on my mouth as long as the wicked are in my presence."*

A muzzle is something you fasten over an animal's mouth to keep its mouth closed. A muzzled animal cannot bite or eat. When David says he will put a muzzle on, that means he will be careful what he says.

David also prayed that God would help him not to say bad things.

Ps 141:3 *Set a guard over my mouth, O Lord; keep watch over the door of my lips.*

The New Testament also has things to say about what comes out of our mouths.

Col 4:6 *Let your conversation be always full of grace, seasoned with salt, so that you may know how to answer everyone.*

Do you think that your conversation is full of grace? After people talk to you, do they leave with a good feeling? If they do, then your conversation is probably full of grace.

Jas 3:9 *With the tongue we praise our Lord and Father, and with it we curse men, who have been made in God's likeness.*

James says that it should not be like this. We should praise God, and we should bless people, not curse them or say bad things about them.

We should control our tongues and what we say.

SEPTEMBER 26

Good Words Welcome

The things we say have a lot of power. That is why we should learn to control our tongues.

Isaiah said that God gave him wisdom to know the right things to say, things that would encourage people.

Isa 50:4 *The Sovereign LORD has given me an instructed tongue, to know the word that sustains the weary. He wakens me morning by morning, wakens my ear to listen like one being taught.*

Isaiah was God's prophet. He spent time praying and listening to God. Because he did so, God gave him the right words to say to people. When people were tired or discouraged he would speak words of encouragement. He would make the people feel better.

The Book of Proverbs tells us about how important the things we say are.

Prov 25:11 *A word aptly spoken is like apples of gold in settings of silver.*

That means a word spoken at just the right time is a very beautiful thing.

Prov 12:25 *An anxious heart weighs a man down, but a kind word cheers him up.*

Your words can cheer people up, even if they are having a bad day.

Prov 15:23 *A man finds joy in giving an apt reply—and how good is a timely word!*

You can cheer people up with what you say. When you say the right thing at the right time, it makes someone else happy. It also makes you happy.

SEPTEMBER 27

Eating Contest

Have you ever heard of a hot dog eating contest? People compete to see who can eat the most hot dogs in a certain amount of time. Do you think it is right to do this? God gives us food to nourish our bodies, but when people eat more than they should, it is called the sin of gluttony.

You might not have seen or been part of an eating contest, but you may have overeaten a time or two. How does a person know when she has eaten too much? She usually feels uncomfortable afterward. She might say that she feels "stuffed."

So how does a person know when she has eaten *enough*? If you eat slowly, your body will let you know. The feeling of hunger is no longer there and you feel good. If you eat too fast, you won't feel full until it's too late.

It takes self-control not to eat too much. It takes self-control to eat slowly. It takes self-control not to eat between meals. It takes self-control to choose healthy foods. We should use self-control in taking care of our bodies.

Rom 6:11 *In the same way, count yourselves dead to sin but alive to God in Christ Jesus.* **Rom 6:12** *Therefore do not let sin reign in your mortal body so that you obey its evil desires.* **Rom 6:13** *Do not offer the parts of your body to sin, as instruments of wickedness, but rather offer yourselves to God, as those who have been brought from death to life; and offer the parts of your body to him as instruments of righteousness.* **Rom 6:14** *For sin shall not be your master, because you are not under law, but under grace.*

Paul says if we are Christians, then sin does not rule us, Jesus does. When Jesus rules in our lives we eat so that we can do his will. When Jesus rules in our lives, our thoughts are taken up with him, not with what we are going to eat next.

SEPTEMBER 28

Stomach is God

Paul tells the Philippian Christians that many people are enemies of the cross of Christ. He means they are not true Christians even if they might say they are. Christians should love Jesus. If they love Jesus they should not be living sinful lives. Paul says these people have their stomach as their god, not Jesus.

Phil 3:19 *Their destiny is destruction, their god is their stomach, and their glory is in their shame. Their mind is on earthly things.*

The people Paul was writing about were probably involved in the sin of gluttony. He said that their god is their stomach.

The Book of Proverbs has a warning for those who have a weakness in eating too much.

Prov 23:1 *When you sit to dine with a ruler, note well what is before you.*

Why should a person be careful about what they are eating when they sit down with a ruler? It is probably because rulers were wealthy people. That means they would have a lot of food on the table. If someone were to write this passage today they might write, "When you go out to a restaurant that serves 'all you can eat,' be careful."

Prov 23:2 *And put a knife to your throat if you are given to gluttony.*

This scripture says put a knife to your throat. Some Bibles say this expression means "use self restraint," self-control. You should be very careful to exercise self-control when a lot of food is available and you have a weakness with eating too much.

Prov 23:3 *Do not crave his delicacies, for that food is deceptive.*

If you know that food controls many of your thoughts, or you know that you lack self-control in the area of food, you should ask your parents for help. Parents can set up stricter guidelines about how much, when, and what you eat.

SEPTEMBER 29

Righteous Anger

When we talk about self-control, we often think of being able to control our anger. Anger is not always a bad thing. If anger was always sinful, then Jesus would never have gotten angry. Jesus did become angry. Do you remember what made Jesus angry? He was angry that people didn't want him to heal on the Sabbath.

Mk 3:1-2 *Another time he went into the synagogue, and a man with a shriveled hand was there. Some of them were looking for a reason to accuse Jesus, so they watched him closely to see if he would heal him on the Sabbath.* **Mk 3:3** *Jesus said to the man with the shriveled hand, "Stand up in front of everyone."*

Mk 3:4 *Then Jesus asked them, "Which is lawful on the Sabbath: to do good or to do evil, to save life or to kill?" But they remained silent.*

Mk 3:5 *He looked around at them in anger and, deeply distressed at their stubborn hearts, said to the man, "Stretch out your hand." He stretched it out, and his hand was completely restored.*

Jesus was angry that people did not accept God's way in their lives. They thought they were doing the right thing by "keeping the Sabbath." They would say, "Doesn't one of the Ten Commandments say, 'Remember the Sabbath, to keep it holy'?" Jesus taught that if we love God and our fellow man we will be obeying all of God's commands. The Jews had become focused on "keeping the law" rather than loving God. Because of this, Jesus was angry with them. The Bible says the people had "stubborn hearts."

What Jesus had is called "righteous anger." When we get angry because we see someone doing something wrong, that is righteous anger. Righteous anger can cause us to try to right the wrong. Jesus told the Pharisees that they were wrong about healing on the Sabbath. He tried to make them see that God allowed healing on the Sabbath.

Not *all* anger is bad. Righteous anger can be a good thing.

EXERCISE SELF-CONTROL

SEPTEMBER
30
Temper Tantrum

Pedro saw the M&Ms as he walked with his mom down the aisle of the grocery store. He asked his mom if he could have some. His mom said, "No." Pedro really wanted the M&Ms. He began to cry. The crying got louder and louder, and then Pedro lost control. He threw himself down on the floor and began kicking and screaming. He wanted some M&Ms!

Mom knew it was time to go. She was glad that she had not yet put anything in her basket. She picked Pedro up and took him kicking and screaming to the car. When they got home Dad gave Pedro a good spanking and sent him to his room.

Have you ever seen someone do what Pedro did? When someone kicks and screams like that it is called a temper tantrum. Pedro let himself get so angry that he lost control of himself. He made a scene.

The next time Pedro and his mom went in the store, Pedro saw the M&Ms again. Pedro remembered what happened last time. He didn't want to get spanked again so he used his self-control. He looked away from the M&Ms and started to think about something else.

The Bible tells us to be self-controlled.

I Pet 5:8 *Be self-controlled and alert. Your enemy the devil prowls around like a roaring lion looking for someone to devour.*

I Thes 5:6 *So then, let us not be like others, who are asleep, but let us be alert and self-controlled.* **I Thes 5:8** *But since we belong to the day, let us be self-controlled, putting on faith and love as a breastplate, and the hope of salvation as a helmet.*

Paul tells us that the grace of God teaches us to live self-controlled lives.

Tit 2:12 *It teaches us to say "No" to ungodliness and worldly passions, and to live self-controlled, upright and godly lives in this present age.*

OCTOBER 1

The Wrong Crowd

Dad came home one day and said about the neighbor's son, "I think Cody is starting to hang out with the wrong crowd."

What is "the wrong crowd?" It could mean a group of people who don't do their best in school. The wrong crowd could be children whose parents allow them to do most things your parents don't allow you to do. The wrong crowd could also be a group of people who are mean to others. God says choosing our friends is important.

I Cor 15:33 *Do not be misled: "Bad company corrupts good character."*

Even if we are usually "good people," when we hang around with people who aren't good we might start acting like them.

In the Book of Deuteronomy, Moses warns people about turning away from God.

Deut 13:6 *If your very own brother, or your son or daughter, or the wife you love, or your closest friend secretly entices you, saying, "Let us go and worship other gods" (gods that neither you nor your fathers have known,* **Deut 13:7** *gods of the peoples around you, whether near or far, from one end of the land to the other),* **Deut 13:8** *do not yield to him or listen to him. Show him no pity. Do not spare him or shield him.*

God says that some people will try to make us do things we shouldn't be doing. He says we should not listen to them or do the things they say. It is good not to make friends of people who try to make us do bad things.

Children are wise when they choose friends that help them to be good.

OCTOBER 2

Salvation for All

All through Old Testament history God made himself known to his people, the Jews. Every once in a while he would also reveal himself to a non-Jew. These non-Jews were called Gentiles.

When Jesus began preaching, he proclaimed that he was the savior not just of the Jews, but of the Gentiles also. Jesus brought salvation for all people.

The Jews had a hard time accepting that idea. They knew that *they* were God's people and that God had promised to send *them* a savior.

After Jesus' resurrection, many Gentiles were trusting Christ as their savior. Paul and Barnabas, at their church in Antioch, witnessed how God was doing miracles among the Gentiles.

Some people from Judea came to the Antioch church. They said that the Gentiles would have to keep all the Jewish laws if they wanted the salvation that God offered.

Paul and Barnabas disagreed. They made a trip to Jerusalem to speak with the church leaders there. They debated the topic and then Peter said what he thought.

Acts 15:7 *After much discussion, Peter got up and addressed them: "Brothers, you know that some time ago God made a choice among you that the Gentiles might hear from my lips the message of the gospel and believe.* **Acts 15:8** *God, who knows the heart, showed that he accepted them by giving the Holy Spirit to them, just as he did to us.* **Acts 15:9** *He made no distinction between us and them, for he purified their hearts by faith.* **Acts 15:10-11** *Now then, why do you try to test God by putting on the necks of the disciples a yoke that neither we nor our fathers have been able to bear? No! We believe it is through the grace of our Lord Jesus that we are saved, just as they are."*

Peter, as the leader of the church in Jerusalem, made a wise decision: since God accepted the Gentiles without them having to follow the Jewish laws, the church should also accept the Gentiles without requiring them to follow Jewish law.

OCTOBER 3

Knowledge & Wisdom

Knowledge means knowing about things. Wisdom is knowing the right things to do. I will give you five statements and you tell me if each is an example of knowledge or wisdom. Remember knowledge means knowing about things, and wisdom means knowing the right things to do.

Does it take knowledge or wisdom to:

#1. Give the answer to 3 x 4?	Knowledge
#2. Decide to tell the truth?	Wisdom
#3. Know who the president is?	Knowledge
#4. Know the meaning of the word "ruse?"	Knowledge
#5. Decide to do your schoolwork before playing?	Wisdom

Earlier in this book we talked about "fearing" God. To fear God means to respect God and to realize how great God is. When someone fears—reveres—God, he has the fear of the Lord. The Bible says this fear of the Lord is the beginning of knowledge.

Prov 1:7 *The fear of the Lord is the beginning of knowledge, but fools despise wisdom and discipline.*

The Bible also says the fear of the Lord is the beginning of wisdom.

Ps 111:10 *The fear of the Lord is the beginning of wisdom; all who follow his precepts have good understanding. To him belongs eternal praise.*

Prov 9:10 *The fear of the Lord is the beginning of wisdom, and knowledge of the Holy One is understanding.*

The Bible says the fear of the Lord is the beginning of knowledge and wisdom. It also says the fear of the Lord is wisdom.

Job 28:28 *And he said to man, "The fear of the Lord—that is wisdom, and to shun evil is understanding."*

People who believe in God and live good lives are people who fear God. They are growing in knowledge and wisdom. God says knowledge and wisdom begin with the fear of the Lord.

OCTOBER

4

Choose Rightly
Bible

Jesus told many parables. A parable is a story that is used to teach a lesson. We find the parable of the two sons in Matthew, chapter 21.

Mt 21:28 *What do you think? There was a man who had two sons. He went to the first and said, "Son, go and work today in the vineyard."*

Mt 21:29 *"I will not," he answered, but later he changed his mind and went.*

Mt 21:30 *Then the father went to the other son and said the same thing. He answered, "I will, sir," but he did not go.*

Mt 21:31 *Which of the two did what his father wanted?*
"The first," they answered.

Jesus said to them, "I tell you the truth, the tax collectors and the prostitutes are entering the kingdom of God ahead of you."

Even though the first son said he would not go, he changed his mind and went.

Jesus wanted people to learn a lesson from this parable of his. He wanted people to know they cannot just say they will obey God, and then God will be happy with them. They must actually do what God asks them to do.

This parable can teach us about getting into heaven. If bad people repent, trust Jesus as their Savior and change their lives, they are obeying God. They will be allowed into heaven. Other people who think they are good people won't get to heaven because they refuse to obey God. They refuse to trust Jesus as their Savior.

This parable can also teach us a lesson about being people who do the right thing. If you are a wise person, you are one who knows right from wrong and then chooses the right.

OCTOBER 5

Knowledge Puffs Up

Everyone in Jose's class knows that Jadin is the smartest boy in their grade. He gets all A's and he always knows the answers to the teacher's questions. But Jadin is not the boy that people want to talk to when they have a problem; people want to talk to Demetrius. Everyone likes Demetrius; he is kind to all and he listens to what they have to say. He really cares. Often Demetrius is asked to settle arguments between two children. You could say that Demetrius is wise.

Jadin is a smart boy. He has a lot of knowledge. God warns us about knowledge.

I Cor 8:1 *Now about food sacrificed to idols: We know that we all possess knowledge. Knowledge puffs up, but love builds up.*

The apostle Paul is telling the people that they have knowledge about God's law. They know God's law says his people should not eat food sacrificed to idols. Paul says the people are "puffed up" or proud because they have this knowledge of God's law. Paul says the people who know so much about God's law don't understand God very well.

I Cor 8:2 *The man who thinks he knows something does not yet know as he ought to know.*

Paul tells the Corinthians that love for God is far more important than knowledge.

I Cor 8:3 *But the man who loves God is known by God.*

Paul says that even if we possess "all knowledge," but we don't have love, we are nothing.

I Cor 13:2 *If I have the gift of prophecy and can fathom all mysteries and all knowledge, and if I have a faith that can move mountains, but have not love, I am nothing.*

Knowledge is not a bad thing. But love is more important than knowledge is.

WISDOM

OCTOBER 6

Daniel is Wise
Bible

Daniel had been raised in a Jewish home in Judah. He worshipped the God of Abraham, Isaac and Jacob. He learned God's law and tried to live his life for God.

One day the Babylonians captured the land where Daniel lived. Daniel, three of his friends, and many other young Israelite men were taken to the country of Babylon.

Dan 1:3 *Then the king ordered Ashpenaz [ash pea naz], chief of his court officials, to bring in some of the Israelites from the royal family and the nobility—* **Dan 1:4** *young men without any physical defect, handsome, showing aptitude for every kind of learning, well informed, quick to understand, and qualified to serve in the king's palace. He was to teach them the language and literature of the Babylonians.* **Dan 1:5** *The king assigned them a daily amount of food and wine from the king's table. They were to be trained for three years, and after that they were to enter the king's service.*

Daniel and his friends refused to eat the king's food and instead asked to be fed just vegetables and water. After ten days they looked healthier than any of the other young men.

At the end of three years the king talked with all the young men. He found Daniel and his three friends were the best among all the Israelite young men. They were not only better than the other young men of Israelite descent; they were better than the magicians of Babylon!

Dan 1:20 *In every matter of wisdom and understanding about which the king questioned them, he found them ten times better than all the magicians and enchanters in his whole kingdom.*

Daniel and his friends lived according to God's law. They became wise young men. If we live according to God's law we become wise.

OCTOBER 7

Tell a Dream
Bible

King Nebuchadnezzar had some dreams. They were such bad dreams that he was worried about them; he couldn't sleep. The king wanted his "wise men"—his magicians, enchanters, sorcerers and astrologers—to tell him what his dream was. Then he wanted them to tell him what it meant. The wise men asked the king to tell them about his dream and then they would interpret it for him.

The king would not tell them the dream. He thought they should be able to tell him the dream. If they could do that, then he knew their interpretation of the dream would be correct. The wise men said that no one could do what the king asked. The king became angry. He was going to have all the wise men of Babylon killed. Arioch [*air* ee ahk], the commander of the king's guard, went to carry out the king's order. (Remember, Daniel and his three friends were considered wise men.)

Dan 2:14 *When Arioch, the commander of the king's guard, had gone out to put to death the wise men of Babylon, Daniel spoke to him with wisdom and tact.*

Daniel asked why this was happening. Arioch explained and then Daniel asked for some time. He told Arioch that he could interpret the king's dream. Daniel asked his three friends to pray that God would show him what the king had dreamt. God answered their prayers.

Dan 2:19 *During the night the mystery was revealed to Daniel in a vision. Then Daniel praised the God of heaven* **Dan 2:20** *and said:*

"Praise be to the name of God for ever and ever; wisdom and power are his. **Dan 2:21** *He changes times and seasons; he sets up kings and deposes them. He gives wisdom to the wise and knowledge to the discerning."*

Daniel had a lot of wisdom. He spoke with wisdom. He was able to interpret dreams. Daniel said that God is the one who gives wisdom.

WISDOM

OCTOBER 8

Wise Deacons

Do you go to a school that has a lot of Spanish-speaking children? If you do, you probably notice that the people who speak English talk to each other and look out for each other. The people who speak Spanish often talk to each other and look out for each other.

That's how it was in the early church. There were Gentile Christians who spoke Greek and there were Hebrew, Jewish, Christians who spoke Aramaic [air uh *may* ik]. The Greek people complained; they said the church was taking care of the Hebrew widows,* but neglecting the Greek widows.

The twelve apostles saw this problem. They made a wise decision.

Acts 6:2 *So the Twelve gathered all the disciples together and said, "It would not be right for us to neglect the ministry of the word of God in order to wait on tables.*

Acts 6:3 *Brothers, choose seven men from among you who are known to be full of the Spirit and wisdom. We will turn this responsibility over to them* **Acts 6:4** *and will give our attention to prayer and the ministry of the word."*

The apostles knew their job was to pray and teach God's Word. They made a wise decision. The apostles chose wise people to take care of other things, like making sure the widows were taken care of.

If you have a problem and need to make a wise decision, ask God for help. God promises to give us wisdom.

Jas 1:5 *If any of you lacks wisdom, he should ask God, who gives generously to all without finding fault, and it will be given to him.*

Widows—women whose husbands have died

OCTOBER 9

Tired Puppies
Marigny

The Marigny family raised Brittany Spaniels. Their mother dog, Charlotte, had a litter* of eleven puppies. The Marignys had seen a picture of a litter of four puppies in a basket. The picture had been taken in a studio by a professional photographer. Since this was intended to be Charlotte's last litter of puppies, the Marignys decided to take their puppies to the studio for a picture.

Mommy Marigny thought they should do a practice session. The family brought all the puppies from the backyard kennel and put them on a blanket on the living room floor. Eleven puppies were not about to stay in one place, much less pose, for a picture.

Mommy had an idea. A couple of hours before the studio time, they would give the puppies a bath and then keep them playing so they would be sleepy at picture time. The idea worked; it was easier trying to keep the puppies awake than it was trying to keep them from running off. Mommy showed wisdom in her idea. (The cover picture for this book is one of the pictures taken at the studio.)

God tells us how we can become wise:

Prov 2:1 *My son, if you accept my words and store up my commands within you,* **Prov 2:2-3** *turning your ear to wisdom and applying your heart to understanding, and if you call out for insight and cry aloud for understanding,* **Prov 2:4-5** *and if you look for it as for silver and search for it as for hidden treasure, then you will understand the fear of the LORD and find the knowledge of God.* **Prov 2:6** *For the LORD gives wisdom, and from his mouth come knowledge and understanding.*

Litter—a group of animals born at the same time from the same mother

WISDOM

OCTOBER 10

Jesus is Wise
Bible

Jesus is someone who is wise. This scripture in Luke is talking about Jesus when he was young:

Lk 2:40 *And the child grew and became strong; he was filled with wisdom, and the grace of God was upon him.*

Jesus was filled with wisdom. Luke also tells us that Jesus grew in wisdom.

Lk 2:52 *And Jesus grew in wisdom and stature, and in favor with God and men.*

People traveled great distances to hear Jesus teach. They were amazed that he was such a wise man. They knew Jesus had a special gift because he could heal people. The people wondered where Jesus had gotten so much wisdom.

Mk 6:2 *When the Sabbath came, he began to teach in the synagogue, and many who heard him were amazed.*

"Where did this man get these things?" they asked. "What's this wisdom that has been given him, that he even does miracles!"

Mt 13:54 *Coming to his hometown, he began teaching the people in their synagogue, and they were amazed. "Where did this man get this wisdom and these miraculous powers?" they asked.*

When Jesus lived on this earth, he was wise.

OCTOBER 11

Spiritual Things

The scriptures we read last night from Matthew and Mark tell how amazed the people were that Jesus had such great wisdom. The gospel of John also tells us how the people were surprised at Jesus' wisdom.

Jn 7:14 *Not until halfway through the Feast did Jesus go up to the temple courts and begin to teach.* **Jn 7:15** *The Jews were amazed and asked, "How did this man get such learning without having studied?"*

Jn 7:16 *Jesus answered, "My teaching is not my own. It comes from him who sent me."*

Jesus was sent by God; he said his teaching came from God. Yet Jesus is God; he is the second person of the Trinity, God the Son. He was full of the wisdom of God because he is God.

The Jews knew that Jesus didn't go to college. They were amazed that he knew so much.

We can be like Jesus. All of us who have asked Jesus to be our Savior have the Holy Spirit living inside of us. That Holy Spirit is full of wisdom. He will give us wisdom.

When Paul was preaching about Jesus, he said that our wisdom is "not the wisdom of this age or of the rulers of this age." He said it was a different kind of wisdom.

I Cor 2:7 *No, we speak of God's secret wisdom, a wisdom that has been hidden and that God destined for our glory before time began.*

This secret wisdom is the wisdom we have about spiritual things because we have trusted Jesus.

OCTOBER 12

Avoid the Trap

Some of the religious leaders of Jesus' day regularly tried to catch Jesus saying or doing something wrong. Do you remember we read that the chief priests and scribes tried to trap Jesus about paying taxes? They probably thought he was going to say that people shouldn't pay taxes. If Jesus would have said that, he could have been arrested by Roman officials. Jesus knew the question was a trap. He answered it wisely; the people asking the question didn't know what to say.

The chief priests and elders came to Jesus another time and asked him who gave him the power to heal. Jesus could have said his power came from the fact that he was the Son of God. If Jesus had said that, he would probably have been arrested right then by Jewish religious officials. Jesus knew it was not yet time for him to be arrested so he asked the leaders a question.

Mt 21:24 *Jesus replied, "I will also ask you one question. If you answer me, I will tell you by what authority I am doing these things.* **Mt 21:25** *John's baptism—where did it come from? Was it from heaven, or from men?"*

They discussed it among themselves and said, "If we say, 'From heaven,' he will ask, 'Then why didn't you believe him?' **Mt 21:26** *But if we say, 'From men'—we are afraid of the people, for they all hold that John was a prophet."*

Mt 21:27 *So they answered Jesus, "We don't know."*

Then he said, "Neither will I tell you by what authority I am doing these things."

Jesus knew it was not time yet for him to be arrested. He kept from answering the chief priests' question by asking them a question. If the priests would admit that John was sent by God, they would have to admit that Jesus was also, for John had said that Jesus was the Messiah. The chief priests didn't want to admit that Jesus was sent by God, so they said they didn't know who sent John.

Jesus wisely avoided this trap of the chief priests and elders just as he wisely answered the question about the taxes.

OCTOBER 13

He's a Fool

The Bible tells us that Nabal [nay buhl] was a mean man.

I Sam 25:3 *His name was Nabal and his wife's name was Abigail. She was an intelligent and beautiful woman, but her husband, a Calebite [kay leh bite], was surly and mean in his dealings.*

"Surly" means "rude and unfriendly." Nabal was surly and mean. He was also very wealthy.

I Sam 25:2 *A certain man in Maon [may on], who had property there at Carmel, was very wealthy. He had a thousand goats and three thousand sheep, which he was shearing in Carmel.*

Nabal's wealth did not make him a generous man. In fact, he was very stingy.

David and his many followers had been living out in the desert. For a long time they had lived on the edge of Nabal's property. They had protected his flocks by making sure wild animals didn't kill them. They also kept thieves from stealing the livestock. Nabal's men knew this was true. They knew and liked David's men.

One time David wanted to celebrate with his men. They didn't have a lot of possessions, so David sent some men to Nabal to ask if he would spare some of his wealth. Because David's men had protected Nabal's flock they thought surely this rich man would give them a little of what he had. They were surprised at his answer.

I Sam 25:10 *Nabal answered David's servants, "Who is this David? Who is this son of Jesse? Many servants are breaking away from their masters these days.* **I Sam 25:11** *Why should I take my bread and water, and the meat I have slaughtered for my shearers, and give it to men coming from who knows where?"*

The Bible says Nabal's name means "fool."

"Foolish" is the opposite of "wise." Nabal was a fool because he did not care about God or other people. He only cared about himself!

WISDOM

OCTOBER 14

It Brightens the Face

It had been a really close little league game and Pete had made "the play of the game" when he caught the fly ball in left field. Pete's dad was very proud of his son. He wasn't just proud of him because he was a good ball player; he was proud that his son had been chosen to be the team captain.

The position of team captain is often given to the pitcher, first baseman or short stop, because those players are usually the best players on the team. Pete was not the team's pitcher, first baseman or short stop; he played left field. Pete was chosen as team captain because he practiced hard, he encouraged his teammates whether their team won or lost, and he kept his attitude positive.

Prov 29:3a *A man who loves wisdom brings joy to his father.*

Prov 15:20 *A wise son brings joy to his father, but a foolish man despises his mother.*

Pete brought joy to his father; he was wise.

Prov 15:21 *Folly delights a man who lacks judgment, but a man of understanding keeps a straight course.*

Pete was someone who kept a straight course; he knew and did the right thing.

Eccl 8:1 *Who is like the wise man? Who knows the explanation of things? Wisdom brightens a man's face and changes its hard appearance.*

Wisdom inside a person can brighten his face.

OCTOBER 15

Trust & Obey

Deut 34:9 *Now Joshua son of Nun was filled with the spirit of wisdom because Moses had laid his hands on him. So the Israelites listened to him and did what the* L<small>ORD</small> *had commanded Moses.*

Joshua was filled with the spirit of wisdom.

Moses had led God's people out of Egypt, and now Joshua was to be the new leader of God's people. He would need wisdom for such a big job. What are some things Joshua did that show his wisdom?

First, Joshua did what God told him to. God told Joshua to get the people ready to cross the Jordan River.

Josh 1:2 *"Moses my servant is dead. Now then, you and all these people, get ready to cross the Jordan River into the land I am about to give to them—to the Israelites."*

The second thing Joshua did that showed he was wise was to expect great things from God.

Josh 3:5 *Joshua told the people, "Consecrate yourselves, for tomorrow the* L<small>ORD</small> *will do amazing things among you."*

The third thing Joshua did was to trust God even when things were not going well.

One time the Israelites' enemies beat them soundly in a battle. Joshua did not get discouraged; instead he prayed.

Josh 7:6 *Then Joshua tore his clothes and fell facedown to the ground before the ark of the* L<small>ORD</small>, *remaining there till evening. The elders of Israel did the same, and sprinkled dust on their heads.*

Joshua was a wise man because he did what God told him to do and he expected great things from God. Joshua also showed that he was wise by praying and trusting in God even when things weren't going well.

OCTOBER 16

Ezra Knows the Word
Bible

Artaxerxes [ar tuh *zerk* seez] was the King of Persia. He wrote a letter to Ezra the priest. In it he said:

Ezra 7:25 *And you, Ezra, in accordance with the wisdom of your God, which you possess, appoint magistrates and judges to administer justice to all the people of Trans-Euphrates—all who know the laws of your God. And you are to teach any who do not know them.*

The king said that Ezra possessed the wisdom of God. Now where did Ezra get his wisdom?

Ezra 7:6 *This Ezra came up from Babylon. He was a teacher well versed in the Law of Moses, which the LORD, the God of Israel, had given. The king had granted him everything he asked, for the hand of the LORD his God was on him.*

This scripture says Ezra was "a teacher well versed in the Law of Moses." To be "well versed" in something means that you know a lot about it. Ezra had studied and so he knew a lot about the Law of Moses. The Law of Moses is the first five books of our Bible. What are the first five books of the Bible? If you look at the beginning of your Bible you will find a list of the books that are in it. The first five books are:

Table of Contents (OT) *Genesis, Exodus, Leviticus, Numbers and Deuteronomy.*

What does the book of Ezra say that Ezra did with the Law of the Lord?

Ezra 7:10 *For Ezra had devoted himself to the study and observance of the Law of the LORD, and to teaching its decrees and laws in Israel.*

Ezra studied and observed the Law of Moses. He was wise because he did that.

People today can also become wise by studying and practicing God's Word.

OCTOBER 17

Girls Feed Lambs
Marigny

The Marignys went to Uncle Roger's farm. Aunt Sue gave the girls some bottles with big nipples on them. She told them they could feed the lambs. These lambs were very tame because they had been fed with the bottle for a few weeks already.

The lambs came quickly when they saw the bottles. Kerri, Gladys, Reyne and Rachael tipped the bottles so the lambs could suck. The girls had to hold on tight because the lambs sucked hard and sometimes would move. The lambs sure liked the milk. The milk helped them to grow.

Just as those lambs liked their milk, God tells us to want spiritual milk.

I Pet 2:2 *Like newborn babies, crave pure spiritual milk, so that by it you may grow up in your salvation.*

What is the spiritual milk God is talking about? It is the Word of God! Why would God call his Word spiritual milk? It is because by reading our Bibles we grow spiritually. Food makes bodies strong and healthy. When we read God's Word, our souls become strong and healthy.

Moses taught God's laws to the people. He said if they obeyed God's law this would show their wisdom to other nations.

Deut 4:5 *See, I have taught you decrees and laws as the LORD my God commanded me, so that you may follow them in the land you are entering to take possession of it.* **Deut 4:6** *Observe them carefully, for this will show your wisdom and understanding to the nations, who will hear about all these decrees and say, "Surely this great nation is a wise and understanding people."*

Ps 119:104 *I gain understanding from your precepts; therefore I hate every wrong path.*

Understanding is another word the Bible uses for wisdom. We get wisdom from reading God's Word.

OCTOBER 18

Choose to Serve God
Bible

Moses was born in Egypt. During this time Pharaoh was worried that the Hebrew people were growing in numbers. Pharaoh made a law.

Ex 1:22 *Then Pharaoh gave this order to all his people: "Every boy that is born you must throw into the river, but let every girl live."*

Pharaoh thought if he killed the baby boys, then the girls wouldn't have anyone to marry when they grew up. The girls couldn't get married and have children. The Pharaoh thought this was a good way to keep the Hebrews from growing in numbers.

Moses' parents were Hebrew and they didn't want baby Moses to die, so they hid him. The Pharaoh's daughter found Moses. She raised him as an Egyptian.

Acts 7:22 *Moses was educated in all the wisdom of the Egyptians and was powerful in speech and action.*

When Moses was older he found out that he really was a Hebrew. He learned that he had been adopted by the Pharaoh's daughter. He knew that the Hebrews were God's chosen people. Moses made a choice. He decided that even though he had a comfortable life in Egypt, he would rather be known as one of God's people.

Heb 11:24-25 *By faith Moses, when he had grown up, refused to be known as the son of Pharaoh's daughter. He chose to be mistreated along with the people of God rather than to enjoy the pleasures of sin for a short time.* **Heb 11:26** *He regarded disgrace for the sake of Christ as of greater value than the treasures of Egypt, because he was looking ahead to his reward.*

Moses did the right thing by choosing to live as one of God's people. He made a wise choice.

OCTOBER 19

Wise, Old Man

Have you ever seen someone who looked like "a wise, old man?" Well, just because someone is old does not mean that he is wise.

The Bible says,

Prov 9:10 *The fear of the LORD is the beginning of wisdom, and knowledge of the Holy One is understanding.*

A person first begins on the path of wisdom when he fears God. To fear God means to reverence him.

Paul said that Timothy was made wise by the Scriptures that taught him God's plan of salvation.

II Tim 3:15 *And how from infancy you have known the holy Scriptures, which are able to make you wise for salvation through faith in Christ Jesus.*

Psalm 119 tells us that God's Word makes us wise when we read and meditate on it.

Ps 119:98 *Your commands make me wiser than my enemies, for they are ever with me.*

Ps 119:99 *I have more insight than all my teachers, for I meditate on your statutes.*

The person who wrote Psalm 119 says that God's commands make him wiser than his enemies. He says it is because he meditates on God's statutes that he is wiser than all his teachers. We can learn a lot from other people, but God's Word can make us wiser than other people can.

A wise old man is one who has lived his life for God. A wise old man is one who has studied God's Word and tried to do what it says.

You can't tell if someone is wise just by his looks!

OCTOBER 20

Judging Wisely

Roy and Jerry were brothers. Most of the time they played together pretty well. It seemed, though, that at least once a day they got upset with each other. This time Roy said if Jerry threw one more ball so high that he couldn't catch it, Roy would not play catch anymore. Jerry didn't mean to, but there went the ball again, and Roy had to chase it down.

The boys came in the house arguing with each other. Mom didn't like seeing them like this. She sat down with them and helped them get to where they could talk to each other again.

Mom acted like a judge for the boys. Over the years, she had grown in wisdom so she knew how to handle situations like this.

Solomon, in the Book of Proverbs, tells his sons to get wisdom:

Prov 4:5 *Get wisdom, get understanding; do not forget my words or swerve from them.*

Prov 4:6 *Do not forsake wisdom, and she will protect you; love her, and she will watch over you.*

Prov 4:7 *Wisdom is supreme; therefore get wisdom. Though it cost all you have, get understanding.*

Prov 4:8-9 *Esteem her, and she will exalt you; embrace her, and she will honor you. She will set a garland of grace on your head and present you with a crown of splendor.*

God wants us, his people, to desire wisdom.

OCTOBER 21

Wise Men

Some people who have studied the Bible think that Moses led as many as a million people out of Egypt. Moses acted like a judge for God's people. He didn't just have to settle an argument between two boys like the mother in last night's devotion. All day long Moses was settling arguments.

Ex 18:13 *The next day Moses took his seat to serve as judge for the people, and they stood around him from morning till evening.*

Moses' father-in-law, Jethro, asked him why he was doing this.

Ex 18:15 *Moses answered him, "Because the people come to me to seek God's will.*

Ex 18:16 *Whenever they have a dispute, it is brought to me, and I decide between the parties and inform them of God's decrees and laws."*

Jethro saw that Moses was going to wear himself out by judging between the people. The job was just too big for him. Jethro knew that Moses was trying to do too much. He gave Moses some wise advice:

Ex 18:21 *"But select capable men from all the people—men who fear God, trustworthy men who hate dishonest gain—and appoint them as officials over thousands, hundreds, fifties and tens."*

Jethro wanted the leaders to be wise. He knew they would be wise if they feared God. Moses followed Jethro's advice and appointed wise men to help him do the judging.

OCTOBER 22

Solomon is Wise
Bible

The Lord appeared to King Solomon in a dream. He said the king could ask him for whatever he wanted. King Solomon knew that ruling a large kingdom was a big job so he asked God for the wisdom to rule well.

I Ki 3:9 *So give your servant a discerning heart to govern your people and to distinguish between right and wrong. For who is able to govern this great people of yours?*

God was pleased with the king's request. He gave Solomon great wisdom.

I Ki 4:29 *God gave Solomon wisdom and very great insight, and a breadth of understanding as measureless as the sand on the seashore.*

No one can count how many grains of sand are on the seashore. The Bible tells us that the wisdom God gave to Solomon was so much that to measure his wisdom would be like counting that sand.

I Ki 4:30 *Solomon's wisdom was greater than the wisdom of all the men of the East, and greater than all the wisdom of Egypt.*

People in Israel knew there were great kingdoms in the East and in Egypt. They believed some people from these kingdoms were wise. Solomon is said to have had greater wisdom than any of these wise men.

I Ki 4:34 *Men of all nations came to listen to Solomon's wisdom, sent by all the kings of the world, who had heard of his wisdom.*

Solomon asked God for wisdom and God gave it. We can ask God for wisdom and he will also give wisdom to us.

A Baby Story

OCTOBER 23

A story in the Bible tells us about Solomon's wisdom. Two ladies came to the king. The Bible doesn't tell us their names, but let's call them Deborah and Tamar. They were arguing about a baby.

Deborah said, "My lord, this woman and I live in the same house. I had a baby while she was there with me. The third day after my child was born, this woman also had a baby. We were alone; there was no one in the house but the two of us." Deborah then told the king that Tamar's baby died in the night. Deborah said that Tamar came and took her baby.

Tamar said that was not true; she said the living baby was hers. So both women were claiming that the baby that was still living was theirs.

King Solomon listened to their stories and then he decided what he would do.

I Ki 3:24-25 *Then the king said, "Bring me a sword." So they brought a sword for the king. He then gave an order: "Cut the living child in two and give half to one and half to the other."*

I Ki 3:26 *The woman whose son was alive was filled with compassion for her son and said to the king, "Please, my lord, give her the living baby! Don't kill him!"*

But the other said, "Neither I nor you shall have him. Cut him in two!"

I Ki 3:27 *Then the king gave his ruling: "Give the living baby to the first woman. Do not kill him; she is his mother."*

I Ki 3:28 *When all Israel heard the verdict the king had given, they held the king in awe, because they saw that he had wisdom from God to administer justice.*

Solomon was not really going to kill the baby. He knew if he said to have the baby killed, its real mother would want the baby to live. Solomon used the wisdom God had given him to rule justly.

OCTOBER 24

Wise to Obey

DeShawn would be starting sixth grade this year. He was twelve so his parents said he wouldn't need anyone to come and sit with him after school. His parents told him to come straight home after school. It would be an hour later that Mom would get home from work. DeShawn knew the house would be quiet, but he wanted to show his parents how grown up he was. He came straight home from school for the first week.

The second week, some boys asked DeShawn if he could play some ball and then go home. DeShawn almost went with the boys, but then he remembered the rule that he was supposed to go directly home. DeShawn told the guys that maybe he could come tomorrow; he would have to check with his parents first. DeShawn made a wise decision; he made a right choice.

The Book of Proverbs says many things about wisdom.

Prov 3:13-14 *Blessed is the man who finds wisdom, the man who gains understanding, for she is more profitable than silver and yields better returns than gold.*

How can wisdom be better than silver and gold? Silver and gold can make us rich in this life, but wisdom can bring us to eternal life. Let's continue reading what Proverbs says about wisdom:

Prov 3:15-16 *She is more precious than rubies; nothing you desire can compare with her. Long life is in her right hand; in her left hand are riches and honor.*

Here God promises long life to those who live wisely. God also promises long life to those who honor their parents. DeShawn, by honoring his parents, is living wisely.

What else does Proverbs 3 tell us about wisdom?

Prov 3:17 *Her ways are pleasant ways, and all her paths are peace.*

Prov 3:18 *She is a tree of life to those who embrace her; those who lay hold of her will be blessed.*

Wise people live in peace and they are blessed by God.

OCTOBER 25

Not a Wise Choice
Bible

When King Solomon died, his son Rehoboam became the king in Jerusalem. King Solomon had ruled his kingdom firmly. The people came to Rehoboam and asked him to lighten their work load:

I Ki 12:4 *"Your father put a heavy yoke on us, but now lighten the harsh labor and the heavy yoke he put on us, and we will serve you."*

King Rehoboam told the people he needed some time to decide what he would do. He first asked the elders that had worked for his father what they thought he should do.

I Ki 12:7 *They replied, "If today you will be a servant to these people and serve them and give them a favorable answer, they will always be your servants."*

King Rehoboam didn't accept this advice. Instead he asked some young people who had grown up with him what he should do. These young men were Rehoboam's advisers.

I Ki 12:10 *The young men who had grown up with him replied, "Tell these people who have said to you, 'Your father put a heavy yoke on us, but make our yoke lighter'—tell them, 'My little finger is thicker than my father's waist.* **I Ki 12:11** *My father laid on you a heavy yoke; I will make it even heavier. My father scourged you with whips; I will scourge you with scorpions.'"*

Rehoboam took the advice of the young men. He made the Israelites work even harder. That was not a wise choice. Israel rebelled against King Rehoboam. They killed the man who was in charge of forced labor and almost killed the king. The Bible says he escaped to Jerusalem.

How was Rehoboam to know whose advice to follow? If people are giving us different advice, how are we to know whose counsel to follow? Rehoboam should have been praying about this major decision. God would have led him to do the right thing. If we pray for guidance, God will lead us to do the right thing.

OCTOBER 26

Rich Fool

Jesus told a story about a man whom God called a fool. This story is titled "The Parable of the Rich Fool."

Lk 12:16-17 *And he told them this parable: The ground of a certain rich man produced a good crop. He thought to himself, "What shall I do? I have no place to store my crops."*

Lk 12:18-19 *Then he said, "This is what I'll do. I will tear down my barns and build bigger ones, and there I will store all my grain and my goods. And I'll say to myself, 'You have plenty of good things laid up for many years. Take life easy; eat, drink and be merry.'"*

Lk 12:20 *But God said to him, "You fool! This very night your life will be demanded from you. Then who will get what you have prepared for yourself?"*

Lk 12:21 *This is how it will be with anyone who stores up things for himself but is not rich toward God.*

The man in this parable is very rich. He decides he will use his money in a way that will make his life easier and more comfortable in the years to come. What do you think is most important to this rich man? What is at the center of his life? His life is centered on himself and on his money. God says this type of a person is a fool.

Jesus says people should be "rich toward God." That means they should make God the most important thing in their life—they should live to please him. People who make God the most important person in their lives and who live to please God are wise.

OCTOBER 27

Wise to Follow Jesus

Jesus taught about the difference between a wise man and a foolish man. He said a wise man builds his house on a solid foundation. A foolish man builds his house on sand.

Mt 7:24 *"Therefore everyone who hears these words of mine and puts them into practice is like a wise man who built his house on the rock.* **Mt 7:25** *The rain came down, the streams rose, and the winds blew and beat against that house; yet it did not fall, because it had its foundation on the rock.* **Mt 7:26** *But everyone who hears these words of mine and does not put them into practice is like a foolish man who built his house on sand.* **Mt 7:27** *The rain came down, the streams rose, and the winds blew and beat against that house, and it fell with a great crash."*

If we learn how Jesus taught us to live, and we try to live that way, we are wise. Even if bad things happen in our lives, we will continue to believe that God is good, because he sent Jesus to die for us. Trying to live according to Jesus' teaching is building our house on the rock.

If we learn how Jesus taught us to live, and we decide not to live that way, we are foolish. When troubles come into our lives, we have nowhere to turn, because we have rejected Jesus. Not living according to Jesus' teaching is building our house on the sand.

Let's choose to follow Jesus. It's the wise choice.

OCTOBER

28

No Boasting
Bible

Jeremiah was a prophet of God in Old Testament times. God sent him to say some hard things to his people. God told Jeremiah to give the people this message:

Jer 8:8 *"How can you say, 'We are wise, for we have the law of the Lord,' when actually the lying pen of the scribes has handled it falsely?* **Jer 8:9** *The wise will be put to shame; they will be dismayed and trapped. Since they have rejected the word of the Lord, what kind of wisdom do they have?"*

People can know a lot of things and be full of knowledge. They can even have a lot of knowledge about God's Word. They can claim that they know what God's Word means.

In this passage from Jeremiah, God tells the people that the scribes are handling his Word falsely. That means that they are teaching people things that God is not really saying. The scribes think they are wise, but they are not.

Jeremiah tells people that they should not boast about their wisdom.

Jer 9:23 *This is what the Lord says: "Let not the wise man boast of his wisdom or the strong man boast of his strength or the rich man boast of his riches,* **Jer 9:24** *but let him who boasts boast about this: that he understands and knows me, that I am the Lord, who exercises kindness, justice and righteousness on earth, for in these I delight," declares the Lord.*

Our wisdom does not give us a reason to boast. Our wisdom should cause us to try to understand God even more.

OCTOBER 29

Wise Words

Other words in the Bible that mean almost the same as "wisdom" are the words "understanding" and "discernment." Let's look at some verses about understanding.

The writer of Psalm 119 prays for understanding. He says that if he is given understanding, then he will keep and obey God's laws.

Ps 119:34 *Give me understanding, and I will keep your law and obey it with all my heart.*

The psalm writer knows that he needs help to understand God's law. He prays that God will give him understanding.

Ps 119:73 *Your hands made me and formed me; give me understanding to learn your commands.*

God's Word is what gives us understanding.

Ps 119:130 *The unfolding of your words gives light; it gives understanding to the simple.*

The word "discernment" is used in the following passage:

Ps 119:125 *I am your servant; give me discernment that I may understand your statutes.*

We gain understanding and discernment by reading God's Word. We also need the help of God to understand his Word. The writer of Psalm 119 prays that God will give him understanding and discernment. He is really praying for wisdom.

OCTOBER 30

From Idols to God

Celts [selts or kelts] are people who speak the Celtic language. They lived in central Europe 700 years before Jesus was born. Rome conquered most of Europe so the only place the Celtic culture continued was in Scotland, Ireland, Britain and northern France.

It is believed that Halloween first began with the Celts. Their educated people were called Druids. These Druids could be judges, lawmakers or priests.

The Celtic new year began on November first. The people would all put out the fires in their fireplaces. Then the Druid priests built a huge bonfire on which they offered sacrifices to their gods. They offered animals, crops and possibly even human sacrifices. The people would relight their fireplaces with fire taken from the bonfire.

When the Celts became Christians in A.D. 400-500 druidism, their former religion, died out. The Celtic people were wise when they turned from worshipping false gods to worshipping the one true God.

Paul preached that God, the creator, was the true God.

Acts 17:24 *The God who made the world and everything in it is the Lord of heaven and earth and does not live in temples built by hands.*

Paul preached that God commands all people to repent, because God will one day come to judge every person. Paul says Jesus' resurrection proves that this will happen.

Acts 17:31 *For he has set a day when he will judge the world with justice by the man he has appointed. He has given proof of this to all men by raising him from the dead.*

Jesus tells us that there is one true God.

Jn 17:3 *Now this is eternal life: that they may know you, the only true God, and Jesus Christ, whom you have sent.*

Paul said people were reporting how the Thessalonians turned from idols to God.

I Thes 1:9b *They tell how you turned to God from idols to serve the living and true God.*

The Celts likewise began serving the one true God. That was a wise choice.

OCTOBER

Fisher of Men

31

Halloween

The Celts had celebrated November first as their new year for so long that when they became Christians it was hard for them to change those habits. The church knew that druidism was a false religion. In the 800's the church made November first All Saints Day so people could still celebrate the day, but turn their minds to God instead of away from God.

Some Christians use Halloween to teach their children about men and women who have given their lives to God and accomplished great things for him. Let's look at one of those people, the apostle Peter. When Jesus first met Peter, he was a fisherman.

Mt 4:18 *As Jesus was walking beside the Sea of Galilee, he saw two brothers, Simon called Peter and his brother Andrew. They were casting a net into the lake, for they were fishermen.* **Mt 4:19-20** *"Come, follow me," Jesus said, "and I will make you fishers of men." At once they left their nets and followed him.*

Peter left one job and started another. He began following Jesus and was one of Jesus' closest friends. We often read about Jesus taking Peter, James and John with him.

After Jesus' ascension Peter became the recognized leader of the apostles. On the day of Pentecost he addressed a large crowd of Jews. These Jews had traveled from many nations to Jerusalem most likely to celebrate the Jewish "Feast of Weeks." Peter preached boldly to them about how Jesus had died and then risen from the dead. Peter told the people that they needed to repent and be baptized so that their sins would be forgiven.

Acts 2:40 *With many other words he warned them; and he pleaded with them, "Save yourselves from this corrupt generation."* **Acts 2:41** *Those who accepted his message were baptized, and about three thousand were added to their number that day.*

Three thousand people trusted Christ as their Savior that day! Peter truly did become a "fisher of men." For the rest of his life, he continued to spread the gospel.

NOVEMBER

1   Greedy Ahab

There is a story in the Bible about a very selfish man. His name was Ahab [*ay* hab]. He was the king of Israel and even though he lived in a palace and had very nice things, he wanted still more. He wanted a vineyard* that belonged to Naboth [*nay* bahth]. Let's read about it.

I Ki 21:2-3 *Ahab said to Naboth, "Let me have your vineyard to use for a vegetable garden, since it is close to my palace. In exchange I will give you a better vineyard or, if you prefer, I will pay you whatever it is worth."*

But Naboth replied, "The Lord *forbid that I should give you the inheritance of my fathers."*

I Ki 21:4 *So Ahab went home, sullen and angry because Naboth the Jezreelite had said, "I will not give you the inheritance of my fathers." He lay on his bed sulking and refused to eat.*

I Ki 21:5-6 *His wife Jezebel came in and asked him, "Why are you so sullen? Why won't you eat?"*

He answered her, "Because I said to Naboth the Jezreelite, 'Sell me your vineyard; or if you prefer, I will give you another vineyard in its place.' But he said, 'I will not give you my vineyard.'"

I Ki 21:7 *Jezebel his wife said, "Is this how you act as king over Israel? Get up and eat! Cheer up. I'll get you the vineyard of Naboth the Jezreeelite."*

Ahab did get Naboth's vineyard, but God was not pleased with Ahab. Ahab was greedy;* he really wanted Naboth's vineyard. God does not want us to be greedy.

Vineyard—a field where grapes are grown
Greedy—wanting a lot more than you need or deserve

NOVEMBER 2

Sharing Heaven

God is eternal; that means God has no beginning and no end.

When Abraham was blessing his sons he said this to Asher.

Deut 33:27a *The eternal God is your refuge, and underneath are the everlasting arms.*

God is eternal. Another scripture says that he lives forever.

Isa 57:15a *For this is what the high and lofty One says—he who lives forever, whose name is holy.*

Before time began, God the Father, God the Son and God the Holy Spirit lived. Our minds cannot understand that he has always existed. It's hard to imagine, but God never had a beginning nor does he have an end. God was happy in heaven, but he wanted to share heaven with other spiritual beings who could live forever. That is why he created people.

Gen 1:26 *Then God said, "Let us make man in our image, in our likeness, and let them rule over the fish of the sea and the birds of the air, over the livestock, over all the earth, and over all the creatures that move along the ground.*

Gen 1:27 *So God created man in his own image, in the image of God he created him; male and female he created them.*

God is not selfish. He wants to share heaven with people.

DON'T BE SELFISH

NOVEMBER 3

Generosity

It is only the beginning of November but Sandra is already looking forward to Christmas. Christmas is her favorite holiday; she loves to open her presents.

Across town, Ray has been saving his money. He gets paid for taking care of his neighbor's dog when they go on vacation or out of town. Ray asked his mom, dad and big sister what they wanted for Christmas. Then he started to think about when he would be able to buy their gifts. He planned carefully so that his family would be surprised.

Ray's favorite holiday was Christmas, too; but Ray loved to give gifts.

Jesus said that it is more blessed to give than to receive.

Acts 20:35b *. . . remembering the words the Lord Jesus himself said: "It is more blessed to give than to receive."*

Ray felt happy because he focused on the giving at Christmas. Sandra, on the other hand, focused on the receiving.

Here are some more scriptures about giving:

II Cor 9:7 *Each man should give what he has decided in his heart to give, not reluctantly or under compulsion, for God loves a cheerful giver.*

In this scripture, Paul is writing about giving to the church. He says people should not give reluctantly—that means people should enjoy giving; they should not be thinking, "I don't want to give this, but I guess I will." Paul says they should not give under compulsion. He means they should not feel like they have to give. Paul then says that God loves a cheerful giver.

Prov 21:26b *. . . but the righteous give without sparing.*

God's people, the righteous, are generous, not stingy.

Prov 28:27a *He who gives to the poor will lack nothing.*

God promises that if we give to the poor, he will meet our needs.

NOVEMBER 4

Go Home
Bible

The story of Naomi [nay *oh* mee] is found in the Book of Ruth. Naomi, her husband and their two sons lived in Israel until there came a famine in the land, and they had to move elsewhere.

Ruth 1:1 *In the days when the judges ruled, there was a famine in the land, and a man from Bethlehem in Judah, together with his wife and two sons, went to live for a while in the country of Moab.*

Naomi and her family went to live in Moab. Naomi's husband, Elimelech [ee *lim* eh lek], died there.

Ruth 1:3 *Now Elimelech, Naomi's husband, died, and she was left with her two sons.*

Naomi's two sons married Moabite women and then both of her sons died. Naomi was left without a husband, and without her two sons. She just had two daughters-in-law. Their names were Orpah [*or* puh] and Ruth.

Naomi heard that God had provided food for the people back in Israel. She decided to go home. She told Orpah and Ruth to return to their mother's homes.

Ruth 1:8 *Then Naomi said to her two daughters-in-law, "Go back, each of you, to your mother's home. May the LORD show kindness to you, as you have shown to your dead and to me."*

Naomi said that her daughters-in-law had been kind to her. When she said they had shown kindness to their dead, she was talking about how Orpah and Ruth had loved her sons. Naomi wished for them to be able to find other husbands.

Ruth 1:9 *"May the LORD grant that each of you will find rest in the home of another husband." Then she kissed them and they wept aloud.*

Naomi wanted the best for her daughters-in-law. Even though she could use their help and would enjoy their companionship, she thought about what would be best for them. Naomi was selfless.

(to be cont.)

DON'T BE SELFISH

NOVEMBER 5

I'll Stay
Bible (cont.)

Yesterday we read how Naomi lost her husband and her two sons in Moab. She was going back to Israel with her two daughters-in-law when she realized they might be better off in Moab. She told them that they should return.

Orpah and Ruth said they wanted to go with Naomi. They wept **Ruth 1:10** *and said to her, "We will go back with you to your people."*

Ruth 1:11 *But Naomi said, "Return home, my daughters. Why would you come with me? Am I going to have any more sons, who could become your husbands?"*

Naomi insisted that it would be better for them if they would go back to Moab and find husbands who would take care of them. Naomi felt that "the Lord's hand (had) gone out against (her!)" She said they should go home.

Ruth 1:14 *At this they wept again. Then Orpah kissed her mother-in-law good-by, but Ruth clung to her.*

Orpah went back to Moab, but Ruth insisted she would go with Naomi to Bethlehem in Judah.

Ruth 1:16 *But Ruth replied, "Don't urge me to leave you or to turn back from you. Where you go I will go, and where you stay I will stay. Your people will be my people and your God my God."*

Ruth was not just looking out for herself. She knew Naomi was very sad after the loss of her husband and two sons. She decided to take care of her mother-in-law.

We, also, should not always be thinking just of ourselves. We should be thinking about other people as well.

DON'T BE SELFISH

NOVEMBER 6

Giving Up Jesus

Can you think of something that you treasure? Maybe it's a toy or game that is yours; maybe it's a pet that's really special; or it might be a best friend you have. How do you think it would feel if you had to give up that special thing or person for a while?

Well, that's how it was for God. God the Father, God the Son and the Holy Spirit were living in the perfect home—heaven. They, as the Trinity, enjoyed the company of each other. Proverbs, chapter eight, talks about wisdom, but it also describes Jesus.

Prov 8:30 *Then I was the craftsman at his side. I was filled with delight day after day, rejoicing always in his presence.*

This scripture describes how Jesus felt about being with God, the Father: "He rejoiced always in His presence." Even though they loved being with each other, God the Father allowed Jesus to come to earth in order to save us.

Rom 8:32a *He who did not spare his own Son, but gave him up for us all.*

God gave Jesus up for us. He didn't just give up his presence in heaven. He allowed Jesus to die on the cross for our sins.

Jn 3:16 *For God so loved the world that he gave his one and only Son, that whoever believes in him shall not perish but have eternal life.*

God suffered as he watched his Son die for us.

I Jn 4:9 *This is how God showed his love among us: He sent his one and only Son into the world that we might live through him.*

God is selfless. He gave up Jesus' presence in heaven. He also watched him die on the cross. God did those things for us.

DON'T BE SELFISH

NOVEMBER 7 — **Think of Others**

Keith was standing in the street and a car was headed his way. His big brother, Rick, pushed him out of the way, but then Rick got hit by the car. This is a good example of Jesus' teaching:

Jn 15:13 *Greater love has no one than this, that he lay down his life for his friends.*

A lot of people talk about love, but they really don't know what love is. God tells us what love is, in the letter called I Corinthians:

I Cor 13:4 *Love is patient, love is kind. It does not envy, it does not boast, it is not proud.* **I Cor 13:5** *It is not rude, it is not self-seeking, it is not easily angered, it keeps no record of wrongs.*

Love is not self-seeking; that means we should not just look out for ourselves.

When you get up in the morning you might think, "What do *I* want to do today? Where do *I* want to go today? What do *I* want to eat today?" These questions all show us that we are self-seeking.

The Bible says "love is not self-seeking." If we don't want to be self-seeking we should ask questions like these, instead of the ones we asked earlier: "How can I make *Dad*'s day better?" "Where would *my little sister* like to go today?" "Can I help *Mom* make her favorite dessert tonight?"

Phil 2:4 *Each of you should look not only to your own interests, but also to the interests of others.*

NOVEMBER 8

Others above Self

A sixth-grade class was good at raising money. They had put on a carnival for the children in the school gym. They divided the money they earned between the eight classrooms in their elementary school. The money was to be spent on new reading material. The class had also sent money to help the victims of Hurricane Katrina.

Before they went into Junior High, these sixth-graders decided to go on a class trip. They raised the money, but a month before they were scheduled to go one of their classmate's father was diagnosed with cancer. Howard's family had a lot of things to pay for. The class quickly decided to give their "fun" money to Howard's family.

God did not put us on the earth to try to find out what will make us happy. He put us here so that we would honor him by being selfless, by thinking about others. This sixth grade class knows how to be selfless.

I Cor 10:24 *Nobody should seek his own good, but the good of others.*

It's hard not to be self-centered, but if we put God first in our lives, he will teach us how to love others. Jesus said this is how we should live our lives.

Mt 22:37 *Jesus replied, "Love the Lord your God with all your heart and with all your soul and with all your mind.* **Mt 22:38-39** *This is the first and greatest commandment. And the second is like it: 'Love your neighbor as yourself.'* **Mt 22:40** *All the Law and the Prophets hang on these two commandments."*

DON'T BE SELFISH

NOVEMBER 9

Selflessness

When we are sick, it is hard for us to think about others. We might feel uncomfortable or even be in pain.

When Jesus went to the cross, he endured a great amount of pain. He was whipped and had a crown of thorns placed on his head. Then he carried a heavy cross part of the way to Calvary. There, Roman soldiers hung him on the cross. Jesus, even enduring all this, did not think only of himself. All during Jesus' earthly ministry, he cared about the needs of others. When Jesus was suffering, he still showed concern for others. He cared for the women who wept as they followed him to Calvary. He told them to be concerned about their families.

Lk 23:28 *Jesus turned and said to them, "Daughters of Jerusalem, do not weep for me; weep for yourselves and for your children."*

Lk 23:31 *"For if men do these things when the tree is green, what will happen when it is dry?"*

Jesus said "when the tree is green." He meant that when he walked on the earth, God's presence was near to the people. He knew there would be hard times for God's people when he left the earth— "when it would be dry."

Jesus cared about the thief who was crucified with him. When the thief asked Jesus to remember him, Jesus forgave him and promised him a place in paradise.

When Jesus was suffering on the cross, he showed concern for his mother. He told John to take care of Mary.

Jn 19:26 *When Jesus saw his mother there, and the disciple whom he loved standing nearby, he said to his mother, "Dear woman, here is your son,"* **Jn 19:27** *and to the disciple, "Here is your mother." From that time on, this disciple took her into his home.*

Jesus even forgave those who were crucifying him. In the midst of great suffering, Jesus cared about the needs of others. He is a perfect example of selflessness.

DON'T BE SELFISH

NOVEMBER 10

Care for Others

Tyler was going into second grade this year. He had walked the two blocks to school all last year. Now his younger sister was starting kindergarten. Their mom had walked with Suzie her first day, but now Tyler was put in charge of getting her to school. He would make sure she didn't get lost and that she safely crossed the streets.

When we are responsible for others, we learn to be selfless. Tyler knew that he couldn't stop and talk to his friends because Suzie needed him. Tyler was becoming more like Jesus. When Jesus lived on the earth he looked out for other people—he looked out for other people by teaching them about God.

Lk 4:15 *He taught in their synagogues, and everyone praised him.*

Once when the people found Jesus in a quiet place, they wanted to keep him to themselves.

Lk 4:43 *But he said, "I must preach the good news of the kingdom of God to the other towns also, because that is why I was sent."*

Whenever people came to him, Jesus taught and healed them.

Lk 5:15 *Yet the news about him spread all the more, so that crowds of people came to hear him and to be healed of their sicknesses.*

One time Jesus wanted to get away from people and be just with his disciples in the town of Bethsaida, **Lk 9:11** *but the crowds learned about it and followed him. He welcomed them and spoke to them about the kingdom of God, and healed those who needed healing.*

When Jesus was on the earth he spent his time looking out for the needs of other people.

When Tyler is looking out for Suzie, he is acting like Jesus.

DON'T BE SELFISH

NOVEMBER

11

Help Yourself

Callie was "the baby" in her family for four years. Things changed when Mommy brought home her new baby sister. Callie knew something was different and so did the rest of the family. Steven, her 10 year-old brother, understood how Callie felt. He took Callie aside and explained how babies can't do anything for themselves.

Steven told Callie that she had learned to do many things. For example, she could feed herself, change her clothes and even wash her own hands. Steven said the new baby was not able to do any of these things, so Mommy and others in the family would have to do all those things for the baby. Because Callie is older, she can help take care of the baby.

God says that we should serve one another.

Gal 5:13 *You, my brothers, were called to be free. But do not use your freedom to indulge the sinful nature; rather, serve one another in love.*

Callie can serve her family and the baby by doing more to take care of herself. Callie can also serve by helping to take care of her baby sister.

Jesus told his disciples that he did not come to earth to be served, but instead, to serve.

Mt 20:28 *"Just as the Son of Man did not come to be served, but to serve, and to give his life as a ransom for many."*

At the Last Supper, Jesus washed the disciples' feet. Then he explained to them that they should be willing to serve other people in the same way.

Jn 13:14 *"Now that I, your Lord and Teacher, have washed your feet, you also should wash one another's feet.* **Jn 13:15** *I have set you an example that you should do as I have done for you."*

By serving others, like Jesus did, we learn to be selfless. If Callie helps herself and her baby sister, she will show that she is selfless.

NOVEMBER 12

Abraham Tithed

Lin started getting an allowance in her family when she turned six. Her parents gave her one dollar each Saturday so that she could begin to learn how to handle money. Lin's dad wanted her to understand that one tenth of everything she was given, or that she earned, was to be given to God. Giving one tenth of our income to the church is called tithing.

Every Sunday morning Lin tithed by putting a shiny dime in the offering plate as it passed down her pew. Ten cents is one tenth of the allowance she was given each week.

Abraham is the first person whom we know tithed. We can read about how Abraham tithed in chapter 14 of Genesis. Remember, Abraham's name was Abram before God changed it.

The Bible says that Abram defeated the kings that had captured his nephew, Lot. He was returning home when he was met by Melchizedek [mel *kih* zeh dek].

Gen 14:18 *Then Melchizedek king of Salem brought out bread and wine. He was priest of God Most High,* **Gen 14:19** *and he blessed Abram, saying,*

"Blessed be Abram by God Most High, Creator of heaven and earth."

Gen 14:20 *And blessed be God Most High, who delivered your enemies into your hand." Then Abram gave him a tenth of everything.*

Abraham gave to Melchizedek, priest of God Most High, ten percent of all that he had taken in battle.

Abraham giving ten percent is also recorded in the letter to the Hebrews.

Heb 7:2a *And Abraham gave him a tenth of everything.*

We, as God's people, should give ten percent of what we earn to God's work. Six-year-old Lin was learning this lesson early in her life.

DON'T BE SELFISH

NOVEMBER 13

Help the Helpless

Christina was six and her baby brother Lucas was only about a year old. They had been playing together on the den floor. Lucas chewed first on this toy and then on that one; *everything* went in his mouth. Christina got up to tell Mom about something. She barely bumped Lucas, but he tipped over and hit his head. He started to cry. Christina thought Lucas cried way too easily; he had hardly hit his head. Mom came right away. She explained to Christina that Lucas wouldn't always be so helpless, but for right now he was. Mom said taking care of helpless people makes us more like God. In the scriptures we are going to read, God is someone who helps people.

Ps 10:14 *But you, O God, do see trouble and grief; you consider it to take it in hand. The victim commits himself to you; you are the helper of the fatherless.*

God is the helper of the fatherless—those who don't have daddies.

Ps 72:12 *For he will deliver the needy who cry out, the afflicted who have no one to help.*

God takes care of those who have no one.

Heb 13:6 *So we say with confidence, "The Lord is my helper; I will not be afraid. What can man do to me?"*

God is our helper.

Ps 27:1 *The Lord is my light and my salvation—whom shall I fear? The Lord is the stronghold of my life—of whom shall I be afraid?*

When someone says, "The Lord is my salvation," they understand that they are helpless—that they cannot save themselves. God sent Jesus to be our Savior. He helps us because we are helpless.

Mom explained to Christina that soon Lucas would be doing things for himself, but he is helpless right now. His helplessness is a chance for other members of his family to be like God; they can be helpers.

NOVEMBER 14

Christ-centered Lives

There is a well-known illustration used to show people how they are in relation to Jesus. It is a picture of a chair or a throne. The picture shows the cross on the chair or the cross off of the chair. The picture with the cross on the chair means that you have asked Jesus to take control of your life. If the cross is not on the chair, then Jesus is not controlling your life, you are.

When we control our lives, the decisions we make usually center around what we think will make us better or happier. God wants us to step down from the chair and make Jesus the center of our lives. Everything we do should be done because we love God and want to please him. Without Jesus, people tend to be very self-centered. With Jesus as their focus, they become more interested in helping others, because that is what God is like.

Paul tells the Philippians that most people are looking out for themselves.

Phil 2:21 *For everyone looks out for his own interests, not those of Jesus Christ.*

Paul warns Timothy that in the last days people will love themselves.

II Tim 3:2 *People will be lovers of themselves, lovers of money, boastful, proud, abusive, disobedient to their parents, ungrateful, unholy.*

The first thing in Paul's list is "lovers of themselves." We should not love ourselves more than we love God or other people.

Rom 15:1 *We who are strong ought to bear with the failings of the weak and not to please ourselves.* **Rom 15:2** *Each of us should please his neighbor for his good, to build him up.*

If our lives are centered on Christ, then we will be concerned about others not just ourselves.

DON'T BE SELFISH

NOVEMBER 15

Pray for Others
Bible

The prophet Samuel was a man interested in other people. The people asked him to pray for them.

I Sam 12:19 *The people all said to Samuel, "Pray to the Lord your God for your servants so that we will not die, for we have added to all our other sins the evil of asking for a king."*

Samuel was God's prophet, and a man of prayer. This is how he answered the people's request for prayer:

I Sam 12:23 *"As for me, far be it from me that I should sin against the Lord by failing to pray for you. And I will teach you the way that is good and right."*

Samuel was interested in other people. When he prayed he took time to pray for others, not just for himself.

Jesus is also interested in other people. Right now he is in heaven praying for God's people.

Heb 7:24 *But because Jesus lives forever, he has a permanent priesthood.* **Heb 7:25** *Therefore he is able to save completely those who come to God through him, because he always lives to intercede* for them.*

Samuel prayed for God's people. Jesus is praying for his people. One of the best ways we can help others is to pray for them.

Intercede—pray for others

NOVEMBER 16

In the Door
Marigny

Kerri's family was going to take her to a friend's birthday party. Kerri got ready and Daddy helped four year-old Gladys get ready. Mommy had dressed the twins and was now buckling them in their car seats. Daddy belted Gladys in her booster seat.

Kerri had just finished sliding the van door shut, when Mommy closed the front door. Kerri had been holding on to the door jamb and her fingers got slammed in the door. Mommy hurried to open the door. She told Kerri how sorry she was and hugged her tight. They went back in the house to get some ice to put on the fingers. Mommy said there wasn't any ice but the frozen can of orange juice would do. She wrapped the can in a washcloth and Kerri held it on her throbbing fingers.

The outing for the day was cancelled, so Mommy and Daddy began unloading the girls. Daddy could have been upset that the day was "ruined," but he knew Kerri was hurt and that her welfare was most important at the time.

In the same way Daddy cared about Kerri, God cares about people who are in need.

Ps 102:17 *He will respond to the prayer of the destitute;* he will not despise their plea.*

God will answer destitute people who pray to Him.

Psalm 72 was written by King Solomon. He tells how God cares for the needy.

Ps 72:4 *He will defend the afflicted among the people and save the children of the needy; he will crush the oppressor.*

Ps 72:12 *For he will deliver the needy who cry out, the afflicted who have no one to help.*

Ps 72:13 *He will take pity on the weak and the needy and save the needy from death.*

God takes care of his people in their time of need, just like Kerri's dad took care of her.

Destitute—having nothing

DON'T BE SELFISH

NOVEMBER
17

Out the Window
Marigny

In Italy the Marignys lived in an apartment. An American military family lived below them, and an Italian family lived beside them. Mommy could speak a little Italian, but not much.

One day the Italian wife, Mrs. Mori, brought "Bark," our girls' stuffed dog, over. She said the dog had fallen out of our second story window. Mommy couldn't understand Italian very well, so Mrs. Mori showed her the place she had found the dog. Mommy looked up and saw the open window. She hurried upstairs. Daddy had stapled netting over the windows to act as screens. But the bottom of the netting on this window was loose.

Gladys was on the changing table right beside the open window. She could have easily fallen out the window and onto the concrete below.

Mrs. Mori probably saved Gladys' life that day.

Are you looking out for the people you live with, live next to, or go to school with? God tells us we should be.

Phil 2:3 *Do nothing out of selfish ambition or vain conceit, but in humility consider others better than yourselves.* **Phil 2:4** *Each of you should look not only to your own interests, but also to the interests of others.*

I Cor 10:24 *Nobody should seek his own good, but the good of others.*

Rom 15:2 *Each of us should please his neighbor for his good, to build him up.*

Arguing

NOVEMBER 18

Marjorie and Eddie would argue about almost anything. They were especially unhappy with each other when they had to go someplace in the car. At home they might say things like, "Mom, she's taking my things," or "Mom, he's not letting me play."

In the car they would say things like, "Mom, he's touching me," or "Mom, she's looking at me." It seemed that Marjorie and Eddie were just in the habit of arguing.

The letter of James says that people quarrel and fight.

Jas 4:1 *What causes fights and quarrels among you? Don't they come from your desires that battle within you?* **Jas 4:2** *You want something but don't get it. You kill and covet, but you cannot have what you want. You quarrel and fight. You do not have, because you do not ask God.*

When things aren't going right for Eddie he could pray. He might ask God to keep his sister from bothering him. Marjorie could ask God to make Eddie leave her alone. The children could ask for those things, but if they do they are only thinking of themselves. James tells Christians they should pray prayers that help God's kingdom to grow. They should not pray prayers whose answers will just please them.

Jas 4:3 *When you ask, you do not receive, because you ask with wrong motives, that you may spend what you get on your pleasures.*

Eddie could ask God to help him be kind to Marjorie. Marjorie could ask God to teach her how to think more about what Eddie would like to do than what she would like. She could pray that God would help her be a peacemaker in the family, rather than a troublemaker. These are prayers that would help God's kingdom to grow. If God answered these prayers, Eddie and Marjorie would be acting more like Jesus. God wants to answer this type of humble prayer.

Jas 4:10 *Humble yourselves before the Lord, and he will lift you up.*

DON'T BE SELFISH

NOVEMBER
19

Me, Me, Me

Jesus told the Pharisees and the teachers of the law that they were full of greed and self-indulgence:* **Mt 23:25** *"Woe to you, teachers of the law and Pharisees, you hypocrites! You clean the outside of the cup and dish, but inside they are full of greed and self-indulgence."*

A verse in Luke is almost the same. A Pharisee had invited Jesus to eat with him. The Pharisee noticed that Jesus hadn't washed before he ate. He was surprised.

Lk 11:39 *Then the Lord said to him, "Now then, you Pharisees clean the outside of the cup and dish, but inside you are full of greed and wickedness."*

Jesus knew that the Pharisees' hearts were not right with God. He told them that washing their bodies would not make their hearts clean. Jesus was not happy that the Pharisees wanted to show that they were important. Jesus was talking about the Pharisees when he said that **Mt 23:6** *"they love the place of honor at banquets and the most important seats in the synagogues."*

The Pharisees were looking out for themselves. They wanted to be important and to have lots of nice things. But Jesus said they were not teaching the people correctly. Instead, they were keeping people from knowing the truth about God. Jesus said,

Lk 11:52 *"Woe to you experts in the law, because you have taken away the key to knowledge. You yourselves have not entered, and you have hindered those who were entering."*

If the Pharisees were doing their job, they would be leading people to God. They were more interested in having a comfortable life; they were self-centered, not God-centered.

Self-indulgence—eating, using or spending on yourself more than you need or should

DON'T BE SELFISH

NOVEMBER 20

Thanksgiving
Thanksgiving

Thanksgiving, as we know it, is an American holiday that can be traced back to the Pilgrims. After a few hard winters the Pilgrims had a good corn harvest. They gathered with the Indians to thank God and to feast.

The Pilgrims were thankful for something specific God had done in their lives.

King David also was very thankful for how God worked in his life. After God had delivered him from all his enemies, David wrote Psalm 18 as a song of Thanksgiving to God. Let's read the beginning and the end of the psalm.

Ps 18:1-2 *I love you, O Lord, my strength. The Lord is my rock, my fortress and my deliverer; my God is my rock, in whom I take refuge. He is my shield and the horn of my salvation, my stronghold.*

Ps 18:3 & 46 *I call to the Lord, who is worthy of praise, and I am saved from my enemies.*

(vs 46) The Lord lives! Praise be to my Rock! Exalted be God my Savior!

Ps 18:47-48 *He is the God who avenges me, who subdues nations under me, who saves me from my enemies. You exalted me above my foes; from violent men you rescued me.*

Ps 18:49-50 *Therefore I will praise you among the nations, O Lord; I will sing praises to your name. He gives his king great victories; he shows unfailing kindness to his anointed, to David and his descendants forever.*

God gave David victory over other kings. He gave the Pilgrims a good harvest. God is willing to bless us in specific ways as well. He is willing to share with us his goodness.

NOVEMBER 21

Feast of Tabernacles

In the Bible, God set up three seven-day festivals that his people were to celebrate each year: "Passover" or the "Feast of Unleavened Bread" is the first; fifty days later they celebrated "Pentecost," also called the "Feast of Weeks;" then in the fall they celebrated the "Feast of Tabernacles" (or Booths), also called the "Feast of Ingathering."

God wanted his people to be a "celebrating people." Wow! They were to celebrate twenty-one days in every year. In Christian churches most congregations celebrate Easter which is like the Passover, and then Pentecost fifty days later. The Feast of Tabernacles would probably be like our Thanksgiving; except it is celebrated in September or October when *their* harvest occurs. Let's see how the Feast of Tabernacles was to be celebrated. God gave Moses the instructions.

Lev 23:39 *So beginning with the fifteenth day of the seventh month,* after you have gathered the crops of the land, celebrate the festival to the LORD for seven days; the first day is a day of rest, and the eighth day also is a day of rest.*

This feast was a celebration of God's goodness in the harvest.

Lev 23:41 *Celebrate this as a festival to the LORD for seven days each year. This is to be a lasting ordinance for the generations to come; celebrate it in the seventh month.*

This festival happened after their fall harvest. Our celebration of Thanksgiving is also usually celebrated after harvesting is done.

Lev 23:42 *Live in booths for seven days: All native-born Israelites are to live in booths* **Lev 23:43** *so your descendants will know that I had the Israelites live in booths when I brought them out of Egypt. I am the LORD your God.*

God wanted the people to live in booths to remind them of how God had brought them out of Egypt. It was a celebration of thanksgiving.

Seventh Month—the seventh Hebrew month, Tishri, would be the English September or October

NOVEMBER 22

Don't Take Anything
Bible

Joshua led the Israelites in conquering the Promised Land. He was sure that God would help them conquer the land. After they conquered the city of Jericho they sent a small army to take the city of Ai [*ay eye*]. This time the Israelites were defeated. Joshua prayed and asked God what went wrong.

God told him that someone in the camp had stolen some things from Jericho. When they took the city of Jericho, God had told them that everything was to be destroyed, except the silver, gold, bronze and iron—these were to be put in the temple treasury. God told Joshua that someone in the Israelite camp had taken some things from Jericho. God showed the Israelites that Achan [*ay cuhn*] was the man who had taken the goods. Joshua confronted him.

Josh 7:19 *Then Joshua said to Achan, "My son, give glory to the Lord, the God of Israel, and give him the praise. Tell me what you have done; do not hide it from me."*

Josh 7:20 *Achan replied, "It is true! I have sinned against the Lord, the God of Israel. This is what I have done:* **Josh 7:21a** *When I saw in the plunder a beautiful robe from Babylonia, two hundred shekels of silver and a wedge of gold weighing fifty shekels, I coveted* them and took them.* **Josh 7:21b** *They are hidden in the ground inside my tent, with the silver underneath."*

Achan, along with all Israel knew what God had said about destroying everything in Jericho. Achan admitted that when he saw the robe and the silver and gold that he coveted them. Achan coveted those things and then he took them.

When Achan took those things he knew that it was wrong. He was not doing what God had commanded. Achan was thinking only of himself; he was being selfish.

Coveted—really wanted something that didn't belong to him

DON'T BE SELFISH

NOVEMBER 23

The Best Animals
Bible

Samuel, the prophet, anointed Saul as king of Israel. Saul knew that Samuel was a man of God so he listened to his advice. Once Samuel came to Saul and told him that God wanted to punish the Amalekites [uh *mal* uh kites]. The Amalekites had attacked Israel when Israel left Egypt. Samuel had very specific instructions from God for King Saul. Samuel told Saul that when he attacked the Amelekites he was supposed to destroy *all* of the sheep, camels and donkeys. King Saul went and attacked the Amalekites.

I Sam 15:9a *But Saul and the army spared Agag [ay gag] and the best of the sheep and cattle, the fat calves and lambs—everything that was good.* **I Sam 15:9b** *These they were unwilling to destroy completely, but everything that was despised and weak they totally destroyed.*

God was not pleased that King Saul had disobeyed him. God told Samuel that he was sorry he had made Saul the king, because Saul would not obey God.

When Samuel asked Saul why he disobeyed, Saul blamed his army.

I Sam 15:15 *Saul answered, "The soldiers brought them from the Amalekites; they spared the best of the sheep and cattle to sacrifice to the Lord your God, but we totally destroyed the rest."*

Samuel reminded Saul of God's instructions. Saul again blamed the soldiers. When Samuel told Saul that God had rejected him as king, Saul finally confessed that he did wrong. It was too late. Saul wanted Samuel to go with him so he could worship the Lord. Samuel refused. He said again that God had rejected Saul as king.

I Sam 15:26 *But Samuel said to him, "I will not go back with you. You have rejected the word of the Lord, and the Lord has rejected you as king over Israel!"*

Because Saul wanted to keep the nice looking livestock, he lost his kingdom.

The 10th Commandment

NOVEMBER 24

The Tenth Commandment says, "You shall not covet." That is a shortened version of how the Bible says it. The longer versions can be found in Exodus and Deuteronomy:

Ex 20:17 *You shall not covet your neighbor's house. You shall not covet your neighbor's wife, or his manservant or maidservant, his ox or donkey, or anything that belongs to your neighbor.*

Deut 5:21 *You shall not covet your neighbor's wife. You shall not set your desire on your neighbor's house or land, his manservant or maidservant, his ox or donkey, or anything that belongs to your neighbor.*

When we covet the things that belong to other people, we are allowing ourselves to be self-centered. Jesus warned us not to let our lives be caught up in the things we own.

Lk 12:15 *Then he said to them, "Watch out! Be on your guard against all kinds of greed; a man's life does not consist in the abundance of his possessions."*

Instead of trying to get more and more things, or even worrying about having enough to eat, Jesus said, **Lk 12:31** *"But seek his kingdom, and these things will be given to you as well."*

In the New American Bible Luke 12:31 says, "Seek out instead his kingship over you, and the rest will follow in turn."

If we seek God's kingship over us, we will not be self-centered and covet other people's things.

DON'T BE SELFISH

NOVEMBER
25

Dirty Face
Marigny

Kerri's daddy was in the army. Sometimes he would go to the field for training and be gone for as long as two weeks at a stretch. When he came home he was tired and dirty; he would sit in the recliner to rest. Kerri and her sisters pulled the boot blousers* [*blouz* erz] out of the legs of Daddy's uniform pants and then tried to loosen the tightly laced combat boots. They took a long time getting the laces loose enough, and then they tugged hard to get the boots off.

Kerri stood beside the chair her daddy was reclining in. With the wet wipes she began wiping the camouflage paint and dirt from her daddy's face.

Paul told the Galatian Christians that they should serve one another.

Gal 5:13 *You, my brothers, were called to be free. But do not use your freedom to indulge the sinful nature; rather, serve one another in love.*

Then Paul says how important loving others is.

Gal 5:14 *The entire law is summed up in a single command: "Love your neighbor as yourself."*

When Jesus taught the people he said that all the law and the prophets hang on two commandments. He said the first one was to love God with all your heart, soul and mind. Then he said, **Mt 22:39** *"And the second is like it: 'Love your neighbor as yourself.'* **Mt 22:40** *All the Law and the Prophets hang on these two commandments."*

Paul didn't mention the first commandment of loving God. That's because he was trying to correct people who thought that because they were Christians they were free to do anything they wanted to. They thought they could be self-indulgent and just live to please themselves.

Paul is trying to help them think correctly. He says if Christians love their neighbor they will not be breaking the commandments. Serving others is living selflessly.

Boot blousers—elastic bands put in the pant legs of uniforms to hold them in place

DON'T BE SELFISH

NOVEMBER 26

Don't Touch Them

In Matthew, Mark and Luke we find the story of Jesus healing a man with leprosy.

Mt 8:2 *A man with leprosy came and knelt before him and said, "Lord, if you are willing, you can make me clean."*

Mt 8:3 *Jesus reached out his hand and touched the man. "I am willing," he said. "Be clean!" Immediately he was cured of his leprosy.*

This is how it is told in Mark.

Mk 1:41-42 *Filled with compassion, Jesus reached out his hand and touched the man. "I am willing," he said. "Be clean!" Immediately the leprosy left him and he was cured.*

Luke's story is almost the same.

Lk 5:13 *Jesus reached out his hand and touched the man. "I am willing," he said. "Be clean!" And immediately the leprosy left him.*

The stories could all be talking about one man that Jesus healed. It is just told by all three writers, Matthew, Mark and Luke.

They all remembered this event, because it was a miracle. Leprosy was a disease that no medicine could make better. People would just become sicker until they died. All the stories say that Jesus "reached out his hand and touched the man."

If Jesus was self-centered, he would have stayed away from a man who could have made him sick. He would have stayed away and not even looked at someone who probably looked bad because of his skin disease. Jesus did not avoid the man or look away from him. He reached out his hand and touched him.

If we are selfless we will also reach out to those who are sick and to those who don't have any friends.

DON'T BE SELFISH

NOVEMBER

27

Judah is Selfless

Joseph was sold by his brothers to people who sold him as a slave in Egypt. God took care of Joseph, and he was made ruler of Egypt under the Pharaoh. Joseph saved up grain in Egypt because God had shown him there would be a famine. When the famine came, Joseph's brothers came to buy some of the grain Joseph had stored up.

Joseph knew who his brothers were, but they didn't know he was their brother. Joseph said if they came again to get grain, they would need to bring their other brother. Joseph wanted to see Benjamin who hadn't come along on this trip.

Benjamin's father, Jacob, did not want to let Benjamin go; he thought something might happen to Benjamin. When they ran out of food, Jacob finally agreed to let him go.

Benjamin's older brother, Judah, promised he would bring Benjamin safely home.

Gen 43:8 *Then Judah said to Israel his father, "Send the boy along with me and we will go at once, so that we and you and our children may live and not die.* **Gen 43:9** *I myself will guarantee his safety; you can hold me personally responsible for him. If I do not bring him back to you and set him here before you, I will bear the blame before you all my life."*

When the brothers got the grain from Egypt, Joseph ordered someone to put his silver cup in Benjamin's sack. They left to go back to Canaan. Joseph asked his steward to go and bring back the one who had the silver cup—Benjamin. Now remember Judah's oath. He *had* to bring Benjamin back with him. All the brothers went back to see if they couldn't make things right. Judah pleaded that Benjamin be allowed to return home.

Gen 44:33 *"Now then, please let your servant remain here as my lord's slave in place of the boy, and let the boy return with his brothers.* **Gen 44:34** *How can I go back to my father if the boy is not with me? No! Do not let me see the misery that would come upon my father."*

Judah was willing to be Joseph's slave in place of Benjamin. He cared more about his father than he did about himself. Judah was being selfless.

NOVEMBER 28

I Already Told You
Bible

Jeremiah served as one of God's prophets. He was given a message by God to deliver to the people: "The Babylonian army is going to attack Jerusalem. Jerusalem will be captured. If you stay in Jerusalem you will die, but if you surrender to the Babylonians you will live."

Some people didn't like what Jeremiah was saying. The captain of the guard gave orders that Jeremiah be thrown into a dungeon. Jeremiah was there a long time, and then King Zedekiah [zed uh *kie* uh] had him released.

Jer 37:17 *Then King Zedekiah sent for him and had him brought to the palace, where he asked him privately, "Is there any word from the* LORD*?"*

"Yes," Jeremiah replied, "you will be handed over to the king of Babylon."

Some of the officials did not like this message. They told the king that Jeremiah was discouraging the soldiers. Because King Zedekiah was not a strong ruler, he told the officials to do whatever they wanted.

Jer 38:6 *So they took Jeremiah and put him into the cistern of Malkijah* [mal *kie* juh]*, the king's son, which was in the courtyard of the guard. They lowered Jeremiah by ropes into the cistern; it had no water in it, only mud, and Jeremiah sank down into the mud.*

First Jeremiah was thrown into a dungeon and then into a cistern because he spoke the message God had given him. He was released from the dungeon and rescued from the cistern. Do you think he stopped giving the people God's message? The king asked him again what God's message was.

Jer 38:17a *Then Jeremiah said to Zedekiah, "This is what the* LORD *God Almighty, the God of Israel, says: 'If you surrender to the officers of the king of Babylon,* **Jer 38:17b** *your life will be spared and this city will not be burned down; you and your family will live.'"*

Jeremiah spoke the same message even though he knew it might mean trouble for him. He did not think of what was in his own best interest, instead he obeyed God. He was selfless.

DON'T BE SELFISH

NOVEMBER 29

Suffering for Us

What are some things that Jesus suffered so that we might be able to go to heaven?

Pontius Pilate was the governor when Jesus was arrested. He had Jesus whipped.

Jn 19:1 *Then Pilate took Jesus and had him flogged.**

Next, the soldiers put a robe on Jesus and a crown of thorns on his head.

Mk 15:17 *They put a purple robe on him, then twisted together a crown of thorns and set it on him.*

The soldiers made fun of Jesus. They acted like he was a king by kneeling in front of him, but they were just being mean.

Jesus began carrying his cross.

Jn 19:17 *Carrying his own cross, he went out to the place of the Skull (which in Aramaic is called Golgotha).*

Jesus was probably so weak from being whipped that he couldn't carry his cross all the way. The gospels of Matthew, Mark and Luke report that Simon carried Jesus' cross.

Finally, Jesus was crucified.

Lk 23:33 *When they came to the place called the Skull, there they crucified him, along with the criminals—one on his right, the other on his left.*

Because Jesus loves us so much he was willing to die for us. He was whipped and crowned with thorns. He carried his cross and then was crucified. Jesus gave himself for us. Are we willing to give ourselves for other people?

What are some things we could do that would show we are selfless? We could help Mom set the table. We could help clean up the house before Dad comes home. We could share our toys with our brother or sister.

Flogged—whipped

NOVEMBER 30

Care about Souls

The Bible teaches that the only way a person can get into heaven is by believing in Jesus. If we have accepted Jesus as our Savior we are on our way to heaven. If we really care about other people we will want them to go to heaven also. The apostle Paul felt that way about the Israelites.

Rom 10:1 *Brothers, my heart's desire and prayer to God for the Israelites is that they may be saved.*

When you tell other people about God's plan for them to go to heaven, you are being selfless.

You can tell them that God made people.

Gen 1:27 *So God created man in his own image, in the image of God he created him; male and female he created them.*

Then tell them that people turned away from God.

Rom 3:23 *For all have sinned and fall short of the glory of God.*

Tell them that God loved people so much that he sent Jesus to die for their sins. Tell them all they need to do is believe in Jesus and they will be saved. That is what Paul and Silas told some people who asked them what they needed to do to be saved.

Acts 16:31 *They replied, "Believe in the Lord Jesus, and you will be saved—you and your household."*

When we care about people's souls we are being selfless.

DECEMBER 1

Jesus is Coming
Marigny

Christmas is the day we celebrate Jesus' birthday. Advent begins four Sundays before Christmas. During these four weeks God's people look forward to Christmas.

Families have different traditions* during advent. The Marigny family would buy advent calendars for each of their four girls. Each day you would open a little "window" on the calendar and find a piece of chocolate.

Some churches light candles on an advent wreath; three candles are purple and one candle is pink. On the first Sunday of Advent, one candle is lit. The second Sunday two candles are lit. This continues until, on the fourth Sunday, all four candles are lit.

Both of these traditions—advent calendars and advent candles on a wreath—remind us that Christmas is coming.

As we get ready for the coming of Christmas we should also get ready for Jesus' second coming. We should make sure we are ready for his return.

Mt 24:36 *No one knows about that day or hour, not even the angels in heaven, nor the Son, but only the Father.*

Mt 24:42 *Therefore keep watch, because you do not know on what day your Lord will come.* **Mt 24:43** *But understand this: If the owner of the house had known at what time of night the thief was coming, he would have kept watch and would not have let his house be broken into.* **Mt 24:44** *So you also must be ready, because the Son of Man will come at an hour when you do not expect him.*

Traditions—things that people do in a similar way each time, e.g., lighting advent candles

DECEMBER 2

Condi

Condoleeza [kahn dah *lee* zuh] Rice started piano lessons when she was three. She was homeschooled in kindergarten, which gave her a big head start in life; she skipped first grade and seventh grade! By the time she was seventeen she had finished one year of college. When she was twenty-six, she had her PhD in international studies.

Condi was not only hardworking in her studies, she also took figure skating and piano lessons. She worked hard at both of these.

Condoleeza Rice, as Secretary of State for the United States, is probably one of the most powerful people in the world. She is an example of a scripture in Proverbs.

Prov 12:24 *Diligent hands will rule, but laziness ends in slave labor.*

A diligent person is one who works hard. The opposite of a diligent person is a sluggard; a sluggard is someone who is lazy. In the Book of Proverbs God talks about both of these types of people. Sometimes he will talk about both of these types of people in the same verse, like in the verse we just read. Read Proverbs 12:24 again.

Diligent hands will rule, but laziness ends in slave labor.

Diligent people will rule, but lazy people become slaves. In another passage in Proverbs, God tells lazy people to follow the example of the ant.

Prov 6:6 *Go to the ant, you sluggard; consider its ways and be wise!*

Prov 6:7 *It has no commander, no overseer or ruler,*

Prov 6:8 *yet it stores its provisions in summer and gathers its food at harvest.*

Ants are diligent. Condoleeza Rice is diligent. God wants us to be diligent, too.

BE DILIGENT

DECEMBER 3

God Worked

Do you know that God worked? What kind of work did God do? The Bible says God worked six days to create the world and then on the seventh day he rested. Let's read about God's work in Genesis, chapter one.

Gen 1:3 & 6 *And God said, "Let there be light," and there was light.*

After God created light, there was light and dark. *(vs 6) And God said, "Let there be an expanse between the waters to separate water from water."*

This was when God made the sky and earth separate from each other.

Gen 1:11 & 14 *Then God said, "Let the land produce vegetation: seed-bearing plants and trees on the land that bear fruit with seed in it, according to their various kinds." And it was so.*

After God made the dry land appear, he created the plants and trees.

(vs 14) And God said, "Let there be lights in the expanse of the sky to separate the day from the night, and let them serve as signs to mark seasons and days and years.

God created the sun, moon and stars.

Gen 1:20 & 24 *And God said, "Let the water teem with living creatures, and let birds fly above the earth across the expanse of the sky."*

God created the fish and the birds.

(vs 24) And God said, "Let the land produce living creatures according to their kinds: livestock, creatures that move along the ground, and wild animals, each according to its kind." And it was so.

God created all the different kinds of animals.

Gen 1:26 *Then God said, "Let us make man in our image, in our likeness, and let them rule over the fish of the sea and the birds of the air, over the livestock, over all the earth, and over all the creatures that move along the ground."*

God created all the animals and man on that sixth day. It was probably a lot of work.

God worked for six days to create the world and everything in it.

DECEMBER 4

Work to Eat

When Shawn sat down for supper he noticed there was not a plate, fork, or even a glass at his place. There was just a piece of paper with II Thessalonians 3:10 written on it. Shawn's dad told him to get a Bible and look up that verse. Shawn went to his room and got his Bible. He found the verse and read it out loud.

II Thes 3:10 *For even when we were with you, we gave you this rule: "If a man will not work, he shall not eat."*

Shawn remembered how he had slept in that morning. While everyone else got their chores done, *he* was resting between his clean sheets. He knew that every Saturday he was required to clean his room and then help with chores. Today it was his turn to dust the furniture and vacuum the carpets. No one reminded him that he needed to do those things, but he knew well enough.

Shawn looked at his empty place at the table. Dad told him he could eat when the chores were finished. Shawn got up from the table and went to work.

Ever since Adam's sin in the Garden of Eden, people have had to work for a living. After Adam and Eve ate of the forbidden fruit, God spoke first to the serpent, then to Eve and finally to Adam.

Gen 3:17 *To Adam he said, "Because you listened to your wife and ate from the tree about which I commanded you, 'You must not eat of it,'*

> *"Cursed is the ground because of you; through painful toil you will eat of it all the days of your life.* **Gen 3:18** *It will produce thorns and thistles for you, and you will eat the plants of the field.* **Gen 3:19** *By the sweat of your brow you will eat your food until you return to the ground, since from it you were taken; for dust you are and to dust you will return."*

Shawn learned that work is as much a part of living as eating is.

DECEMBER 5

Lazy Person

Abigail's chores this week were to help Mom fold and put away the laundry. Mom looked at the three stacks of neatly folded clothes and noticed that Abigail had only folded four things. Abigail could have worked harder, but she was lazy. The Bible, especially the Book of Proverbs, has a lot to say about laziness. In the Bible, lazy people are often called sluggards. Since people today don't use the word "sluggard," let's replace it with "lazy person." When you read your scripture, if you see the word "sluggard" I want you to say "lazy person" instead.

Prov 21:25 *The (sluggard's) lazy person's craving will be the death of him, because his hands refuse to work.* **Prov 21:26** *All day long he craves for more, but the righteous give without sparing.*

Lazy people want things, but they are not willing to work in order to get them.

Prov 22:13 *The (sluggard) lazy person says, "There is a lion outside!" or, "I will be murdered in the streets!"*

A lazy person is always making excuses for why she didn't get things done. Do you think Abigail told her mother that the reason she didn't fold more clothes was because there was a lion outside? Probably not. She might have said she was tired.

Prov 19:24 *The (sluggard) lazy person buries his hand in the dish; he will not even bring it back to his mouth!*

Now that's lazy, when you can't even feed yourself!

Abigail should be diligent in her chores. We should be diligent in our work.

BE DILIGENT

DECEMBER 6

Undone Chores

Perry was very good at getting out of doing his chores. His brothers and sisters were tired of having to do not only their work, but also his.

Let's use the words "lazy person" for "sluggard" again.

Prov 26:16 *The (sluggard) lazy person is wiser in his own eyes than seven men who answer discreetly.*

A lazy person may begin to think he is better than other people. Perry might think that because his "slaves" were doing the work that he "as prince" didn't need to work.

Prov 20:4 *A (sluggard) lazy person does not plow in season; so at harvest time he looks but finds nothing.*

If a farmer does not plant his crop in the spring, there will be no harvest in the fall. If Perry is as lazy with his school work as he is with his chores, he will get lower grades than he should.

Prov 10:26 *As vinegar to the teeth and smoke to the eyes, so is a (sluggard) lazy person to those who send him.*

I don't know what vinegar does to teeth, but I know that smoke causes eyes to hurt. They feel like they burn.

If you need something done, don't ask Perry to do it. He will let you down.

Prov 18:9 *One who is slack in his work is brother to one who destroys.*

Another translation of the Bible—the English translation for the Deaf—translates this verse: "A person who does bad work is as bad as a person who destroys things."

BE DILIGENT

DECEMBER 7

A Big Job
Bible

God has a plan for your life. He has something for you to do that no other human being can do.

God also had a plan for Nehemiah's life. Nehemiah was someone who cared very much for God's people. Even though he lived in a country far away, he prayed regularly for the Jews in Judea and for Jerusalem. Some people from Judah came to Nehemiah. He asked them how things were going. They told Nehemiah that things were not good. In fact, things were terrible. Nehemiah tells it like this:

Neh 1:3 *They said to me, "Those who survived the exile and are back in the province are in great trouble and disgrace. The wall of Jerusalem is broken down, and its gates have been burned with fire."*

Nehemiah wanted to make things better. He asked his boss, the king, if he could go and rebuild the walls of Jerusalem. Building the walls was a very big job. Nehemiah was the right man for the job, and the king let him go. Nehemiah writes about what happened.

Neh 2:11 *I went to Jerusalem, and after staying there three days* **Neh 2:12** *I set out during the night with a few men. I had not told anyone what my God had put in my heart to do for Jerusalem. There were no mounts with me except the one I was riding on.*

Nehemiah believed that God had put in his heart the desire to rebuild the wall around the city of Jerusalem. Some evil people tried to stop Nehemiah, but Nehemiah sent messengers to them.

Neh 6:3 *So I sent messengers to them with this reply: "I am carrying on a great project and cannot go down. Why should the work stop while I leave it and go down to you?"*

With God's help Nehemiah rebuilt the wall around Jerusalem. It was a lot of work, but Nehemiah was willing to do whatever he could to help God's people.

If we give ourselves to God's service, He will give us a big job to do also.

DECEMBER 8

Embarrassed

Nadia's mom said she could go over to Tara's house to play. Tara took Nadia into her room. Nadia's eyes got big as she walked into Tara's room. The floor was covered with clothes and blankets. Only a sheet half-way covered the mattress. The closet had toys and clothes piled up at the bottom and the dresser drawers were open with clothes hanging from each one.

Nadia could tell that Tara was embarrassed. She volunteered to help Tara straighten things up so they would have a place to play. The girls didn't get a chance to play at all that day. By the time they picked up and sorted everything on the floor, Nadia had to go home.

Tara's mom knew that Tara didn't clean her room. She had told her so many times to clean it that she had grown tired of it. She decided that Tara must keep the door to her room closed if she was going to be so messy.

Some children are so busy with different activities that they don't have time to clean their rooms. That wasn't the case with Tara; she was just lazy. Solomon tells a story in the book of Proverbs. The person he writes about is something like Tara.

Prov 24:30-31 *I went past the field of the sluggard, past the vineyard of the man who lacks judgment; thorns had come up everywhere, the ground was covered with weeds, and the stone wall was in ruins.* **Prov 24:32** *I applied my heart to what I observed and learned a lesson from what I saw:* **Prov 24:33** *A little sleep, a little slumber, a little folding of the hands to rest—* **Prov 24:34** *and poverty will come on you like a bandit and scarcity like an armed man.*

What did Solomon learn? He learned that if you are lazy and all you want to do is sleep, you can become poor in a hurry. He learned that if you are lazy, the place you live can become a mess.

After Nadia's visit, Tara determined that she would try to keep her room looking better; she didn't want to be embarrassed again.

BE DILIGENT

DECEMBER 9

Meditate on the Word

A catechism is a set of beliefs of a church. Many short catechisms are recorded in a question and answer format.

The Westminster catechism was used in many public schools in Scotland. It contains one hundred and seven questions and answers that students were expected to memorize. The first question is "What is the chief end of man?"

Johnny was only six when the teacher read that question. Johnny and his twenty classmates memorized the answer, "The chief end of man is to glorify God and to enjoy him forever."

When Johnny was playing with his dad in the evening, he told him what he had learned. He said to his dad, "I know what the Chief Indian is, Dad."

"What is the Chief Indian, Johnny?" Dad asked.

Johnny beamed as he said, "The Chief Indian is to glorify God and enjoy him forever."

Dad understood right away that Johnny had thought the teacher said "Chief Indian" instead of "the chief end of man."

Johnny's dad explained to him what the teacher had really said. Then Dad told his son how proud he was that Johnny had memorized the answer correctly.

Just like Johnny memorized his answer to the catechism, many people memorize scripture. The writer of Psalm 119 probably memorized a lot of scripture. He says several times that he meditates on God's Word.

Ps 119:15 *I meditate on your precepts and consider your ways.*

Ps 119:23b *Your servant will meditate on your decrees.*

Ps 119:78b *But I will meditate on your precepts.*

Ps 119:148 *My eyes stay open through the watches of the night, that I may meditate on your promises.*

DECEMBER 10

Study the Word

Scottish boys were diligent in memorizing their catechism. The writer of Psalm 119 was diligent in meditating on God's Word. The Bereans [beh *ree* unz] were diligent in checking their Scriptures to see if what Paul was preaching was true.

Luke wrote the book of Acts. In it he says that he is proud of the Bereans because they go back and check Scriptures when they hear preaching.

Acts 17:11 *Now the Bereans were of more noble character than the Thessalonians, for they received the message with great eagerness and examined the Scriptures every day to see if what Paul said was true.*

The Apostle Paul was preaching at Berea. The people there listened to what Paul was preaching. Then the people went home and looked to see if what Paul was preaching was what the Scriptures said. During Paul's time the people only had the Old Testament; the New Testament was not yet written. The Old Testament scriptures were written on scrolls that the people kept at home. That is why the people went home to check if what Paul said was true.

The person that wrote Psalm 119 said:

Ps 119:105 *Your word is a lamp to my feet and a light for my path.*

If the Word of God is to be our guide, we need to know what it says. Paul told Timothy:

II Tim 2:15a *Do your best to present yourself to God as one approved,* **II Tim 2:15b** *a workman who does not need to be ashamed and who correctly handles the word of truth.*

Preachers and the people who listen to them should be diligent in studying God's Word.

DECEMBER 11

Gathering Firewood

Every summer the Kahill family goes camping. Evenings are spent around the campfire telling stories. That is why during the day every family member is required to collect wood for the fire.

The Apostle Paul once was gathering firewood, but his wasn't a normal camping trip. He was on a ship that was wrecked by a storm. The Bible says the ship ran into a sand bar so it didn't make it to the beach. Then the waves pounding on the back of the ship broke it into pieces. There were two hundred seventy-six passengers. The people who could swim jumped into the ocean and swam to shore. The story continues in Acts.

Acts 27:44 *The rest were to get there on planks or on pieces of the ship. In this way everyone reached land in safety.*

Acts 28:1 *Once safely on shore, we found out that the island was called Malta.*

Acts 28:2 *The islanders showed us unusual kindness. They built a fire and welcomed us all because it was raining and cold.* **Acts 28:3** *Paul gathered a pile of brushwood and, as he put it on the fire, a viper, driven out by the heat, fastened itself on his hand.*

Do you remember that a viper is a poisonous snake? Paul was bitten by a snake, but we'll save that for another time. What did Paul do in the first half of that verse? He gathered firewood.

Paul knew he was an apostle of God; he was an important man. However, he didn't sit around waiting for people to meet his needs. He saw a need and helped where he could.

DECEMBER 12

Maker of Tents

In Bible times, people didn't have combines to harvest grain; instead they had a three-step process of cutting, threshing or treading, and winnowing. A sickle was used to cut the grain. The grain was then taken to a threshing floor—a level and hard-beaten plot in the open air. On the threshing floor oxen would break the shell off the kernels by walking on the grain or pulling a heavy machine over the grain. This was also called treading. Winnowing was the last step. On windy days the grain was tossed into the air so the wind could blow the chaff away.

Treading of the grain is the harvesting step mentioned in Deuteronomy 25:4.

Deut 25:4 *Do not muzzle an ox while it is treading out the grain.*

Do you remember that a muzzle is something that will keep an animal from eating? So this scripture really means, "Allow the oxen to eat while they are working."

The Apostle Paul quoted this scripture two times.

I Cor 9:9 *For it is written in the Law of Moses: "Do not muzzle an ox while it is treading out the grain."*

I Tim 5:18 *For the Scripture says, "Do not muzzle the ox while it is treading out the grain," and "The worker deserves his wages."*

Paul was applying this scripture to people who work for God, e.g., pastors, evangelists, etc. He said if these people are helping the church, then the church should pay them for their work. It's the same as the oxen getting "paid" with food for their work.

Even though Paul taught this rule, he kept up his work as a tentmaker for part of the time that he was preaching. Paul says he did this because he didn't want to be a burden on people.

II Cor 11:9 *And when I was with you and needed something, I was not a burden to anyone, for the brothers who came from Macedonia supplied what I needed. I have kept myself from being a burden to you in any way, and will continue to do so.*

DECEMBER 13

Two Jobs
Bible

Paul was sent out by the church at Antioch to be a missionary. Paul could have just let the Antioch church pay for all his expenses, or he could have taken offerings every place he preached to help pay his way.

Paul didn't want to make people pay in order to hear the gospel. He preached for free. Because he did that, he had to have another job. He earned money by making tents.

We can read about Paul being a tentmaker in chapter 18 of Acts. The Bible tells us that Paul went to Corinth.

Acts 18:2-3 *There he met a Jew named Aquila, a native of Pontus, who had recently come from Italy with his wife Priscilla, because Claudius had ordered all the Jews to leave Rome. Paul went to see them, and because he was a tentmaker as they were, he stayed and worked with them.*

Paul earned a living for himself and the other missionaries so they could go and preach for free.

Acts 20:34 *You yourselves know that these hands of mine have supplied my own needs and the needs of my companions.*

Paul said he did accept help, but not from the Corinthians.

II Cor 11:7 *Was it a sin for me to lower myself in order to elevate you by preaching the gospel of God to you free of charge?* **II Cor 11:8** *I robbed other churches by receiving support from them so as to serve you.*

When Paul says he robbed other churches, he simply means that he accepted money from them.

Paul set an example for us that we should be hard workers—"busy as beavers."

DECEMBER 14

Care of Pets
Warren Marigny

Gregory was only about ten when he found a stray puppy. He knew he would have to get permission from Mama before he could bring the puppy home, so he locked it up.

Mama didn't want a dog to take care of. She had nine children and she thought that was enough for her to handle. Gregory kept asking, though, and Mama gave in. She told Gregory he would be the one taking care of the dog.

Most children and many adults like puppies. They are "sooo" cute.

There are a few places in the Bible that talk about taking care of animals. In the book of Genesis, Rebekah is talking to Abraham's servant.

Gen 24:19 *After she had given him a drink, she said, "I'll draw water for your camels too, until they have finished drinking."*

In the Book of Exodus, Moses was sitting by a well.

Ex 2:16 *Now a priest of Midian had seven daughters, and they came to draw water and fill the troughs to water their father's flock.*

In both these scriptures women are making sure the animals get water. All animals need water. They also need food.

Deut 25:4 *Do not muzzle the ox while it is treading out the grain.*

This was one of many laws God gave to his people. He told them to feed their oxen. If they put a muzzle on them, it would keep them from eating. Oxen need food to live; in fact, all animals need food to live, even puppies.

If you get a puppy, or already have one, it needs water and food every day. What else do puppies need? They need to get exercise and they need to be cleaned up after. Proverbs tells us:

Prov 12:10a *A righteous man cares for the needs of his animal.*

DECEMBER 15

Eating Dirt
Warren Marigny

Terry didn't have a lot of friends in school. In fact, he was a loner who kept to himself. He was pushed around a lot and was on the top of the "beat up list" for boys who wanted to "bully" someone. Terry claims that he ate enough dirt to fill a garden plot. Why were those children so mean?

Rom 3:23 *For all have sinned and fall short of the glory of God.* All people are born with original sin.

Heb 5:14 *But solid food is for the mature, who by constant use have trained themselves to distinguish good from evil.*

If children have not been taught about God and have not had their consciences trained to know right from wrong, they can be especially cruel.

Terry's godmother often dressed him in white, and it's possible that the other children were envious of him. They didn't have someone who kept their clothes clean and pressed and their shoes always clean. Terry's godmother was very proud of "her boy" and she worked hard to keep him looking nice.

We also should work hard at keeping ourselves looking nice. It may be difficult to do that, especially if you are part of a large family. Because most people only wear their Sunday shoes once a week, it's so easy for one or even both of them to get lost. It's not easy to keep track of other things either, like hats and mittens.

In order to dress nicely, it might mean that you keep your room tidy so you know where things are. You might have to spend some time every day putting things where they belong. That way when you get dressed you *can* look nice.

I Thes 4:11a *Make it your ambition to lead a quiet life,* **I Thes 4:11b** *to mind your own business and to work with your hands, just as we told you.*

Diligence Rewarded

DECEMBER 16

Jason McElwain was born with autism. He was the manager for his high school basketball team. That means he took care of the towels and water and helped the coach with anything he needed. Because Jason was so dedicated, the coach asked Jason to put on a uniform for their last home game. He might not get a chance to play, but at least he would be a part of the team. When the team had a big lead in the fourth quarter coach put Jason in.

With four minutes to play Jason missed his first two shots, but he didn't give up. After that he made six 3-point baskets and one 2-pointer, for a total of 20 points. At the buzzer his last 3-pointer went in. The crowd cheered and raced off the bleachers to congratulate him.

Jason had worked hard for his team. He was rewarded by being allowed to play in a game.

God will one day reward us for all that we have done for him. Jesus told a parable about how God will reward us. In this parable Jesus said God will tell us we have done a good job if we use our talents for him.

Mt 25:21 *"His master replied, 'Well done, good and faithful servant! You have been faithful with a few things; I will put you in charge of many things. Come and share you master's happiness!'"*

Other Scriptures tell us that God will reward us for the work we do.

Mt 16:27 *For the Son of Man is going to come in his Father's glory with his angels, and then he will reward each person according to what he has done.*

I Cor 3:8 *The man who plants and the man who waters have one purpose, and each will be rewarded according to his own labor.*

Rom 2:6 *God "will give to each person according to what he has done."*

BE DILIGENT

DECEMBER 17

Rewarded for Work

Todd had been doing chores in his family for a while now. Every afternoon his mom assigned him fifteen minutes of chores. Then on Saturday morning, the whole family would work for an hour or two depending on what needed to be done.

When Todd's family moved to a new place, Todd noticed that many boys his age didn't have to do chores. Todd decided he would just not do chores anymore. His afternoon chores were left undone. On Saturday morning, even though Mom woke him several times, Todd dozed off again.

Todd's dad asked him what was going on. Todd told him that no other boys around had to do chores.

Todd's dad said the family was not going to change their rules so that they would be like their neighbors. Todd's dad said God wants his people to spend their time wisely. All people that are able should help with the house chores. Todd's dad said there are several scriptures that say we will be rewarded by God for what we do. If we lie around and do nothing we will lose that reward.

Ps 62:12b *Surely you will reward each person according to what he has done.*

Rev 2:23b *Then all the churches will know that I am he who searches hearts and minds, and I will repay each of you according to your deeds.*

Rev 22:12 *"Behold, I am coming soon! My reward is with me, and I will give to everyone according to what he has done."*

Todd's dad ended the conversation by saying that God does not want us to be like everyone else. In fact, God wants us to be very different from other people. God wants his people to be so different from other people, that everyone will know God is real.

Mt 5:16 *In the same way, let your light shine before men, that they may see your good deeds and praise your Father in heaven.*

DECEMBER 18

Changing Jobs

There are four gospels in the Bible. Do you know their names? They are Matthew, Mark, Luke and John. Do you remember what the word "gospel" means? It means "good news."

Paul and Barnabas went to many Galatian cities **Acts 14:7** *where they continued to preach the good news.* The gospel is good news because it tells us how we can live forever with God in heaven.

Only three of the gospels are called synoptic [suh *nop* tik]. The dictionary says synoptic means "presenting an account from the same point of view." Because Matthew, Mark and Luke have many of the same stories, they are called the "synoptic gospels."

The gospel of John is different from the other three. It contains much material that is not in the other gospels. That's why the gospel of John is not one of the synoptic gospels.

A story that is found in all three synoptic gospels talks about how Jesus called Matthew to a different type of work. This story is not found in the gospel of John. Let's read parts of the story from each of the synoptic gospels.

Mt 9:9-10 *As Jesus went on from there, he saw a man named Matthew sitting at the tax collector's booth. "Follow me," he told him, and Matthew got up and followed him.*

While Jesus was having dinner at Matthew's house, many tax collectors and "sinners" came and ate with him and his disciples.

Mk 2:16 *When the teachers of the law who were Pharisees saw him eating with the "sinners" and tax collectors, they asked his disciples: "Why does he eat with tax collectors and 'sinners'?"*

Lk 5:31-32 *Jesus answered them, "It is not the healthy who need a doctor, but the sick. I have not come to call the righteous, but sinners to repentance."*

Matthew left his job of collecting taxes to become a follower of Jesus. God might be calling us to work full-time for him, also. What job might God have in mind for you?

DECEMBER 19

Be Prepared

Let's read a parable that is in all three synoptic gospels but is not found in the gospel of John.

Mt 21:33-34 *"Listen to another parable: There was a landowner who planted a vineyard. He put a wall around it, dug a winepress in it and built a watchtower. Then he rented the vineyard to some farmers and went away on a journey. When the harvest time approached, he sent his servants to the tenants to collect his fruit.* **Mk 12:3-5** *But they seized him, beat him and sent him away empty-handed. Then he sent another servant to them; they struck this man on the head and treated him shamefully. He sent still another, and that one they killed. He sent many others; some of them they beat, others they killed.*

Lk 20:13-14 *"Then the owner of the vineyard said, 'What shall I do? I will send my son, whom I love; perhaps they will respect him.'*

"But when the tenants saw him, they talked the matter over. 'This is the heir,' they said. 'Let's kill him, and the inheritance will be ours.' **Mt 21:39-41** *So they took him and threw him out of the vineyard and killed him.*

"Therefore, when the owner of the vineyard comes, what will he do to those tenants?"

"He will bring those wretches to a wretched end," they replied, *"and he will rent the vineyard to other tenants, who will give him his share of the crop at harvest time."*

This story is about how God, all through history, has sent prophets to his people. These prophets told the people to turn back to God. Often the people would not listen to the prophets. Finally, God sent his Son, Jesus. Instead of listening to Jesus, the people killed him.

Advent is a time when we are preparing for Christmas. Any day is a good time to begin listening to God and deciding to obey him. If we do that, we will be ready to meet him even if he comes back tomorrow.

DECEMBER 20

Practice, Practice
Marigny

Rachael started learning to play the piano when she was six. Her mom taught her in the beginning, but when she started third grade she took lessons from her teacher, Mrs. Steenson. Mrs. Steenson was a great teacher because Rachael liked her and wanted to play well for her.

Children take lessons for many different activities. Some learn how to swim, dance, skate, play musical instruments, do gymnastics, etc. For all these lessons the most important thing is to practice what you are taught.

If you take lessons every week for a year, that is 52 lessons. If you don't practice between lessons you will probably not be as good as the person who practices every day. If you really want to be good at something you need to practice; you need to be diligent.

Do you remember what a sluggard is? That's right, it's a lazy person.

Prov 13:4 *The sluggard craves and gets nothing, but the desires of the diligent are fully satisfied.*

A diligent person works hard to get what he wants. If you want to be good at the thing you are taking lessons for, you need to practice.

Rom 12:11 *Never be lacking in zeal, but keep your spiritual fervor, serving the Lord.*

This scripture is talking about having zeal, or being excited, about spiritual things. However, it does say we should "*never* be lacking in zeal." Are you excited about practicing?

Col 3:17 *And whatever you do, whether in word or deed, do it all in the name of the Lord Jesus, giving thanks to God the Father through him.*

Col 3:23 *Whatever you do, work at it with all your heart, as working for the Lord, not for men.*

If you are taking lessons, work at it with all your heart. Remember to practice, practice, practice!

DECEMBER 21

Marble Champion
Warren Marigny

As a boy, Terry learned to shoot marbles. He got so good at the game that he had several containers, including two gallon-jars, filled with marbles. When Terry planned on playing, he would fill his pockets with cat eyes, beanies and the big marbles that he called "knuckle fitters."

Terry could flick one of those marbles more than twenty feet. He was able to hit the pile of marbles hard! His knuckle fitter often hit the marble he was aiming for. Terry says if there had been a tournament for marble shooting all over the United States, he would have been able to compete. He was just that good!

The reason Terry became a good marble player was because he played a lot. If we want to be good Christians we need to work at it. We need to take time to study God's Word.

Studying God's Word helps us to know the difference between good and evil.

Heb 5:14 *But solid food is for the mature, who by constant use have trained themselves to distinguish good from evil.*

II Tim 2:15 *Do your best to present yourself to God as one approved, a workman who does not need to be ashamed and who correctly handles the word of truth.*

We need to be students of God's Word to be good Christians.

The apostle Paul said that some people who are teaching God's Word are false teachers. He said they pretend to be apostles, but are not even Christians.

II Cor 11:13 *For such men are false apostles, deceitful workmen, masquerading* [mass kuh *raid* ing] *as* apostles of Christ.*

John tells us how we can know who the real teachers are.

I Jn 4:2 *This is how you can recognize the Spirit of God: Every spirit that acknowledges that Jesus Christ has come in the flesh is from God.*

Masquerading as—pretending to be

Hit the Beanie Out
Warren Marigny

One of the marble games Terry used to play was called bull ring. A large circle, probably fifteen feet across, was made by drawing in the dirt with a stick. In the middle of that large circle a small circle was drawn. In this small circle were placed an equal number of marbles from each player; usually there were three to five players. The object was to knock the marbles out of not just the inside ring, but also the outside one. If you knocked the beanie, the small marble, out you won all the marbles. If you knocked other marbles out you got to keep just the ones you knocked out.

The beanie was the smallest marble so it was the hardest one to hit. If you could hit the beanie out of the large circle, you would win the game.

Being a Christian is kind of like shooting for that small marble. Jesus said it like this:

Mt 7:13 *Enter through the narrow gate. For wide is the gate and broad is the road that leads to destruction, and many enter through it.*
Mt 7:14 *But small is the gate and narrow the road that leads to life, and only a few find it.*

People get into heaven by believing in Jesus. Jesus said he is that small gate:

Jn 10:9 *I am the gate; whoever enters through me will be saved. He will come in and go out, and find pasture.*

Someone asked Jesus if only a few people would be saved. He said,

Lk 13:24 *Make every effort to enter through the narrow door, because many, I tell you, will try to enter and will not be able to.*

Becoming a Christian is an easy enough thing to do. But living a Christian life is a very difficult thing to do. Jesus said the gate to get into heaven is narrow. Following Jesus is hard work, but it is worth our effort.

DECEMBER 23

Santa Claus

Did you know that the name Santa Claus comes from the Dutch name for Saint Nicolaus? In Dutch, it sounded a little different than Santa Claus; it was "Sinter Klaas."

There is a legend about Saint Nicolaus. It goes like this:

Three girls couldn't afford a dowry. In earlier times and even now in some countries girls need a dowry in order to get married. A dowry is some money saved up by the girl and her family to give to her husband.

Nicolaus met these three girls. He gave each of them some gold. Now they had a dowry so that they could get married.

Nicholas was a bishop who is said to have performed many miracles. He was busy doing God's work. We also should be busy doing God's work.

Gal 6:9 *Let us not become weary in doing good, for at the proper time we will reap a harvest if we do not give up.*

Paul knows people can get tired of doing good works. He encourages them to keep doing good things.

Col 3:23 *Whatever you do, work at it with all your heart, as working for the Lord, not for men,* **Col 3:24** *since you know that you will receive an inheritance from the Lord as a reward. It is the Lord Christ you are serving.*

When Paul says we will "receive an inheritance" he means that God will reward us for the good things we do.

Heb 6:10 *God is not unjust; he will not forget your work and the love you have shown him as you have helped his people and continue to help them.*

God doesn't forget the good things we do. He also knows about all the good things St. Nicolaus did in his lifetime.

DECEMBER

24

God's Elves
Christmas Eve

Some people say that Santa's elves are very busy at Christmas time. If you have seen pictures of them, or have seen them in movies, they are often busy making all kinds of toys.

Do you know that everyone who is a Christian is like one of God's elves? Well . . . we are not elves, but we are God's helpers. Do you remember the greatest thing that God has ever done? By Jesus' death on the cross he provided salvation for all people. That is the greatest thing God ever did.

God saved mankind and he wants people to share in that great work. He lets people help him—be his "elves"—in that work. If we are Christians, then we are made "new" in Christ.

II Cor 5:17 *Therefore, if anyone is in Christ, he is a new creation; the old has gone, the new has come!*

God has forgiven our sins. After we are forgiven, God wants us to tell other people that they can have their sins forgiven, too.

II Cor 5:18 *All this is from God, who reconciled us to himself through Christ and gave us the ministry of reconciliation:* **II Cor 5:19** *that God was reconciling the world to himself in Christ, not counting men's sins against them. And he has committed to us the message of reconciliation.*

God reconciled us to himself. That means he made peace between us and himself by forgiving us. God goes on to call us ambassadors. That's another word for elves.

II Cor 5:20 *We are therefore Christ's ambassadors, as though God were making his appeal through us. We implore you on Christ's behalf: Be reconciled to God.*

Paul says we are Christ's ambassadors. That means we are the people Jesus sends to speak for him. Paul, as Christ's ambassador, begged the Corinthians to ask Jesus to forgive their sins and then trust Jesus as their Savior. We also, as Jesus' "elves," should be sincerely asking people to accept Jesus' forgiveness and salvation.

DECEMBER 25

Follow Advice
Christmas

A most wonderful thing happened on the very first Christmas. God became a man. Jesus was born. God becoming man is called "the incarnation." The Bible tells the Christmas story in Luke, chapter two.

Joseph and Mary had to go to Bethlehem to register. They were engaged to be married, but Mary was pregnant by the Holy Spirit. Her baby was about to be born. The trip from Nazareth to Bethlehem was about eighty miles, so Mary must have been very tired. When they got to Bethlehem there was no room for them to stay in the inn. The innkeeper let them use the stable where the animals were housed. Mary gave birth to baby Jesus there.

The Bible says Jesus' birth was announced to some shepherds.

Lk 2:8-9 *And there were shepherds living out in the fields nearby, keeping watch over their flocks at night. An angel of the Lord appeared to them, and the glory of the Lord shone around them, and they were terrified.*

Lk 2:10-11 *But the angel said to them, "Do not be afraid. I bring you good news of great joy that will be for all the people. Today in the town of David a Savior has been born to you; he is Christ the Lord.* **Lk 2:12-13** *This will be a sign to you: You will find a baby wrapped in cloths and lying in a manger."*

Suddenly a great company of the heavenly host appeared with the angel, praising God and saying,

Lk 2:14 *"Glory to God in the highest, and on earth peace to men on whom his favor rests."*

The shepherds were excited about what had happened; they hurried off to go see the baby. They followed the angel's instructions; they found Jesus just like the angel had said.

Have you followed God's instructions on how to get to heaven? If you have trusted Jesus to be your Savior, you are on your way.

DECEMBER 26

Work, Work, Work

Have you ever heard of a workaholic? A workaholic is someone who works all the time. They work every day and they work all day. They might stop to eat, but then they are right back at work.

God does not want people to be workaholics. He wants us to work hard, but he also wants us to rest. God set up for his people the rule that every seventh day would be a day of rest. The fourth commandment says, "Remember the Sabbath, to keep it holy."

The fourth commandment in the Bible is a lot longer than that. It explains how God wants us to keep the Sabbath holy. He said he wanted his people to do all their work in six days. On the seventh day everyone in the family should take a day off of work. God said he even wanted the servants who worked for the Israelites to rest on the Sabbath.

Ex 20:8 *Remember the Sabbath day by keeping it holy.* **Ex 20:9** *Six days you shall labor and do all your work,* **Ex 20:10** *but the seventh day is a Sabbath to the Lord your God. On it you shall not do any work, neither you, nor your son or daughter, nor your manservant or maidservant, nor your animals, nor the alien within your gates.* **Ex 20:11** *For in six days the Lord made the heavens and the earth, the sea, and all that is in them, but he rested on the seventh day. Therefore the Lord blessed the Sabbath day and made it holy.*

God wanted his people and everyone that worked for them—even their animals—to rest one day each week. He said that when he created the earth he worked for six days and then rested. We should also rest one day a week.

DECEMBER 27

Study Hard

Many of you young people are learning to read and write. You are either in school or being homeschooled. That means you are students. Right now your job in life is to learn.

Some young men in the Old Testament were diligent in their studies. Even though they were taken to a strange land they studied hard.

Moses is the first example. He was a Hebrew, but he was raised by the Pharaoh's daughter in Egypt.

Acts 7:22 *Moses was educated in all the wisdom of the Egyptians and was powerful in speech and action.*

Daniel and his three friends are the second example. They also were Israelites. They were taken captive to Babylon. The king of Babylon ordered his chief of court officials to take some of the Israelites who were from the royal family—**Dan 1:4a** *young men without any physical defect, handsome, showing aptitude for every kind of learning, well informed, quick to understand, and qualified to serve in the king's palace.* **Dan 1:4b** *He was to teach them the language and literature of the Babylonians.* **Dan 1:5** *The king assigned them a daily amount of food and wine from the king's table. They were to be trained for three years, and after that they were to enter the king's service.*

At the end of the three years Daniel and his friends were tested by the king. They were ten times better than the magicians and enchanters of Babylon.

Moses, Daniel and Daniel's friends were diligent in their studies. They did great things for God. If you are diligent in your studies, you also can do great things for God.

Making the Bed

DECEMBER 28

Breanna knew that her family required her to make her bed every morning. She got tired of making her bed. She decided that if she slept on top of the covers, instead of between the sheets, she wouldn't have to make the bed. All she would have to do is straighten out the blanket a little bit.

Would you say Breanna is lazy? Maybe you would say she is wise for figuring out a way to do things faster and quicker.

Mom didn't think she was wise. Mom said it was much easier to wash sheets than it was to wash blankets. Breanna might be doing less work, but she was making more work for Mom. Mom told Breanna she could not sleep on top of her bedspread. Breanna started making her bed again.

If you take shortcuts so that you don't have to do so much work, make sure other people are not having to make up for it.

These are some scriptures on diligence:

Prov 13:4 *The sluggard craves and gets nothing, but the desires of the diligent are fully satisfied.*

Prov 10:4 *Lazy hands make a man poor, but diligent hands bring wealth.*

Prov 14:23 *All hard work brings a profit, but mere talk leads only to poverty.*

Some people like to talk a lot and not work very much. God says that will lead to poverty.

Prov 21:5 *The plans of the diligent lead to profit as surely as haste leads to poverty.*

If we hurry to finish things we will probably do a sloppy job. If we plan well, we shouldn't have to hurry.

BE DILIGENT

DECEMBER 29

Brushing Your Teeth

Ashley was only three when she started brushing her teeth. Dad would help her. She stepped up on the stool that made her tall enough to reach the bathroom sink. She squeezed out the toothpaste—sometimes too much—and then began to brush. When she was finished Dad brushed them once more just to make sure they were "shiny." At age five Ashley didn't need Dad's help anymore; she brushed her own teeth. She could reach the sink now without the stool.

When Ashley was thirteen she needed braces. The dentist explained to her that she needed to be extra careful when she brushed so that she would not ruin her teeth. The dentist showed pictures of children who had braces and didn't take time to brush well.

Ashley got her braces off a year later. Her parents felt terrible because Ashley's teeth had lines where the braces had been. Even though her teeth were straight, she did not have the pretty smile that everyone had hoped for.

Ashley's dad went and talked to the dentist. The dentist said that some people at the dentist's office knew that Ashley was not taking good enough care of her teeth. The dentist said some children just will not listen to the warnings. Ashley's dad wished the dentist had talked to him and to Ashley's mom so they could have possibly prevented the tooth decay that happened.

God has given us only two sets of teeth, our baby teeth and then our permanent teeth. We need to be diligent in taking care of them.

The Bible says God created us inside our mothers and that we are wonderfully made.

Ps 139:13 *For you created my inmost being; you knit me together in my mother's womb.*

Ps 139:14 *I praise you because I am fearfully and wonderfully made; your works are wonderful, I know that full well.*

Ps 139:15 *My frame was not hidden from you when I was made in the secret place. When I was woven together in the depths of the earth,* **Ps 139:16a** *your eyes saw my unformed body.*

We need to be diligent in taking care of the wonderful bodies God has given us.

DECEMBER

Jesus Likes Order

30

Dad McGregor was getting so frustrated. He had told his children several times that they should not leave their tricycle and roller skates in the drive. Here he was, leaving the car running in the street again. He put the tricycle and roller skates in the garage. Then he was able to pull the car in the drive.

That was only a small part of the problem. Dad went in the front door and found coats and book bags left in the front entry way. In the living room toys were scattered all over the floor. He knew the children's bedrooms didn't look any better. Why couldn't his children learn to put things where they belonged?

Jesus liked things to be orderly. When he fed five thousand people one day, he made sure it was not a mob of people all racing to get the food. He instructed the disciples to have the people sit in groups.

Mk 6:39 *Then Jesus directed them to have all the people sit down in groups on the green grass.* **Mk 6:40** *So they sat down in groups of hundreds and fifties.*

Luke's gospel just says they grouped in fifties.

Lk 9:14 *(About five thousand men were there.) But he said to his disciples, "Have them sit down in groups of about fifty each."*

After the five thousand were fed Jesus didn't want the leftover food littering the ground. Jesus told his disciples to gather the leftovers.

Jn 6:12 *When they had all had enough to eat, he said to his disciples, "Gather the pieces that are left over. Let nothing be wasted."*

Dad decided he wanted the house more orderly. He and mom talked about what could be done. They made a new rule about all toys. Any toys that were left out with no one playing with them, would be put away for one week. Mom made sure that the children had a place to put away all their toys.

(to be cont.)

BE DILIGENT

DECEMBER 31

God Likes Order
(cont.)

Last night we talked about the McGregor family. Dad and Mom decided how they would handle the "toy problem." Toys were not something their children needed. They decided that when toys were left out, they would be taken away for a time.

Backpacks, books, lunchboxes and clothes were another thing. The children needed their school things and they needed to have clothes to wear. Dad made a shelf for all the school things. When the children were done with homework, the books would go back in the backpacks on the shelf. Mom cleared a place in the kitchen cupboard for the children's lunchboxes. They were to put them there when they came home from school.

Mom and Dad decided that the best place for hats, gloves and coats was in the front closet. If Dad would put in a coat rack that wasn't so hard to reach, the children could hang up their own coats. He put in a shelf right above that for their hats, gloves and scarves. When everything had its proper place the McGregor house was much more orderly.

Did you know that God likes things to be orderly? When he made the world he didn't put stars in the oceans or trees in the sky. He put everything in its proper place. Stars he put in the sky and trees he had grow in the ground. God did not put fish in the forest and birds in the rivers; he put fish in rivers and birds in the air.

David wrote about how God made the world an orderly place.

Ps 8:3 *When I consider your heavens, the work of your fingers, the moon and the stars, which you have set in place . . .*

David was amazed at the greatness of God's creation. He said God put man in charge of **Ps 8:7** *all flocks and herds, and the beasts of the field,* **Ps 8:8** *the birds of the air, and the fish of the sea, all that swim the paths of the seas.*

When David saw how orderly God had made the world, he praised God.

Ps 8:9 *O Lord, our Lord, how majestic is your name in all the earth!*

BE DILIGENT

CLOSING REMARKS

Thank you for taking the time to share these devotions with your children. I hope that your family has grown in understanding of what the Bible teaches and how it applies to everyday life. May God richly bless you for faithfully teaching His truth.

Lauretta Marigny

INDEX

Aaron, 55, 195
Abraham, 95, 317
Achan, 327
Adam and Eve, 1, 3, 161
Adon and Adonai, 208, 209
Adulterous generation, 204
Advent, 336
Afflicted, 109
Ahab, 306
Ambassador, 359
Ascribe to the Lord, 208, 211
Avenge, 222
Bear with each other, 63
Belshazzar, 145
Birthright, 76
Blue-collar workers, 142
Born again, 4
Bribe, 240
Brood, 8
Catechism, 127, 344
Celts, 304, 305
Cistern, 79
Clergyman, 61
Compassion, 112, 116
Confess our sins, 42, 89
Conscience, listen to your, 42
Content, 29
Covet, 167, 327, 329
Crucifixion, 81

Cushite, 71
Daniel, 145, 189, 280, 281, 362
Daughter of Zion, 138, 153
David, 21, 104, 105, 106, 120, 123, 247
Deceive, 90, 225, 227, 229
Denarius, 221
Deny self, 62, 258
Destitute, 321
Diligent, 337
Discern, 23
Discernment, 303
Dorcas, 165
Dressing with propriety, 32
Easter, 83
El, Elah, Eloah & Elohim, 208, 209, 210
Elijah, 53
Elise, 20, 131
Elisha, 54
Eloquent, 249
Epaphroditus, 173
Ephah, 231
Ephod, 55
Eternal, 307
Ezra, 290
Failed to restrain, 191
False prophets, 219
False testimony, 81, 232

Famine, 94
Fear God, 73, 194, 203, 277, 293
Feast of Tabernacles, 326
Flee, 42
Flogged, 334
Foolish, 287
Gentiles, 5, 276
Gideon, 24
Godmother, 57
Gospel, Good News, 78, 353
Gossip, 39
Grace, 132, 149
Grazing, 143
Greedy, 306
Greivances, 63
Hannah, 198
Herod, King, 124
Hin, 231
Holy, 40
Holy Thursday, 80
Honor your parents, 156
Humble, 122
Idol, 252
Incarnation, 360
Indignant, 137
Inheritance, 144
Intercede, 320
Irrevocable, 125
Isaac, 97, 224
Israel, 253
Jacob, 75, 76, 99, 226, 253
James and John, 25, 137
Jehoshaphat, 28
Jeremiah, 222, 302, 333
Jeroboam son of Nebat, 147, 176, 177, 178
Jeshurun, 27
Jesus, 2, 4, 8, 13, 49, 60, 67, 78, 80, 81, 83, 139, 142, 160, 236, 273, 286, 331, 334
John Mark, 70
Jonah, 117
Jonathan, 104, 105
Joseph, 22, 100
Joshua, 289
Judah, 332
Justified before God, 151
King, Jr., Martin Luther, 14, 15
Knowledge, 277, 279
Last Supper, 80
Law of Moses, 290
Leprosy, 71, 249
Levites, 242
Lincoln, Abraham, 231
Lord, 208, 209, 210
Made themselves contemptible, 202
Manger, 140
Mantle, 54
Mardi Gras, 167
Martyred, 45
Masquerading as, 356
Matthew, 353
Maundy Thursday, 80
McElwain, Jason, 351
Mephibosheth, 106
Mincing steps, 48
Moses, 126, 195, 196, 238, 249, 292, 295
Nabal, 287
Nathanael, 216
Nebuchadnezzar, 143
Nehemiah, 342
Nicodemus, 4
Nicolaus, St., 358
Numbered, 157
Omniscient, 157
Oppressed, 109
Parable, 278, 300
Paralyzed man, 67
Passover, 80
Patriarchs, 100
Paul, 175, 347, 348
Persecuted, 175

Peter, 64, 165, 276, 305
Pharisee, 4, 8, 175, 263, 324
Plunder, 28, 48
Pray, 320
Pride, 124
Prodigal, 144
Producing good fruit, 91
Prophecy, 138
Prophet, 38
Rebekah, 225
Rebuke, 86
Recompense, 153
Refrain from anger, 260
Rehoboam, 147, 299
Repent, 5, 88
Ressurection, 35
Reveal, 66, 200, 201, 220, 276
Righteous anger, 273
Ruth, 309, 310
Sackcloth, 61
Samuel, 198, 199, 200, 201, 202, 203, 320, 328
Sanctify, 36
Sarah, 24
Saul, King, 104, 250
Saw through their duplicity, 221
Segregation, 14, 15
Self-control, 245, 247
Self-indulgence, 324
Selfless, 332
Seraphs, 186
Shun, 31
Sin, 1, 3

Sinful nature, 1
Sluggard, 337, 340, 355
Solomon, 174, 204, 296, 297
Sovereign, 248
Subdue the earth, 158
Submit, 191
Synagogue, 159, 190
Synoptic, 353, 354
The Day, 163
The law, 37, 254
Timothy, 18
Traditions, 336
Transfigured, 207
Transgressions, 3
Uncircumcision of your sinful nature, 3
Understanding, 291, 303
Veil covers their heart, 127
Vile, 41, 43
Vineyard, 306
Viper, 8, 346
Walk as Jesus did, 139
When Moses is read, 127
When the tree is green, 314
White-collar workers, 142
Widows, 282
Wisdom, 277, 294
With confidence, 262
Woe, 87
Wretched, 129
Yahweh, 208, 210
Zacchaeus, 218